SPIRITUAL AND VISIONARY COMMUNITIES

Based uniquely on the experience and knowledge of notable communal residents and scholars, this anthology offers rich insights into the visions and workings of modern spiritual communities worldwide. Timothy Miller's analytic introduction successfully ties together the threads of communal history and utopian communal usage. Nowhere else is such a penetrating wide-angle-view of contemporary spiritual intentional communities available.
    Donald E. Pitzer, University of Southern Indiana, USA

Once again Timothy Miller has brought together an impressive set of papers that highlight contemporary communities in Spiritual and Visionary Communities: Out to Save the World. *International in scope, this collection of communities presented within the context of their common mission to forge a better life, together present a refreshing assessment of the world of community and spirituality that thrives in the midst of so much global chaos.*
    Susan Love Brown, Florida Atlantic University, USA

Exploring religious and spiritual intentional communities active in the world today, *Spiritual and Visionary Communities* provides a balanced introduction to a diverse range of communities worldwide. Breaking new ground with its focus on communities which have had little previous academic or public attention, the authors explore a part of contemporary society which is rarely understood. Communities studied include: Israeli kibbutzim, Mandarom, the Twelve Tribes, The Farm and the Camphill movement. Written from a range of perspectives, this collection includes contributions from members of the groups themselves, former members, and academic observers, and as such will offer a unique and invaluable discussion of religious and spiritual communities in the U.S., Europe, and beyond.

Ashgate Inform Series on Minority Religions and Spiritual Movements

Series Editor: Eileen Barker,
London School of Economics, Chair and Honorary Director of Inform

Advisory Board:
Afe Adogame, University of Edinburgh, UK,
Madawi Al-Rasheed, King's College, London, UK,
François Bellanger, Université de Genève, Switzerland,
Irena Borowik, Jagiellonian University, Krakow, Poland,
Douglas E. Cowan, University of Waterloo, Ontario, Canada,
Adam Possamai, University of Western Sydney, Australia,
James T. Richardson, University of Nevada, Reno, USA,
Fenggang Yang, Purdue University, USA

Inform is an independent charity that collects and disseminates accurate, balanced and up-to-date information about minority religious and spiritual movements. The Ashgate Inform book series addresses themes related to new religions, many of which have been the topics of Inform seminars. Books in the series will attract both an academic and interested general readership, particularly in the areas of Religious Studies, and the Sociology of Religion and Theology.

Other titles in this series:

Prophecy in the New Millennium
When Prophecies Persist
Edited by Sarah Harvey and Suzanne Newcombe

Spiritual and Visionary Communities
Out to Save the World

TIMOTHY MILLER
University of Kansas, USA

LONDON AND NEW YORK

First published 2013 by Ashgate Publishing

Published 2016 by Routledge
2 Park Square, Milton Park, Abingdon, Oxon OX14 4RN
711 Third Avenue, New York, NY 10017, USA

Routledge is an imprint of the Taylor & Francis Group, an informa business

Copyright © Timothy Miller 2013

Timothy Miller has asserted his right under the Copyright, Designs and Patents Act, 1988, to be identified as the editor of this work.

All rights reserved. No part of this book may be reprinted or reproduced or utilised in any form or by any electronic, mechanical, or other means, now known or hereafter invented, including photocopying and recording, or in any information storage or retrieval system, without permission in writing from the publishers.

Notice:
Product or corporate names may be trademarks or registered trademarks, and are used only for identification and explanation without intent to infringe.

British Library Cataloguing in Publication Data
Spiritual and visionary communities : out to save the
  world. -- (Ashgate Inform series on minority religions and
  spiritual movements)
  1. Collective settlements--Case studies. 2. Religious
  communities--Case studies. 3. Communitarianism--Religious
  aspects.
  I. Series II. Miller, Timothy, 1944-
  307.7'7-dc23

The Library of Congress has cataloged the printed edition as follows:

Spiritual and visionary communities : out to save the world / edited by Timothy Miller.
    p. cm. -- (Ashgate inform series on minority religions and spiritual movements)
  Includes index.
  ISBN 978-1-4094-3902-8 (hardcover) -- ISBN 978-1-4094-3903-5 (pbk.) -- ISBN 978-1-4094-3904-2 (ebook) 1. Religions. I. Miller, Timothy, 1944-
  BL80.3.S685 2013
  307.77--dc23
                                                                                            2012026629

ISBN 13: 978-1-4094-3903-5 (pbk)
ISBN 13: 978-1-4094-3902-8 (hbk)

Contents

List of Contributors   *vii*

Introduction: Persistence Over Millennia:
The Perennial Presence of Intentional Communities   1
Timothy Miller

1   Damanhur: Sustaining Changes in an Intentional Community   15
     Etta M. Madden

2   Mandarom and the Limitations on *Liberté* in the *Laïcité*   29
     Susan J. Palmer

3   Henpecked to Heaven?
     My Life in a Brahma Kumaris Retreat Center   51
     Neville Hodgkinson

4   Realizing the Guru's Intention:
     Hungry Humans and Awkward Animals in a
     New Kadampa Tradition Community   65
     Carol McQuire

5   Tamera, a Model for the Future   83
     Leila Dregger

6   Spirituality in the Camphill Villages   103
     Jan Martin Bang

7   The Farm   121
     Albert Bates

8   A Tradition of Innovation and the Innovation of Tradition:
     The Cultural Developments of the Twelve Tribes Community   139
     Torang Asadi

9	The Family International: The Evolution of a Communal Society *Claire Borowik*	157
10	How Many Arks Does It Take? *Chris Coates*	177
11	Religious Communes in America: An Overview *Timothy Miller*	191
12	The Intersection of White-Racist Communes and the American Legal System *H.C. Lazebnik*	207
13	Communes and Kibbutzim: Towards a Comparison *Henry Near*	225

Select Bibliography *237*
Index *243*

List of Contributors

Torang Asadi holds a dual BA in Mathematics and Art and is currently a religious studies graduate student at the University of Kansas. Her main interests include American religion and communal groups as well as the psychology and sociology of religion. She is engaged in international studies of The Twelve Tribes and the Baha'i Faith, and is exploring film as a medium for the study of religion.

Jan Martin Bang is a qualified Permaculture Designer and teacher. He was active in the English Cooperative and Trade Union movements in the 1970s. He moved to Israel in 1984 and was a kibbutz member for 16 years. He represented the "Global Ecovillage Network" in Israel, and helped build up the Israel Permaculture Group. He was a co-worker at Camphill Solborg in Norway for seven years. He has written *Ecovillages – A Practical Guide to Sustainable Communities*, published in 2005, *Growing Eco Communities – Practical Ways to Create Sustainability* (2007), *Sakhnin – A Portrait of an Environmental Peace Project in Israel* (2009), and *The Hidden Seed – The Story of the Camphill Bible Evening* (2009). He has been connected with the International Communal Studies Association since its founding conference in 1985, and in 2010 was elected President of the Association. He can be contacted at jnbng49@gmail.no.

Albert Bates has been a member and resident of The Farm since 1972. He is a retired attorney, paramedic, and graphic artist, and director of the Ecovillage Training Center, a project that teaches skills for regenerative ecological design of the built environment. He founded the Ecovillage Network of the Americas and is a past president of the Global Ecovillage Network. He travels, teaching permaculture, and serves as an advisor to community sustainability projects on six continents. Among the books he has written are *Climate in Crisis: The Greenhouse Effect and What We Can Do* (1990), *The Post-Petroleum Survival Guide and Cookbook: Recipes for Changing Times* (2006), and *The Biochar Solution: Carbon Farming and Climate Change* (2010).

Claire Borowik has served as the international director of public affairs for the Family International since 2006. She also managed legal and media affairs for the organization in South America for four years, and in North America for 10 years. She is the co-director of the non-profit web-based WorldWide Religious News Service, providing religious news to the academic and legal community. She has been a member of the Family International for 33 years, and has served in several countries of Central and South America for 20 years.

Chris Coates spent 20 years involved in a small commune before moving to Lancaster where he works as a construction project manager for community-based building projects. He is a councillor on both the City and County Councils for the Green Party. He has edited *Diggers & Dreamers*, a biannual guide to communal living in Britain, since its inception in 1989. In 2000 he published *Utopia Britannica*, a history of British Utopian experiments, and has been a member of the International Communal Studies Association since 2003. He is currently part of a group building a cohousing community in Lancaster.

Leila Dregger is a German journalist and has been a member of the Tamera community since 2003. She is the former publisher of the magazine *The Female Voice – Politics of the Heart*, writer of the books *I Am Not in Peace Yet – Perspectives for a New Women's Solidarity* (in German, 2005) and *Tamera – A Model for the Future* (available in English, Portuguese, and German, 2010), and co-author of *Desert or Paradise* (2012) with Sepp Holzer. Her main interests are ecology, community, and peace initiatives worldwide. She has visited those initiatives in all continents and reported about them, thus making connections between them. She hopes to help establish a worldwide network for change with her work, and aims to build a House of Writers for Peace which hosts writers and journalists from different countries, including crisis areas, to share the stories that may help humanity to survive.

Neville Hodgkinson is a writer and journalist who worked for more than 20 years as medical and science correspondent of several national newspapers in the UK. His first book, *Will To Be Well – The Real Alternative Medicine* (1984), was one of the first to describe the intimate links between health and happiness in terms of modern scientific findings. His 1996 book, *AIDS: The Failure of Contemporary Science*, argued for a much wider view of the origins of the syndrome than conventional theory allows. He has been a student for 30 years with the Brahma Kumaris World Spiritual University and is chairman of the Janki Foundation for Global Health Care, a UK-based charity which encourages research and awareness in the field of spirituality and health. He now lives and works at the Brahma Kumaris Global Retreat Centre near Oxford, UK.

H.C. Lazebnik is a graduate student at the University of Kansas, USA; she took undergraduate majors in Religious Studies and Anthropology at the same institution. Her primary research interests include Aryan communities and medieval Norse literature and folklore, with Old Norse as one of her research languages. More broadly, she is interested in newly emergent religious movements in the United States and the world.

Etta M. Madden is a Professor of English at Missouri State University. Her books include *Bodies of Life: Shaker Literature and Literacies* (1998) and *Eating in Eden: Food and American Utopias* (2006). Recently, her research and teaching has focused upon contemporary narratives of healing and of disaffiliation from intentional communities, as well as upon women's visions of utopia and mobility in American culture and literature. In 2009 she served as a Fulbright Commission Senior Lecturer in American Literature at the Università degli Studi di Catania, Italy.

Carol McQuire trained as a social anthropologist at Cambridge University in the 1970s, then spent 20 years working as a classical and pop/rock musician in Mexico. She encountered the New Kadampa Tradition (NKT) in 1994, was ordained in 1999 as Kelsang Shraddha, and lived within an NKT centre in the UK as Company Secretary, Bookings Manager, student on the Teacher Training Programme, and NKT Dharma teacher until 2006. She supports NKT survivors wherever possible.

Timothy Miller is Professor of Religious Studies at the University of Kansas, USA. He teaches American religious history, with specializations in new religious movements and communal groups. Among his books are *The Quest for Utopia in Twentieth-Century America* (1998), *The 60s Communes* (1999), and *American Communes, 1860–1960: A Bibliography* (1990), and *The Encyclopedic Guide to American Intentional Communities* (2013).

Henry Near (d. 2011) was a historian of the kibbutz movement in Israel. His two-volume work, *The Kibbutz Movement: A History* (1992, 1997), is considered the standard work on the topic. Among his other books are *The Kibbutz and Society* (1984) and *Where Community Happens: The Kibbutz and the Philosophy of Communalism* (2011). He was a member of Kibbutz Ha'emek and was Professor Emeritus of Jewish History and Education at Oranim College, University of Haifa. He was an active member of the International Communal Studies Association and of the Utopian Studies Society (Europe).

Susan J. Palmer is a researcher and writer in the field of new religious studies. She lives in Montreal, Quebec, and teaches in the Religious Studies departments of Dawson College and Concordia University (where she received her PhD). Her best-known books are *Moon Sisters, Krishna Mothers, Rajneesh Lovers* (1994); *Millennium, Messiahs and Mayhem* (co-authored with Thomas Robbins, 1998); *Children in New Religions* (1999); and *Aliens Adored: Rael's UFO Religion* (2004). Her most recent book is *The New Heretics of France* (2011). She is currently researching government raids on religious minorities for a book co-authored with Stuart Wright.

Introduction:
Persistence Over Millennia:
The Perennial Presence of
Intentional Communities

Timothy Miller

Human beings (or at least the overwhelming majority of them) are not, by their nature, solitary individuals. They have lived in the company of others for as long as the human race has existed, and for thousands of years some have withdrawn from the larger society to form focused communities of like-minded persons, groups that today we call intentional communities. For millennia the basis of most communities appears to have been religious, but in the last two centuries secular communities have also played major roles in the larger communities movement.

The institution that is probably the oldest human voluntary organization, the Buddhist Sangha, is a set of intentional communities still going strong after some 2,500 years. In subsequent years thousands of other intentional communities have appeared as well. Some 2,000 years ago, for example, a group of ascetic Jews appears to have lived in a communal retreat known as Qumran, near the Dead Sea. The Book of Acts tells us that the very first Christians operated on a communal economy:

> And all who believed were together and had all things in common; and they sold their possessions and goods and distributed them to all, as any had need. And day by day, attending the temple together and breaking bread in their homes, they partook of food with glad and generous hearts, praising God and having favor with all the people. And the Lord added to their number day by day those who were being saved.

> There was not a needy person among them, for as many as were possessors of lands or houses sold them, and brought the proceeds of what was sold and laid it at the apostles' feet; and distribution was made to each as any had need. Thus Joseph who was surnamed by the apostles Barnabas ... sold a field which belonged to him, and brought the money and laid it at the apostles' feet.[1]

That early experiment has not been further attested, either in the Bible or in other early Christian writings, so it must not have lasted for long. Nevertheless, informal communities of the devout within the larger Christian movement were appearing as early as the third century. The largest grouping of such communities in the Western (and Near Eastern) world consists of the monastic orders, of which thousands exist in the Catholic, Eastern Orthodox, and other branches of the faith. In the West, those Christian monasteries dominated the world of intentional communities for well over 1,000 years after Benedict of Nursia (480–537) gave firm structure to what had been a scattering of loose ensembles some 1,500 years ago. In the Middle Ages, Western Christian monasticism became a mighty enterprise, with large institutions that often had extensive real estate holdings and other wealth, and in many cases were the major intellectual centers of their day.

Long before the Protestant Reformation, some groups dissenting from Catholic orthodoxy took up communal living, either out of Christian idealism or as a defensive move against a hostile world. The Bogomils, who appeared in Bulgaria in the tenth century and spread to several other countries, were egalitarians devoted to simple living; their most devoted members were not allowed to own private property and seem to have lived in community. The Cathari, or "pure ones", Christian dissenters with roots in Bogomilism, were active by the eleventh century and were occasionally communitarian, as at the castle of Monteforte near Asti, Italy, where a group of them was discovered and given the chance to repent of their heresies, which included celibacy, vegetarianism, and community of goods. Most declined and were burned at the stake at the direction of the Archbishop of Milan. In 1176 one Peter Waldo, a merchant in Lyons, France, distributed his wealth to the poor and gathered followers who sought to return to apostolic simplicity and community. The Waldensian movement spread to a number of other places

---

[1] Acts 2:44–47 and 4:33–37, Revised Standard Version.

in Europe, and in some localities the believers lived communally, often for self-protection against hunters of heretics.

The Czech dissenter John Hus first rose to prominence in Prague, but looming persecution made him retreat to Tabor, a communal base for his followers, where he did much of his important writing before he was burned at the stake in 1415. For many years Tabor operated as a peasant commune and spawned offshoot communes, in all of which residents pooled their assets and income and redistributed resources equally. But even the dissident Tabor commune spawned its own dissidents, a group that announced that the millennium had come and therefore that human laws had been abandoned. Some hundreds of them, expelled from Tabor, wandered naked, claiming to have recaptured the innocence of Adam and Eve, and eventually set up their own communal settlement on an island in Bohemia. But these Adamites went too far even for the more staid religious reformers and were eventually rounded up and destroyed.

Other spiritual descendants of Hus survive and have had a strong heritage of communal organization. Eventually the main body of Hussites became known as the Moravian Church, and within that body some members formed the communal Unitas Fratrum, or Unity of the Brothers. In the eighteenth century groups of Moravians migrated to America, and there in 1741 they established Bethlehem, Pennsylvania, which operated as a communal settlement for over 20 years. Soon Bethlehem had satellite communities as well, and in 1753 the thriving movement purchased a large tract of land they called Wachovia in North Carolina. There the Moravians founded several more communities, most notably Salem, now part of Winston-Salem. Several American towns are still predominantly Moravian, although they are no longer economically communal.

When Protestantism proper arrived on the scene in the sixteenth century, it was not as favorable to monasticism as Catholicism had long been, and Christian communitarianism in the West saw its footprint reduced, especially when Henry VIII dissolved many of the English monasteries in 1536. That is not to say that Protestants, however, never had communal groups among their diverse denominations. Radical reformers established communal centers in many places as they sought to return to biblical purity and simplicity. The Anabaptists, whose descendants include the Amish and Mennonites, emerged in the first decade after Martin Luther's initial protest against Catholic practices, challenging authority by advancing such doctrines as pacifism, adult baptism, and separation of church and state. They soon spawned a number of communal settlements. One of the most famous emerged when one group of Anabaptists took over the town of Münster and, with millennial fervor, pooled their earthly goods and declared the city the New Jerusalem. The following year the city was retaken by more moderate forces and the rebel leaders were executed.

But the Anabaptists had other early movements, both more fully communal and vastly longer-lived. The Hutterites, in fact, became one of the most notable communal religious movements in history. In 1528 the members of this faction of the larger Anabaptist movement, named after its early leader Jacob Hutter, pooled all of their earthly possessions and embarked on a communal course. Like other Anabaptists they suffered severe persecution (Hutter himself was tortured and then burned at the stake in 1536). But in the fluid geopolitical world of sixteenth-century Europe there were safe havens, and the Hutterites settled in Moravia and Slovakia. There they flourished, reaching a population of perhaps 40,000 in more than 70 communal settlements by the 1570s. This period went down in Hutterite history as the Golden Years, but other persecutions ensued, and Hutterites' fortunes variously waxed and waned until about 1770, when the remnant Hutterite population settled in Russia with guarantees of exemption from military service and the right to educate their own children. A century later those guarantees were withdrawn, and the Hutterites moved again, this time to North America. There, Golden Years blossomed again, and today the Hutterites number 40 to 50 thousand in over 400 colonies in the United States and Canada, constituting one of the largest and longest-lived communal societies ever.

Several English communal movements burst forth during and after the Civil War (1642–1651). The best-known of them was the group that began cultivating common land in Surrey in 1649, seeking to enact a vision of a world without private property and without money. These Diggers, as they were soon known, were evicted from that initial tract of land, but moved a short distance to a new site near Cobham, where again common farming was begun and several homes were built. Other Digger-inspired communities grew up in several other English locations, but in every case they were ferociously opposed by landowners who saw their interests imperiled. The Diggers were short-lived, disappearing in 1651.

Communitarianism was not confined to Europe over those many centuries. Several communal societies were created in the Middle East from time to time, as in the case of the Sufis, the Muslim mystics who in the eighth and ninth centuries began to create communal centers for their spiritual explorations. Soon thereafter came the Qarmathians, or Carmathians, who inaugurated a utopian communal experiment in 899 in eastern Arabia. Although Shi'ite Muslims in origin, they saw some Islamic practices, including the hajj, or pilgrimage, as ignorant superstition, and in 930 plundered Mecca, stealing, among other things, the Black Stone, the most sacred object in Islam. Beyond their violent proclivities, however, they were vegetarians who sought to establish an egalitarian, rational society. The Qarmathians dominated a good deal of the Persian Gulf area through much of the tenth century, finally declining after military defeats in the latter years of the century. At their peak they probably controlled more territory than any other communal group in history.

Better known than the Qarmathians, and perhaps the best-known Islamic communal group of all, were the Assassins, who were active in the eleventh through thirteenth centuries. From a communal headquarters called Alamut in what is now northwestern Iran they deployed expert terrorists who were feared throughout the region. Exacting tribute from those who feared them, the Assassins were, somewhat like the Qarmathians before them, communitarians whose prosperity came at the expense of those they governed or intimidated.

Farther east and several centuries later came another communal group, the Doukhobors of Russia. They emerged in the seventeenth or eighteenth century, taking issue with many practices and doctrines of the Russian Orthodox Church and even rejecting the authority of the government itself. Pacifists, they resisted military service, and were eventually resettled in Ukraine, and then the Caucasus. By the late nineteenth century they had established community of property, and in 1895 they burned their weapons as an outward sign of their pacifism, an act that brought more repression down on them. Exasperated, the Russian government agreed to let them emigrate if they would agree never to return, and in 1899 thousands of them moved to Canada, where they settled in Saskatchewan in three colonies. Later, some of them moved to British Columbia, where they continued their strenuous resistance to civil government. One faction, the Sons of Freedom, became known for their protests that involved arson and group nudity.

Over time they have given up communal living, but tens of thousands of Doukhobors continue to live in Canada and the United States, and a small remnant population remains in Russia and (formerly Soviet) Georgia.

A good deal of the European communal enterprise migrated to the American colonies and then the United States once settlement was possible. I will not recapitulate the survey that constitutes most of my chapter later in this volume, but such groups as the Ephrata Community, the Shakers, the Harmony Society, and the Hutterites were established by immigrant Europeans of various nationalities. As the nineteenth century progressed, other domestically produced American spiritual communities emerged as well – the Oneida Community, the Mormon United Order, and the Koreshan Unity, to name only three. All of these and many more are characterized in Chapter 11.

Meanwhile, international migration of communitarians was not all in one direction. Just as Europeans journeyed to the United States to establish their communal homes, some Americans went elsewhere in search of congenial environments for their own communities. One such migration was undertaken by Mormons, who by the 1880s had come under severe pressure by the federal government because of their practice of polygamy. Many American Mormons had experience with communal living, their church's United Order experiments having flourished in the 1870s, and some of them decided to leave the country. Beginning in about 1885, groups of them began to found what eventually became a string of eight colonies in northern Mexico, not far from the international border. The first of them was Colonia Juárez, established in Chihuahua province. Although many of the Mormon colonists returned to the United States during the Mexican revolution of 1912 and 1913, Colonia Juárez survived and remains an enclave of Americans in Mexico. One other of the Mormon settlements, Colonia Dublán, which was founded at about the same time as Colonia Juárez, has also remained in existence. Another Mormon-oriented Mexican colony not a part of the main Mormon church (officially the Church of Jesus Christ of Latter-day Saints), Colonia LeBaron, which was founded in the 1920s by church members who refused to give up polygamy, also continues. And dwarfing the Mexican colonies are the fundamentalist Mormon colonies of the United States and Canada, where polygamy continues to flourish.

At about the same time, another group of believers set out from America to establish a colony in India. Helena Blavatsky and Henry Olcott had founded the Theosophical Society in the United States in 1875, but after a tour of India in which they were enthusiastically received they decided to move the headquarters to that country. They established a colony at Adyar, near Madras (now Chennai), and it has continued since. Members of various Theosophical organizations also created intentional communities in other countries, including the United States. One major branch of the movement, under Rudolf Steiner's inspiration and leadership, became known as Anthroposophy, and its members founded a great many more communities, most notably ones affiliated with the Camphill movement, which provides communal homes for mentally and physically disabled persons. The movement has grown to over 100 communities in some 23 countries, and other Theosophically based communities continue to operate as well.[2] One chapter in this volume provides a look at Camphill life.

When the original Theosophists moved to India they were entering a land with a strong communal tradition. Spiritual teachers there have gathered followers into ashram communities for millennia. No one could ever compile a comprehensive list of them in the past or present, but the genre has been sufficiently attractive that some of them have reached beyond Hinduism to attract interfaith and international residents. Shantivanam, meaning Forest of Peace, was founded by two French Catholic priests who welcomed followers of diverse religious traditions. The English Catholic monk Bede Griffiths arrived in 1968 to take over the work, and Shantivanam, located in Tamil Nadu state, has continued since as a notable communal center where East meets West. Moreover, one of the world's most ambitious projects in intentional community has arisen from the work of Sri Aurobindo, whose ashram in Pondicherry continues to attract thousands of international visitors. Aurobindo's successor, Mirra Alfassa, known as the Mother, founded Auroville in the countryside outside Pondicherry in 1968 as an ideal town dedicated to the unity of humanity. Some 2,000 residents from several dozens of nations are actively engaged in bringing the Mother's vision to full realization.

In the early twentieth century the land that is now Israel became a leading center of intentional community living. The modern Zionist movement arose in Europe in

---

[2] *Camphill Around the World, 2012.* Available online at http://www.camphill.net/where-we-are, accessed August 16, 2012.

the 1890s among Jews who thought a territorial homeland was essential to Jewish security, and even survival. A principal vehicle of Jewish return to Palestine was the kibbutz, a communal home for the socialist Zionist pioneers. The first kibbutz, Degania, was founded in 1909, and others followed until there were nearly 300 of them. Economically the kibbutzim were fully communal, serving all the needs of their members, until recently, when privatization has come to many of them. They remain important cooperative villages, however, and have developed various industries to supplement the agricultural base upon which they typically rested.

Mennonites, descended from the Anabaptist faction of the Protestant Reformation of the sixteenth century, have in many cases taken up communal living. Most Mennonites are not communal, but in several countries some groups of them have established intentional communities. The Old Colony Mennonites constitute one such group; they originated in Russia and, like many other Mennonites of the day, moved to Canada in the 1870s. Searching for greater isolation and freedom to preserve their traditional institutions (including their own schools) and exemption from military service, they secured guarantees for their special needs from the Mexican government and several thousands of them moved there, where they settled in colonies that eventually numbered more than a dozen. They gradually spread into several other Latin American countries as well. Other Mennonites beyond the Old Colony movement have also taken up communal living. The Sommerfelder Mennonites have colonies in Bolivia, Paraguay, and Mexico, and the Kleine Gemeinde ("Little Church") has them in Belize, Canada, and Mexico. There are others as well. The communal Mennonite presence in Latin America, especially Mexico and Paraguay, is well established.

The twentieth century has seen the growth of many new Catholic communities outside the traditional canonical structures. One notable communitarian movement within Catholicism has been the Catholic Worker movement. Dorothy Day was a recent convert to the faith when she encountered the French grassroots philosopher Peter Maurin, who envisioned religiously based social reform and founded the Catholic Worker movement in 1933. The Workers are known for their leftist political activism and for their communal Houses of Hospitality that provide social services to the poor as well as for their communal farms. From a modest beginning in New York City the movement has spread and has hundreds of communal houses and farms worldwide.

One force driving many relatively recent Catholic communities is Pentecostalism. Initially a Protestant phenomenon, Pentecostalism emerged among Catholics in the 1960s and now, with millions of Catholic participants, it has the official approval of the Church. Most Catholic Pentecostals are involved in fellowship groups within regular Catholic parishes, but a few have formed intentional communities of like-minded faithful. France has been an especially active fountainhead of Pentecostal Catholic communalism, with many centers operating in the country. Notable among them is the Communauté du Chemin Neuf, which has hundreds of members in dozens of communities that have been created in France and several other countries.

More recently, Traditionalist Catholic communities have risen up in several locations. Ecclesiastical reforms and innovations are always controversial, and in Catholicism the Second Vatican Council (1962–1966) instituted reforms that some found scandalous, or even heretical. In their desire to continue in the old ways, with a Latin mass and traditional religious disciplines, some Traditionalists have founded intentional communities of the faithful. Many of them are small and localized, but a few have hundreds of members. The largest, probably, is the Order of the Magnificat of the Mother of God (*L'Ordre du Magnificat de la Mère de Dieu*), or Apostles of Infinite Love (*Les Apôtres de l'Amour Infini*). It is located in a remote area of Quebec, Canada. Other traditionalist communities are scattered around the Catholic world.

Many kinds of Protestants in addition to those mentioned earlier similarly live communally around the world. There are communal groups of Lutherans, Presbyterians, Quakers, Pentecostals, and independent evangelicals and fundamentalists. There are also a great many communities that press the boundary between "religious" and "secular". Findhorn, in Scotland, for example, and several communities elsewhere based on its precepts, is not a conventionally religious community (it has no guiding doctrine or creed), but its spiritual basis is explicit. Its hundreds of members by and large are interested in various spiritual pursuits and disciplines, including meditation, and the founders took an active interest in interaction with the world of the spirit, and in particular the "nature devas", or spirits, to which were attributed the crops of huge vegetables that first brought Findhorn to the world's attention. Co-founder Eileen Caddy also claimed to receive daily messages from God, and her published spiritual writings continue to guide the community after her death.

Many intentional communities today are dedicated to social reform projects, and in many cases their members are driven by religious or spiritual commitments, even if the community as a whole does not have a specific religious basis. The Movement for a New Society (MNS), initially made up of activists against the American war in Vietnam, had a broad social-change agenda and eventually had over 20 communal houses, the majority of them in Philadelphia, Pennsylvania, USA, but some elsewhere as well. (Most of the MNS houses are defunct, although a few survive.) Many of the most active MNS members were Quakers (Friends), and thus also members of a faith community that has long had strong social-activist commitments. MNS itself was not specifically religious in basis, but religious commitment drove many of its most active members.

Similarly on the borders of spiritual community are the many service communities around the world. One of the largest networks of such communities is Emmaus International, whose hundreds of local communal outposts serve the poorest members of society, providing them with housing and food, but also advocating their cause with governmental agencies and the public at large, seeking not only to ameliorate poverty but to eradicate its fundamental causes. Reminiscent of the Catholic Worker movement in its combination of service and activism, Emmaus was founded in 1949 by the French Catholic worker-priest Henri Grouès, known in the movement as Abbé Pierre. It considers itself a secular movement, but the religious foundations of its work are inescapable.

In similar fashion the ecovillages, which collectively have represented one of the cutting edges of communitarianism since the 1990s, are mostly organized on secular principles, but have members with spiritual commitments and undertake work with spiritual implications. The ecovillages are demonstration projects that seek to show the world how the human race can live sustainably, engaging in alternative energy projects, permaculture, and earth-friendly building construction, among other things. Ökodorf Sieben Linden (Seven Lindens Ecovillage) of Poppau, Germany, has environmental projects ranging from organic gardening to straw-bale building, but in its listing in *Eurotopia*, the European guide to intentional communities, its self-description includes "spiritual, inner growth, meditation, yoga".[3] What are the boundaries here? What, exactly, are the realms of ecological consciousness and spirituality? How much do they overlap? No universally applicable answer is possible.

It is also the case that spiritual intentional communities often have an impact on secular movements for social change. Some communities are quite inward in focus and seek to keep the outside world at bay, but many more have members committed to a wide variety of social-reform causes. Not only do they provide support for the activism of their own members, but sometimes they provide resources (often food and housing) for activists. Occasionally, supporters of a social movement undertake a lengthy march, often the length of a country or more, or an extended encampment to call attention to their cause. In case after case they are fed and housed by members of intentional communities. For two decades pacifists and social-justice activists have demonstrated against the School of the Americas (SOA), located in Georgia, USA, which is a training school for mainly Latin American military leaders. Only an hour's drive away by car is the Koinonia Community, which was founded in 1942 to promote racial equality. Koinonia often hosts the SOA demonstrators and supports their work, even though Koinonia is not formally part of the protest movement against SOA.

As the twenty-first century progresses, change is afoot in intentional communities just as it is everywhere else in modern society. The rise of electronic communication has already had a great impact on intentional communities, and promises to have more in the future. When email first became popular, it was a godsend to the many communities that were geographically isolated. Until then communication was by letter (slow) and telephone (expensive), and many communities jumped at the chance to improve their contacts with the outside world. What the long-term effect of that shift will be, though, remains to be seen. Many communities, especially certain religious ones, have found a good deal of strength in their isolation. Children, for example, are likely to stay in touch with a community's central values when the allures of the outside world are far away, but being in touch may change all of that. Hutterite colonies have always been rural, and historically most members have not frequently journeyed into modern

---

[3] *Eurotopia: Intentional Communities and Ecovillages in Europe* (Poppau, 2005), p. 167.

cities. Now, however, colonies have computers and the colonies' young people have email and Facebook accounts and are fairly suddenly immersed in the culture at large. The effects of that outside contact on traditional Hutterite life are likely to be deep.

So what is happening to the intentional communities movement as a whole? Is it growing? Declining? Changing form? Increasing (or decreasing) its influence on society? Those questions do not yield easy answers. The communities movement is hardly a "movement" at all in the sense of something somewhat cohesive, with identifiable patterns of thought and action and lifestyle. And it is an exceedingly hard part of society to measure. No one can come close to counting communal groups in any one country, or even one state or province or county. More than a few of them deliberately try to keep their profiles low for a variety of reasons, perhaps because they fear ideological contamination from the corrupt outside world, or because they are violating certain laws (such as constructing certain buildings without proper permits), or because they fear that those who see them will consider them eccentric and perhaps even dangerous. The people who maintain the various communal directories, including the ones kept by the Fellowship for Intentional Community at www.ic.org and the *Eurotopia* team at www.eurotopia.de/english. html, may list hundreds or even thousands of communities, but they know that far more than that choose not to be listed. Public presence is only the tip of the communal iceberg.

As a result, it is hard to say what the trends are. Are the numbers of communities increasing, or decreasing? And the same for the numbers of members? I would argue that no one really knows. Some have seen surges of commune building from time to time, but I don't think they have provided us with a complete picture of the communal presence in society. In 1984 Michael Barkun argued that American communalism had seen four major surges in history in the early and late nineteenth century, in the Depression years of the 1930s, and in the 1960s era.[4] In the early 1990s Brian J.L. Berry expanded on Barkun's argument, finding surges of communal growth to correspond to economic downturns.[5] But both of them

---

[4] Michael Barkun, "Communal Societies as Cyclical Phenomena", *Communal Societies* 4 (1984): pp. 35–48.

[5] Brian J.L. Berry, *America's Utopian Experiments: Communal Havens from Lone-Wave Crises* (Hanover, 1992).

focused their analyses on the numbers of new communities that were founded in a particular time period, and the creation of new groups hardly measures the communal presence in society as a whole. To assign Hutterite influence only to the group's arrival in North America in 1874 is to overlook its enduring and growing presence ever since.

Every now and then a reporter calls me, telling me that s/he has come to understand that there is increasing interest in communal living these days, and asking me whether that might be the case. I have to start my answer by saying that I have absolutely no way of figuring out whether the hypothesis might be true or not. No one really knows how many communities are out there, and even less how many people populate them.

What we do know certainly, however, is that communitarianism burns brightly in many a human breast. Contemporary society has produced a great deal of alienation, and it's a fair guess that huge numbers of people would like to have more connections, more community in their lives. Although only a tiny fraction of one per cent of the population goes so far as to found or join intentional communities, many more join non-communal religious organizations or are involved in any of a thousand cooperative social organizations. Human society was long a tribal phenomenon, and the instinct to band together is far from defunct.

***

This book is one of a series emanating from INFORM, the Information Network Focus on Religious Movements, based at the London School of Economics and Political Science. Since 1988 INFORM has been presenting public seminars in which members of new religious movements make presentations on their respective movements and scholars provide analyses of them based on their research, which often includes fieldwork with the group(s) in question. The goal of the seminars (indeed, of INFORM as a whole) is to expand public understanding of new and alternative religions, to look past stereotypes and diatribes. Some of these papers were originally presented at INFORM seminars; the rest are here published in that spirit.

The subtitle of this volume, "Out to Save the World", was inspired by Stephen Gaskin of the Farm, an interview with whom is included here. Never modest in his aspirations, Stephen once wrote: "That phrase comes from the old thing, 'Well, I ain't out to save the world, but …'. We are. Out front. I don't know anything else to do that seems worthwhile … Want to help?"[6]

---

[6] [Stephen Gaskin], *Hey Beatnik! This Is the Farm Book!* (Summertown, 1974), unpaginated.

Chapter 1

Damanhur: Sustaining Changes in an Intentional Community

Etta M. Madden

The Federation of Damanhur, located today primarily in the Piedmont region of Italy, certainly exhibits determining characteristics of "intentional communities" as delineated by scholars such as Timothy Miller: members share a common vision; they have some degree of economic sharing; the community consists of at least five adults not biologically related to one another; and the members share living spaces.[1] Within the Federation approximately 1,000 members and supportive friends center their lives around several rural sites north of Torino, in the Val Chiusella and the Alto Canovese, as well as in locales elsewhere in Italy and the world. In addition to their official "Welcome Center" and classroom space, Damanhurians share more than a dozen housing structures, where 10 to 20 members live in units called "*nuclei*"; an outdoor temple, used for worship during Solstice, Equinox and other rites of communal importance; a center for growth, creativity, art, and wellness, known as the Crea, which includes eating establishments, health clinics, a grocery store, and shops where books, jewelry for healing, and art may be purchased; and their renowned underground Temples of Humankind. Damanhurians circulate their own currency, the "credit", "based on ethical values of co-operation and solidarity", and membership in the community requires committed contributions in both currency and labor for the common

---

[1] Timothy Miller, *The Encyclopedic Guide to American Intentional Communities* (Clinton, 2012), p. 2.

good.² Of course, Damanhurians possess a shared vision, stated on their website: the community, "an eco-society based on ethical and spiritual values, ... promotes a culture of peace and equitable development through solidarity, volunteerism, respect for the environment, art, and social and political engagements."³

More important to determine than the Federation's status as an "intentional community", though, is an understanding of how the intentions of this community are practiced and how the community has survived for more than a quarter century. The two topics are complicated as well as integrally related. Damanhur's practices are difficult to describe because they have changed numerous times since the community's formative years in the mid 1970s. As Professor Maria Immacolata Macioti of Università degli Studi Roma "La Sapienza" has noted, and Damanhurians often quote, the only constant about Damanhur is change.⁴ This chapter, then, will not attempt to describe in detail the community's theology and practice but instead defer to others that have, recognizing all the while that life at Damanhur has changed in some degree since each was published.⁵ These changes are crucial to understanding the second topic, Damanhur's survival, which is the focus and assertion of this chapter: it is precisely Damanhur's adaptability which has sustained it. More specifically, Damanhur has responded to points of communal crisis with creativity and growth. Some outsiders, including former members, have seen these crises as events that might cause the community to crumble or as contributing to a less-than-utopian status. Those previously affiliated with Damanhur describe deception by leadership, destruction of personal agency

---

² "17/2/2009 Monetary Sovereignty", *Virtual Damanhur Journal*, Year XXXIV (January–February 2009): p. 3. Available online at http://www.damanhur.org/index.php/about-us/news/virtual-damanhur-journal, accessed July 15, 2011.

³ http://www.damanhur.org/.

⁴ [R.O.], Interview, June 24, 2011 and [E.B.], Interview, June 24 2011. Interviewees' names are not given to protect their anonymity; instead, each has been given a set of false initials.

⁵ See Massimo Introvigne, "Damanhur: A Magical Community in Italy". *Communal Societies*, 16 (1996): pp. 71–84; Massimo Introvigne, "Children of the Underground Temple: Growing Up in Damanhur," in Susan J. Palmer and Charlotte Hardman (eds), *Children in New Religions* (New Brunswick, 1999), pp. 138–149; Jeff Merrifield, *Damanhur: The Story of the Extraordinary Italian Artistic and Spiritual Community* (Santa Cruz, 2006); Silvia Buffagni (Esperide Ananas), *Damanhur: Temples of Humankind* (Berkeley, 2006); Esperide Ananas and Stambecco Pesco, *The Traveler's Guide to Damanhur: The Amazing Northern Italian Eco-Society* (Berkeley, 2009). The community's website, virtual journal, and numerous other publications also provide a wealth of details denoting changes.

among members, and depletion of bank accounts among devotees; as they tell it, the Damanhurian story is one of despair and depression among those afraid to leave as well as those who have; and it is a story of lawsuits, payment of damages, and negative press. While this chapter is not the appropriate venue for such accounts, it does recognize these alternative views to the sustained changes.[6] Yet the community seems to have successfully used crises as healthy points of change.

This case study, then, depicts how Damanhur illustrates ideas expressed by Arthur Bestor and Donald Pitzer. Bestor described utopian communities a half-century ago as "experimental", rather "insulated laboratories" in which social reform methods might be tested and their ideas used as "lever[s]" to exert change upon the world.[7] As Pitzer has noted, the willingness to change the experiments within these communal laboratories is key to their survival; those that are unable to sustain shifts inevitably come to closure or dissolution.[8] Interestingly, Damanhur labels itself on its website as "A Laboratory for the Future of Humanity". When asked about the image of the community as a laboratory, one longtime member responded, "We are no more *an* experiment, but we continue *to* experiment."[9]

---

[6] This story of what David G. Bromley would call "defectors" and "whistleblowers", who contribute to the changes in the community, also deserves to be told. David G. Bromley, "The Social Construction of Contested Exit Roles: Defectors, Whistleblowers, and Apostates," in David G. Bromley (ed.), *The Politics of Religious Apostasy: The Role of Apostates in the Transformation of Religious Movements* (Westport, 1998). For access to a range of materials by and about defectors, see *Damanhur Inside Out*, available online at http://damanhurinsideout.wordpress.com, accessed November 1, 2011; and Gianni Del Vecchio and Stefano Pitrelli, *Occulto Italia* (Rizzoli, 2011).

[7] Arthur E. Bestor, *Backwoods Utopias: The Sectarian and Owenite Phases of Communitarian Socialism in America, 1663–1829* (Philadelphia, 1950), pp. 18, 3.

[8] Pitzer refers to the flexibility contributing to success as "developmental communalism". Donald E. Pitzer, "Developmental Communalism: An Alternative Approach to Communal Studies", in Dennis Hardy and Lorna Davidson (eds), *Utopian Thought and Communal Experience* (Middlesex 1989), pp. 68–76. Restated in Donald E. Pitzer, "How the Harmonists Suffered Disharmony: Schism in Communal Utopias", *American Communal Societies Quarterly*, 5/2 (2011): pp. 55–75, p. 63. Such shifts within communities over time have also been discussed by numerous others. See Jonathan Andelson, "Food and Social Relations in Communal and Capitalist Amana", in Etta M. Madden, and Martha L. Finch (eds), *Eating in Eden: Food and American Utopias* (Lincoln, 2006), pp. 143–161; Etta M. Madden, *Bodies of Life: Shaker Literature and Literacies* (Westport, 1998). Likewise, Brian J. Berry has discussed how utopian communities flourish because of their responses to external social crises in his *America's Utopian Experiments: Communal Havens from Long-Wave Crises* (Hanover, 1992).

[9] [E.B.], Interview, June 24, 2011.

It would be impossible to describe here all the changes Damanhur has sustained since its inception – in membership, location, housing, economic status, business ventures, social structure, and recruitment, for example. Rather, after discussing more extensively Damanhur's philosophies of change, the chapter delineates some major changes in the community's early years, as indicated by both Damanhurians and former Damanhurians, and then several shifts of the last few years.

Upholding Philosophies of Change

In addition to the oft-quoted statement by Professor Macioti about change at Damanhur, members and former members speak frequently of the importance of individuals' willingness to undergo transformation. Philosophically, that is, Damanhur promotes change on several levels. First, it upholds a view not atypical among utopian, intentional communities – that of improving the world, as noted on the website and in Federation publications. Recently, for example, the website has added that it "endorses the Earth Charter", which "is a declaration of fundamental principles for building a just, sustainable, and peaceful global society for the 21st century". Such continually existent-albeit-revised utopian visions have drawn numerous curious visitors and hooked several longtime Damanhurians.[10] But another significant level of change for Damanhurians occurs on a personal level. Again not atypical in intentional communities, individuals are changed – "remade" or "reborn". They take on new names, both animal and vegetal, signifying elements within themselves that have been recognized as developing. Yet these names might be considered minor – mere outer signs compared with the inner changes individuals undergo as they are transformed within the Federation. As one founding member stated, the most important change is to a spiritual life, "putting an emphasis on the spirit, not on the machine".[11] Another longtime member explained, "change is important – not to make a big difference [in the community or world] but to make a difference in ourselves". This smaller type of internal change in the individual who chooses the Damanhurian life may be "less evident [to the

---

[10] [Q.F.], Interview, October 2010; [R.O.], Interview, June 2011; [L.L.], Interview, June 30, 2011.

[11] [E.E.], Interview, June 24, 2011.

public, but it is] revolutionary for the people". This same member described the Game of Life, which has been prominent in the community since the early 1980s, as continually asking members to question themselves, "Am I ready to live this life? Am I ready to change? To grow?" The Game started in a period of difficulty, the member explained, when the community was becoming rigid. Founder Oberto Airaudi, "just a man, but ... a wise man", began to ask of everyone these challenging questions of change. "When people become rigid," the interviewee explained, "they start having trouble." "Stress" sometimes associated with change, however, "can be positive".[12] Airaudi himself explained, "change energizes people".[13] Damanhur asks everyone who comes in to give what they have, to take responsibility, to use their talents to help. According to several members, Airaudi is excellent at encouraging them to develop their ideas and to build upon their strengths, rather than to force his ideas upon them. A concrete example of Airaudi's encouragement is the new center in Reggello, which is discussed later in this chapter.[14]

And then, finally, there is the level of change in communal practices, which impacts individuals and the community as a whole. These might be messages about a living arrangement undergoing transformation, a labor role that's needed, or the gradual introduction of a new practice, such as a class, or the abandonment of any of the above. The individuals' and the community's responses to these are essential to continuing the experiments within the "laboratory". Some of these changes are discussed below.

Significant Past Changes: Going Communal, Going Public

The most significant changes in Damanhur's first two decades have been named rather consistently by Damanhurians and former Damanhurians alike. I note three

---

[12] [E.B.], Interview, June 24, 2011.
[13] Question and Answer Session at Damanhur, June 24, 2011.
[14] [E.B.] and [R.Q.], Interview, June 24, 2011; [K.K.], Interview, June 30, 2011. Conversely, some former members have stated that Airaudi saps people for all they're worth – economically, emotionally, and physically. Del Vecchio and Pitrelli, *Occulto Italia*, p. 25.

of those changes here.[15] First, the visionary and charismatic Airaudi decided with a handful of others to purchase land in the rural Piedmont region so that participants in his successful "school" might live communally, fully acting upon the principles of spiritual growth they embraced. Second, after many years of literally building community on this land, a new project called "the Game of Life" was instituted.[16] This "game" included at that time what might be called an itinerant caravan ministry, resulting in population growth, mostly consisting of young people, who were attracted to this alternative lifestyle in a period of political upheaval in Italy. They came from cities and towns throughout Italy, and several of them remain at Damanhur today. Third, and most significant in the early years, was the discovery of the underground Temples of Mankind (now known as the "Temples of Humankind", the new name reflecting change to more gender inclusiveness instigated by external changes in the larger culture).

In each of these cases, the introduction of change provoked a sense of excitement for some and was unsettling for others. Leaving home and family in a city to live with a new, adopted family in rugged and uncivilized terrain had very real challenges, such as the lack of readily available water and heat. "The Game of Life" erupted as a threat to older members who were happy with the status quo that had been established before energetic young newcomers arrived on the scene. And the discovery of the underground temples in 1992 by the Italian authorities – prompted by the dissatisfaction of a defector – was, as one member recently described it, "the revelation of our greatest secret". As he explained, a common secret provides a powerful bond; the dissolution of the secret created a major change in the community.[17]

The revelation of the Temples of Humankind suggests most clearly the creative response Damanhur has consistently presented in these moments of crisis. As Damanhurians tell the story, Airaudi (known within the community by the animal

---

[15] These events have been selected from interviews with members and former members as well from Damanhurian publications, such as Ananas and Pesco, *The Traveler's Guide*. The specific list and rankings are my own.

[16] E.V.A. Meijerink, "The Game of Life: The Significance of Play in the Commune of Damanhur", *Journal of Contemporary Religion*, 18/2 (2003): p. 155; Ananas and Pesco, *Traveler's Guide*, p. 110, and repeated in the unpaginated "graphic narrative" within the volume.

[17] [R.O.], Interview, June 24, 2011. [Q.F.], Interview, October 2011.

name "Falco", or Falcon) decided that rather than act upset and unsettled by state officials who came to investigate – behavior that would suggest Damanhur was hiding something – the community would invite officials inside for a tour. As the story goes, the officials were so moved by the beauty of what they saw that they became advocates for the preservation of the extensive site.[18]

Thus began a major new phase of Damanhur's existence – a phase in which they were introduced to the public. No longer secretly cloistered, they began fully marketing both their beliefs and their physical community to the world.[19] Visitors were and still are able to tour the Temples, and these phenomenal hand-excavated and decorated cavernous rooms have been featured on *Good Morning, America*, as well as on the BBC and Italian television in 2009.[20] As the video marketing and website demonstrates, Damanhur's emphasis on earth-centered and syncretic spiritual practices, along with their interest in sustainability, have been a draw for visitors from around the world.[21]

Numerous other changes have occurred and been noted: the creation of a constitution; revisions to the constitution; development of the somewhat parliamentary forms of government, including the King Guides and a judicial body; abolition of rules barring sexual relations among members; and the like.[22] Yet following the revelation of the temples, the emphasis upon marketing and environmental sustainability, along with the ongoing emphasis on the importance of change, have been most significant.

---

[18] Ananas and Pesco, *Traveler's Guide*, n.p. Some former members see the entire event as a creative staging on the part of Airaudi. Del Vecchio and Pitrelli, *Occulto Italia*, p. 96.

[19] Fifteen years ago Introvigne wrote of this transition, forecasting a potential dark "Future of Damanhur". Introvigne, "Damanhur," pp. 202–203. Yet he is still able to write about Damanhur in a positive light, highlighting its efforts on behalf of the environment. See "La Religione di Avatar nata in Piemonte", Libero-news.it, available online at http://www.liberoquotidiano.it/news/339744/La_religione_di_Avatar_nata_in_Piemonte.html, accessed August 16, 2012.

[20] Chris Cuomo, Alberto Orso, and Imaeyen Ibanga, "Mystery Behind the Damanhur Temples", January 31 2008, available online at http://abcnews.go.com/GMA/story?id=4216350&page=1, accessed October 24, 2011. For specifics on the features on BBC and RAI 1 in December 2009, see Del Vecchio and Pitrelli, *Occulto Italia*, pp. 15–20.

[21] Del Vecchio and Pitrelli also make this point, *Occulto Italia*, pp. 31, 96–97.

[22] Ananas and Pesco, *Traveler's Guide*; Giuseppina Alemanno, "Dal Segreto della Meditazione alle Donne che Racccontano di Sé", Istituto Richerche di Gruppo Lugano (2009).

The Environment and Recent Changes

Indeed, the most notable recent change is Damanhur's emphasis upon sustainability – an umbrella for numerous smaller changes. In addition to participating actively in the Global Ecovillage Network (GEN), with one member serving as its President, the community claims to have been recognized "by an agency of the United Nations" for these practices and, when outsiders visit, the marketing of sustainability and the role of ecotourism become obvious.[23] For example, in 2007 when the International Communal Studies Association (ICSA) conference met at Damanhur, participants were encouraged to eat at the Crea café, which features organic and vegetarian items, and to shop at the market which sells organic food and health products. They were also served several delicious meals prepared by the community and featuring Damanhurian produce. One conference option was an evening meal at the community cheese factory, at some distance from the Federation Welcome Center and Crea, where participants were served multiple courses consisting primarily of Damanhurian-produced cheeses – at the time, a new venture in "*agricoturismo*". The head cheese-maker presided over the table, providing an explanation (via a translator) of the offerings brought to the table by his wife and partner in the venture. (In a brief conversation after the meal, she explained that this role was her third while at Damanhur: previously, she had been an esthetician and a seamstress. She and her husband had also been in the community long enough to have undergone numerous transformations associated with raising a child there, including seeing him choose to leave.) When asked in 2011 about the cheese factory, a guide responded that it was no more. The facility housing it had only been leased, and it was an experiment deemed not feasible. This Damanhurian food venture in "*agricoturismo*" represents and reveals the community's desire to make good marketing decisions, pragmatically as much as ethically and spiritually based.

Also during the 2007 conference, for example, participants could not help but notice the extensive construction underway on the hillsides of the verdant valley where Damanhur Crea is located. These buildings, participants were told, were a real estate venture envisioning friends and family members of Damanhurians

---

[23] What the UN actually has said about Damanhur has been debated. See also Del Vecchio and Pitrelli, *Occulto Italia*, p. 116.

who might be interested and willing to live in close proximity to and interact with the community as "friends" but not wanting to join the Federation. The idea seemed to be that many people coming to visit Damanhur would be attracted to the locale and choose to settle in the beautiful valley. In 2011 the idea seemed to have been transformed to an emphasis upon affordable space and convenience for aging family members of Damanhurians, who realize the advantages of having needy parents nearby. The venture was described as an "important investment ... new in 2007" with hopes for hosting parents and relatives. While it is "going well", the interviewee explained, "we're changing it". Family members will be given priority and perhaps lower prices, but it is available for others as well. (The price differential was not consistently noted by interviewees, when they were asked about it.) In fact, for many years one Damanhurian was assigned a 50 per cent time role of researching and overseeing potential real estate investments. That project has since slowed but, as he explained, the real estate development up to the present has been important to allow the community to grow. Now the goal is "to conquer who we are", to "settle and breathe".[24] Another view of these investments is described in light of the Damanhurian version of the game of Risk, as a strategic attempt to gain political seats throughout the Piedmont.[25]

Another notable element of Damanhur's sophisticated and ever-changing marketing strategy, related to its emphasis on global sustainability, is its multilingual nature. In 2007, in addition to the ICSA conference hosts providing English-speaking translators from among their membership (as well as a community friend who translated information for Hebrew-speaking guests) for most activities, the Federation website and its glossy, professional magazine, *Qui Damanhur Futuro*, were fully bilingual – obviously reaching out beyond the Piedmont and Italy. This bilingual marketing technique has changed significantly since 2007. Today, the website lists 11 language options in addition to Italian and English.[26] A public "Question and Answer" session, hosted weekly in order to give visitors opportunities to ask questions of Airaudi, is translated into English, German, or Romanian, for example, as guests need. *The Traveler's Guide To*

---

[24] [E.B.], Interview, June 24, 2011; [O.E.], Interview, June 24, 2011.
[25] Del Vecchio and Pitrelli, *Occulto Italia*, pp. 135–143.
[26] These include Spanish, French, German, Dutch, Romanian, Chinese, Japanese, and Korean.

Damanhur (2009), published in English and advertised on the website, was clearly designed to aid potential visitors in preparing for a visit. It includes not only a graphic-novel-type historical account of the community but also information on where to stay and what to see (other than the Federation) in the Piedmont region.

Marketing for visitors is designed to appeal to a wide range of interests and cultures as well as those with varying amounts of leisure and freedom for travel. The website and *The Traveler's Guide* explain that the "New Life" project – note the name that embraces change – allows people to join for three months. Shorter sessions are also available – one day, three days, and seven days. These "short term citizens" stay within the *nuclei*, whenever possible, placed strategically to meet their needs. For example, among the newest Federation experiments are two *nuclei* at some distance from the Val Chiusella in the Alto Canavese, each with different purposes. One called "Aval di Cuceglio" is a sustainably built straw-bale structure, with solar panels, a unique furnace, and cisterns for water collection both for consumption as well as for heating and cooling. The structure, a showcase for sustainability and community (members built it in a record number of months and at a relatively low price), was featured in a 2009 *National Geographic* article,[27] and it often houses groups of Japanese who come for temporary stays.

The second *nucleo* in the Alto Canavese, called "La Prima Stalla", focuses on organic and sustainable agriculture, harvested for the community as well as for outsiders. After meeting and speaking with the lead farmer and observing the tomatoes and other vegetables at this site, we were guided to the cattle barns. The overseer of the livestock proudly explained that this protected breed of cattle, Razza Piemontese, draws a high price and is well known among non-vegetarian foodies. The cattle breeding and care, we were told, is gentle and "free range" – especially the harvesting of veal – different from what might be found elsewhere. Members placed in this *nucleo* are interested in farming, and few seem to be English speakers.[28] Another *nucleo*, Magilla, although it has been in existence for some time, continues to implement experiments in sustainable living.

---

[27] Marco Pinna, "Verde Speranza," *National Geographic Italia* (March 2009): pp. 34–39.

[28] The former cheese-maker, for example, now lives and works at La Prima Stalla.

"*Damanhur è Qui*": Centers and the Center

The *nuclei* in the Alto Canavese, several kilometers from the Federation Welcome Center, the Crea, and the temples in the Val Chiusella, point to the ongoing experiments with satellite "centers" which help to sustain the intentional community. Posters on site, ads in community publications, and previous postings on the website list or have listed several Damanhurian sites around the world: in San Francisco and Zagreb, Croatia, for example, as well as in Palermo, Sicily, and elsewhere in Italy. (Bologna, Faenza, Firenze, Milano, Modena, Verona, Oderzo, Palermo, and Torino were listed in the 2007 magazine, *Qui Damanhur Futuro*. Centers outside Italy were noted as being in Vienna, Zagreb, Berlin, Japan, Delft, Algarve, Ljubljana, Spain, California, Georgia, and North Carolina. Schedules for activities at most of the Italian sites were also published.) They give the impression of an active "missions" effort, reinforced by activities such as the website, the "New Life" project, and weekly public sessions with Airaudi. Yet even these "centers" are somewhat fluid. When asked about them in 2011, one longtime member responded that there was no longer a center in Palermo, and in San Francisco there were only occasional classes hosted by friends of Damanhur. Other centers were described as being in Modena, Bologna, Firenze, and Reggello, Italy, as well as in Croatia and Japan. All of these sites are important to teaching the Damanhurian life and vision to those interested, he explained. He was headed that day to the active center in Zagreb, and he would also help me arrange to visit the centers in Tuscany.

Classes at these centers have been crucial to many who join Damanhur, according to several of those interviewed about their lives in the Federation and observations of changes within it. The centers in Tuscany provide a case in point for the importance and fluidity of these sites. On the north side of Florence, what was once a typical small store in a relatively quiet residential neighborhood on Via Bardazzi is now a nicely renovated space consisting of rooms for reception, classes and workshops, research, and healing.[29] A member proudly showed me the center, explaining what had been accomplished completely by the labor of citizens such as himself, who had never before tried to lay tiles or to put up walls. Notably, this

---

[29] The website, only available in Italian, is http://www.damanhurfirenze.it/, accessed November 27, 2012. It does not mention the living space at Reggello.

center features no living space. The Tuscan Damanhurians, part of an effort begun in the latter 90s, have recently undergone a transition in this regard. Previously, there was common housing for about two dozen near the center. Now, seven adults and two children live just above Reggello, a small city of 16,000, approximately 40 kilometers from Florence. What prompted the change? An idea born of one imaginative member, who shared his thoughts of farm life and "*autosufficienza*" (self-sufficiency) – including knowledge of a beautifully renovated farmhouse and estate, available for lease – with Airaudi. Airaudi encouraged the experiment. Today the Tuscan group works to maintain this property, to learn more about sustainable agriculture and olive production, to invite interested groups to stay at the site, to participate in classes, and to learn more about Damanhurian life. Formerly a B&B, the property includes six apartments with shared living spaces in the main building, a guest house with multiple rooms, and a sparkling swimming pool – as well as approximately six hectares for olives and other cultivation.

The changes necessitated by the move to rural Tuscany have not all been easy, the citizen and two of his colleagues explained. When the decision was made to make the move from the urban center to the Tuscan hills, several opted out of the transition. Some left the community; others went back to the Damanhur of the Piedmont. Reasons varied – the new, longer commute to jobs in Florence, schooling changes for children, or decisions that the Damanhurian life was not quite right, for example. Certainly this transition is a test, one explained, and they have seen some falling off of energy with the loss in numbers. They would like to have another half-dozen or so adult members, but they must have patience. Courses continue to be taught in Florence, and hopefully will continue to bring in citizens. Also, members now invest extensive energy in developing contacts in Tuscany, such as participating in the "Terra Futura" show on sustainability at the Fortezza da Basso in Florence and publicizing activities in *Firenze Città*, a monthly events magazine.

When asked about the distance from the Piedmont and the impact on daily life near Reggello, these members acknowledged that trips to the Val Chiusella once or twice a month sustain them. "The totality of Damanhur is always there … but our idea is that the Damanhurian life is portable." Damanhur may be carried elsewhere. Members are able to participate in evening events via the Internet and, they explained, the Damanhurian life is carried inside each of them.

Also, they maintain more frequent contact with Damanhurians in Modena and Bologna, who are much closer to Tuscany and are also living the "satellite" life.[30]

While the existence of centers such as these has been a constant for many years, the centers themselves fluctuate just as life in the Val Chiusella does. However, when asked about the role of these centers, a longtime member adamantly and conclusively repeated, as he sat a few hundred yards from the outdoor temple in the Piedmont – "*Damanhur è qui. Damanhur è qui.*"[31] This statement echoed one of his points about important changes at Damanhur – the problem of division which occurred in the early years when the "Game of Life" was instituted and the community population grew too quickly. He continued, stating the importance of remembering that this particular place was "*terra scelto da Falco*" – land chosen by Falco. It is "*sempre un posto centrale, una scelta importante*" – always a central place, an important choice.

Conclusion

This member's comments reflect that even in the midst of changes there are consistencies for the Federation of Damanhur. Among those is a connection to place – the place where communal living began, where shared worship sites were first constructed. This keen sense of history and place, as well as of key moments of transition and ongoing philosophies of change, have led Damanhur to where it is today.

The community frequently makes decisions about communal changes, yet the basis for decision-making, such as the closing of the cheese factory or the opening of a new center in the hills of Tuscany, does not always appear obvious; it is rarely detailed with supporting evidence. That is, when Bestor commented on communal "laboratories" and their experiments, he elaborated that "experiment implies a well-formulated hypothesis, and the inventions of methods to test it".[32] Yet examination by outsiders of changes at Damanhur indicate that the hypotheses and methods of testing those hypotheses are not always carefully or

---

[30] [L.L.], Interview, June 30, 2011; [K.K.], Interview, June 30, 2011.
[31] "Damanhur is here." [R.O.], Interview, June 24, 2011.
[32] Bestor, *Backwoods Utopias*, p. 14.

well-formulated – or at least the supporting data and rationale are not readily available to outsiders. Rather, decision-making at Damanhur seems to occur in what appears to be more spontaneous, fluid, and less-methodical ways, although rationales for decisions about transitions are and have been articulated after the fact, analyzed both by those inside and outside of the community.[33] Nonetheless, these decisions – the communal laboratories' responsiveness to change – are essential to survival. During the past few years and today it appears that ecotourism and earth-centered spirituality enable Damanhur to survive. Tomorrow it may be something different.

Anyone interested in speculating may examine these changes and suggest where the community may be tomorrow or in months and years to come. While this chapter has delineated some points of change, it does not attempt to forecast the fate of Damanhur.[34] As a longtime member commented, throughout the years and even recently, some unhappy Damanhurians have left. Unable to sustain the transitions, their roles within the experimental laboratory have drawn to a close. Regarding a recently publicized lawsuit by a former member, for example, a community newsletter announced that Damanhur had "won" the legal battle. The Damanhurian explained that it is not that Damanhur has "won" – rather, the defector plaintiff has "lost". The same citizen noted that positive changes in the community today include the freedom and energy of newly arrived youth from around the world. These young people who arrive today are able to follow their dreams and pursue their interests; Falco's involvement and the structure of community life are not as fixed and rigid as they once were.[35] As the world around Damanhur constantly changes – exerting external forces upon it – so, too, do the citizens. Thus, the experiment called Damanhur continues.

---

[33] One former member refers to the "*Governo di emergenza*" upheld within the community, which emphasized quickness of action or "exigency": "first to do and then to discuss". Alemanno, "Dal Segreto della Meditazione", p. 15.

[34] Others have attempted such crystal ball gazing. In addition to Introvigne, "Damanhur," p. 203, for example, one weblog posting prophesied that Damanhur is "going into a big black hole".

[35] [R.O.], Interview, June 24, 2011. See also Del Vecchio and Pitrelli, *Occulto Italia*, p. 86.

Chapter 2
Mandarom and the Limitations on *Liberté* in the *Laïcité*

Susan J. Palmer

In June 1990, the cover of *Paris Match* featured a photograph of the messianic leader of Aumisme, a new religion situated in the French Alps. It was hardly flattering. Hamsah Manarah was photographed in the act of crowning himself the "Cosmoplanetary Messiah" who would unite the world's faiths and usher in the Golden Age. He was a handsome man, born in Martinique as Gilbert Bourdin, with noble East Indian features. But somehow the photographer managed to catch him at an off moment, sneezing or twitching his nose, looking slightly cross-eyed, his cosmoplanetary crown askew. The message to the French public was clear: "This man is a fanatical cult leader, possibly dangerous. Watch out, he is *fou*!"

Mandarom is the holy city of Aumisme, which combines advaita Hinduism with Western esotericism. In this chapter I will describe the turbulent relationship between Aumisme and France's mass media, and will examine the effects of stigmatizing media reports on its "Holy City", its prophet-founder, Gilbert Bourdin, and the Aumistes. Recently, in an extraordinary turn of fortune, Aumisme was granted recognition as a *culte* (a legitimate form of public worship) by the French state. But the history of the Aumistes' struggle for legitimacy is an eloquent testament to the limits of religious liberty in France. In order to understand the fierce battle between a new religion and the mass media it is necessary to place the conflict in the context of the rise of France's *antisecte* movement.

France and the Rise of *Antisectisme*

The French have a clever word for what happened to Mandarom – *mediabolization*. This refers to the "diabilization" or demonization of a person or group through stigmatizing reports in the media. The Aumistes claim they were the victims of *mediabolization* – but so were many other new religions of that era, after the rise of the French *antisecte* movement in the 1990s.

In France, growing concern over the dangers of *sectes* or cults reached a peak after the 1994–95 series of mass suicides/homicides in Switzerland, Quebec, and France conducted by the Ordre du Temple Solaire (OTS). This concern led to the rise of a government-sponsored anticult initiative, to the 1996 published Guyard Report and its list of 173 *sectes*, and to the launching of a series of watchdog interministerial missions, established to "fight cults".[1] During the 1990s and well into the new millennium, Aumisme's exotic symbols, its bizarre, eclectic architecture, and the colorful costumes of its monks were ubiquitous in the media. Soon Aumisme became one of the most notorious "sectes" in France, simply because it was so photogenic. When the About-Picard law (known as the antisect law) was first proposed in the National Assembly in 2000, the articles in the major newspapers covering this event would feature photographs of Aumisme as the quintessential *secte*, although this law has never been applied to Aumisme.

The History of Aumisme

After studying law and medicine, Gilbert Bourdin found employment in the French civil service. He became interested in esoteric spirituality, and toured the world investigating Tibetan Buddhism, advaita Hinduism and African shamanism, then visited Rishikesh, India, where he became a disciple of Swami Sivananda. On the 13th of February 1961, his guru initiated him into *sannyas*, or renunciation, and gave him the title of Shri Swami Hamsananda Sarasvati ("Felicity of the Absolute").

---

[1] "La premiere loi antisecte", *le Parisien* (22 June 2000); "La loi secticide est toxique", *France Soir* (23 June 2000); "Les sectes dans le collimateur des deputes", *Nice-matin* (23 June 2000); "Les religions critiquent la loi antisectes", *Le Figaro* (23 June 2000).

In 1962 he moved to France and lived alone in a cave in the Vaucluse (in the French Alps) for a year. Announcing his attainment of *samadhi* or enlightenment, he began to accept disciples. He established an ashram in the area and taught yoga.

In 1967 Swami Hamsananda Sarasvati and his disciples founded the Association of the Knights of the Golden Lotus. In 1969 they purchased land in the high mountains near the town of Castellane and commenced the building of the Holy City of Mandarom Shambalasalem. They invited distinguished spiritual masters from various religious traditions to visit and participate in their rituals.

Hamsah Manarah chose this spectacular location because in 1969 he had received a revelation that the Messiah would arrive in the midst of three lakes. There, he believed, all the world's faiths would unite.[2] Thus, the architecture of Mandarom was designed to serve a millenarian purpose.

Between 1969 and 1990, the Aumistes contributed their money and labor in constructing their Holy City. Each temple represented one of the world's great religious traditions. In 1977 the Lotus Temple (where their spiritual master resided) was finished. In 1989 the Mosque, the Hindu Temple, and the Jewish Temple were all completed. Statues of the Buddha, the Cosmic Christ, and the Cosmoplanetary Messiah were erected "to facilitate spiritual exercises and increase concentration in meditation".[3] For Aumistes, the purpose of this building project was – and still is – the revelation of unity of all the world's religions.

During the late 1980s, Bourdin became reclusive and spent most of his days alone in the Lotus Temple. At nightfall he would retire to his bed inside a golden cage and lock himself in with a golden key.[4] According to his disciples, he was preoccupied during this period with the task of warding off demons who threatened to destroy the earth.[5]

Bourdin studied the writings of spiritual masters from many traditions, and his eventual realization of his own messianic role was forged out of a long intense process of study, wrestling with inner demons, and experiencing mystical noetic

---

[2] S. Hamsah Manarah, *Les combats du Messie attendu pour sauver la terre et la creation* (La Baume-de-Castellane, 1990).

[3] Pierluigi Zoccatelli, "Notes on the Aumiste Religion", in James R. Lewis and Jesper Peterson (eds), *Controversial New Religions* (New York, 2004).

[4] Interview with an Aumiste nun, April 2001.

[5] S. Hamsah Manarah, *Je suis l'avatar lumineux de synthese. Voici pourquoi* (La Baume-de-Castellane, 1991), p. 298.

states. In his book *La Revolution du monde des vivants et des morts*, he announced that it will be himself who would usher in the Golden Age as the Messiah of all messiahs.[6]

Bourdin unveiled himself first as Shri Swami Hamsananda Sarasvati, then as the Lord Hamsah Manarah, then as the Hierokarantine, and finally as the Cosmoplanetary Messiah. The latter, the Aumistes believe, has come to Earth at the end of time to unite all the world's religions, to reveal the Unity of the Face of God, and to usher in the Golden Age.[7]

The 1990 Coronation

The Aumistes' ill-fated relationship with the French media commenced in May 1990, when they decided to hold a press conference at their Holy City to announce the glad tidings of the advent of the Cosmoplanetary Messiah to the world. The public was invited to attend a series of climactic coronations during the Buddhist full moon celebration.

In May 1990, Lord Hamsah Manarah sat enthroned as his devotees performed five hours of circumambulations, prostrations, genuflections, and chanting, with drums, bells, and cymbals. One by one, the guru placed a series of elaborate crowns on his own head, each representing one of the major faiths: Hindu, Buddhist, Jewish, Christian, and Muslim. At the climax of the ceremony, accompanied by drums, clashing cymbals and chanting, the guru placed the crown of the Cosmoplanetary Messiah upon his own head, symbolically enacting the Unity of all religions and the advent of the Golden Age.

The Coronation at Mandarom yielded a veritable arsenal of exotic photographs which were employed by UNADFI (Union nationale des associations de defense des familles et du l'individu – France's major "anticult" organization) and by the media in the coming years to illustrate the dangers of *sectes*. Journalists had been given free rein to wander about and take pictures, and the major television

---

[6] S. Hamsah Manarah, *La Revolution du monde des vivants et des morts: La justice divine* (La Baume-de-Castellane, 1993).

[7] See the Aumiste pamphlet: *Aumisme: Religion Universelle de l'Unité des Visages de Dieu* (n.d.).

networks, France 2 and TF1, had prowled around the temples, interviewing the Aumistes in their orange and yellow tunics and mirrored headbands. But when their faces appeared in magazines or on television, many of these Aumistes were summarily dismissed from their jobs. UNADFI had sent out faxes to employers "unmasking" them as members of the "most dangerous sect in France".[8]

Leaders in the *antisecte* movement were quick to exploit the situation. Janine Tavernier, the president of UNADFI, attended the Coronation with Père Trouslard, a Catholic Abbé and fervent heresiologist who worked tirelessly to expose "fake" religions. They came in disguise, posing as a television team. On 24 October 1991 they were guests on a TV talk show. The talk show host commended their "courage" in using fake press cards to spy on Mandarom, and all the other guests on the show concurred that Aumisme was a *secte*.[9]

The persecution that resulted from this negative media coverage was so intense, according to one Aumiste nun, that:

> As the result of the actions of the French government and the unrelenting negative portrayal of our religion in the media, the average Frenchman thinks of Aumisme as a dangerous, bizarre, and secretive cult. The situation in France has gotten increasingly worse and it has become impossible for me to practice my religion openly without shame, or to live at Mandarom without fear.[10]

A Network of Cultural Opponents

In the Mandarom case we find the local journalists cooperating closely with ecologists, an anticult group, politicians, and law enforcement. Thus the media actually played a major role in "bringing down the cult leader" and in the assault on Mandarom's sacred architecture. UNADFI's professional concern was to warn

---

[8] During my visit in June 2001, I interviewed the nun who was guarding the front gate, but she refused to let me take her photograph, explaining that she had almost lost her job as a public school teacher when the parents complained to the school director after seeing her in orange and red robes on television.

[9] Comment of Vedhyas Divya, a Canadian Aumist Bishop, who was present at the time.

[10] Interview with an Aumiste.

the public about the dangers of sects in their midst. The journalists' concern was to produce entertaining stories that would sell newspapers. The zoning officials' job was to impose rules and limitations on local building projects. Each of these groups collected and shared its own negative portraits with the others, and the final product was an image of Mandarom as a *secte dangereuse*. The media broadcast this image to the public.

The network of cultural opponents to Mandarom began to form after the Coronation. In 1992 an ecologist named Robert Ferrato joined forces with anticult activists such as Janine Tavernier and Père Trouslard, and he also began to work with Roger Reybaud, the mayor of the nearby town, Saint-Julien-du-Verdon. Reybaud later became the President of the Victims' Protection Association of Verdon, who awarded a Victims Compensation fund to two alleged "victims" of Hamsah Manarah. In 1994 Alain Delcourt, the father of an Aumiste, joined their network. In November 1994 Delcourt appeared on a talk show with his wife, and they complained bitterly of losing access to their little granddaughter, since their daughter had moved into the "concentration camp" that was Mandarom.

In 1995 a psychoanalyst, Dr Jean-Marie Abgrall, joined the network. Dr Abgrall was appointed by the Court of Digne to investigate the doctrines and practices of the Mandarom and their connection (if any) with the alleged facts of the rape case against M. Bourdin.[11] In his publications Abgrall refers to the leader of Mandarom as "paranoid" and as a "fraud". He described the religion of Aumisme as a "clownesque caricature of a cult".[12]

Dr Abgrall had requested a private meeting with Hamsah Manarah several times before the latter's arrest, but he was consistently refused. Undeterred, he went on to write a psychoanalytic portrait of Gilbert Bourdin for the Court of Digne. Aumiste Dr Christine Amory wrote to the Medical Association to ask if it were consistent with their *déontologie* (code of professional ethics) for a doctor to write a diagnostic report that claimed mental illness of a person he had never met or spoken to. The Order stood by their fellow, but subsequently rewrote its code.[13]

---

[11] Massimo Introvigne, "Holy Mountains and Anti-Cult Ecology: The Campaign against the Aumist Religion in France", in James T. Richardson (ed.) *Regulating Religion* (New York, 2004), p. 76.
[12] Jean-Marie Abgrall, *La Mécanique des sectes* (Paris, 1996), pp. 31, 91.
[13] Interview with Christine Amory, February 2006.

On 11 December 1994 the Delcourts participated in a march organized by Ferrato to protest at the building of the Pyramid Temple. Mayor Reybaud and several officials from ADFI joined them, and the Delcourts were filmed standing against the backdrop of Mandarom's exotic temples. Delcourt wept for the cameras and suggested his granddaughter was being held prisoner in Mandarom.[14]

Mandarom as a Focus of "Moral Panic"

Sociologist Stanley Cohen, in his 1972 book *Folk Devils and Moral Panics*, argues that the labeling of a group as deviant can be a response to a collective sense of social anomie and chaos, which he terms "moral panic".[15] This he defines as "a condition defined as a threat to societal values and interests; its nature is presented in a stylized and stereotypical fashion by the mass media". The sociologist Neil Smelser also considers "moral panic", suggesting that it is an effective strategy for opposing groups that some find offensive, for it invokes "a collective sense of immediate, powerful, ambiguous threat to deeply held norms or values, the preservation of which it is seen as urgent to take some action".[16]

It is clear that the media painted a portrait of Hamsah Manarah as a kind of "folk devil". A fluctuating portrait of deviance was created through collaboration between different interest groups, each with their own agenda for opposing the Aumistes' millenarian enterprise. The relationship between UNADFI and the media was, in James Beckford's terms, a "symbiotic relationship" that was a bit too "cosy" to conform to ethics in journalism.[17] Thus, it appears reasonable to suggest that negative news reports may have over-dramatized an ambiguous situation and raised the public's fears, and may have influenced the decisions made by public officials, paving the way for the public's unquestioning acceptance of

---

[14] The Aumistes claim he was lying, since he had just enjoyed a visit with his granddaughter, and was perfectly aware that her mother did not live at Mandarom, but in Carpentras. They also noted that the Delcourts neglected to mention that they had closed their doors on their daughter once they found out she was living with a man of colour, who would become their granddaughter's father.

[15] Stanley Cohen, *Folk Devils and Moral Panics* (London, 1972).

[16] Neil Smelser, *Theory of Collective Behaviour* (London, 1962).

[17] James Beckford, "The Mass Media and New Religious Movements", in Bryan Wilson and Jamie Cresswell (eds), *New Religious Movements* (London, 1999), pp. 103–119.

the raids on Mandarom and the detonation of the statue and other overreactions to a perceived *secte* threat.

Social Control of a *Secte* – or Religious Persecution?

In the years following the 1990 Coronation, not only the monks who lived at Mandarom but also the rank-and-file members who were scattered throughout France were continually harassed and subjected to arbitrary arrests, detentions, police raids on their private property, and the seizures of office documents and computers. Many were "exposed" as members of a "dangerous sect" to their employers by their local ADFI chapter, whose custom was to send out faxes to the workplace of known Aumistes. Many Aumistes were fired, demoted, or refused promotions. Some experienced the forcible removal of their children by social workers or, in divorce cases, the loss of custody of their children or the cancellation of visiting rights.

After Aumisme was featured on the Guyard Report list of 173 *sectes* presumed dangerous, the Aumistes were blocked each time they tried to lease a public space for one of their conferences. "ADFI would always find out and would phone the hotel, who would cancel our reservation," one Aumiste told me. Even after they found a more tolerant hotel manager in Nice who was not intimidated by ADFI, the conference was cancelled at the last minute due to an anonymous bomb threat.

Mandarom was placed under constant surveillance by law enforcement. Helicopters hovered overhead daily, sent by the federal government, the local police – or sometimes the media. The army regularly unleashed small aircraft to perform military exercises right over Mandarom, swooping down as if to dive-bomb the monastery. A nun who answered the telephone at Mandarom claimed she often received death threats.

The Aumistes were forced to close down their 100-odd centroms (ashrams or meditation centers) in France, and many fled (or returned if they were Canadian citizens) to French-speaking Quebec. Several French citizens applied for political asylum in Canada or the US on grounds of religious persecution.[18] In Quebec

---

[18] I was asked by one of these Aumistes to write an affadavit supporting her claim.

they opened a centrom in the small village of St Lucie, which became a center of worship for around 500 members.

Media-Generated Rumors

There were five main rumors that swirled around Mandarom, disseminated by news reports. The first was about money, that the leader bilked his followers of their money to support his lavish life style while they provided the free labor. The second was that Mandarom was a spy network, a "Trojan Horse" for foreign political interests. The third claimed Mandarom was a dystopia of child abuse and molestation. The fourth was that the Aumistes were planning a mass suicide, as a "copycat" response to the Solar Temple – or that they might even be a secret branch of the now defunct Solar Temple! The fifth rumor was of the rapes of young girls allegedly perpetrated by the "Lord of Manadarom".

Mandarom's Money

According to Mandarom's press release,[19] the income of the Association du Vajra Triomphant (AVT) derives from five sources: membership annual dues (800 francs); the sale of tickets to summer visitors; the sale of books written by Hamsah Manarah; fees for food and board during festivals; and members' donations. These resources are quite legal for voluntary associations. The Aumistes pay various taxes to les *controles fiscales*, including the TVA (value added tax, roughly 19 per cent), "social taxes", professional tax, and the annual forfeiture tax.

The AVT had no serious problems – until the *administration fiscale* suddenly demanded a tax of 60 per cent of all money donated towards the building of the Pyramid Temple. Because Aumisme was not recognized as a *culte*, the AVT was taxed 60 per cent of the members' donations. When it refused to pay what it deemed an unreasonable and illegal tax, the amount was increased to 108 per cent.[20]

---

[19] *La Verité sur l'Argent du Mandarom*, Mandarom press release (22 October 2001).
[20] The Aumistes have challenged the legality of this new tax in court, and are appealing it. Their case is very similar to the landmark case of the Jehovah's Witnesses in France.

Mandarom, a Trojan Horse?

Appearing on a television show called *Pièces à conviction*, the deputy J.P. Brard referred to Mandarom as a "dangerous *secte*" that was "involved in money laundering and had links with the Mafia".[21] Roger Reybaud, appearing on 1 May 2001 in an "investigative" documentary called *Sects and Big-Time Espionage*, proposed that that some *sectes* could actually be used as front-groups for international espionage.[22] Reybaud reported seeing cable plugs and antennas in statues belonging to the nearby Mandarom: "Could these be disguised transmission devices of some foreign country, spying on the acoustic detection laboratory for submarine warfare down below the mountain by Lake Castillon?"

The Children of Mandarom

Between 1995 and 1996 sinister rumors were circulating in the media regarding the "children of Mandarom". Several newspapers and magazines carried stories about the abused and sequestered "children of Mandarom". The Aumistes demurred that theirs was a religion for adults. The monastery housed celibate monks and nuns, all adults. Children were not eligible for initiation until they reached the age of 18. Minors were permitted to visit the premises during the festivals, but only if they were accompanied by their parents. Thus, children had never actually *lived* in the monastery.[23] Nevertheless, the rumor of the abused and disadvantaged children of Mandarom persisted.

Perhaps the most insidious example of this rumor appeared in a 1997 article in *L'Express* titled "The violinist recruiting children for Mandarom". It appears that what actually happened is that a 19-year-old violinist with the Monaco Philharmonic Orchestra was waiting for his rehearsal with a youth choir in a cathedral in Nice. He struck up a conversation with two teenagers, a brother and sister in the choir,

---

[21] Bruno Fouchereau, "Les sectes, cheval de Troie des Etats-Unis en Europe", *Le Monde Diplomatique*, May 2001, p. 1.

[22] Benjamin-Hugo Leblanc, "No Bad Sects in France!", *Religion in the News* 4, 3 (Fall 2001).

[23] Amory claimed that in the summer of 2007 they had 189 members attending the seminar, with 30 children and adolescents. ("When our spiritual master was here, we had 40 children.")

and spoke enthusiastically of his religion, Aumisme. He explained some of its symbols to the curious siblings and invited them to visit Mandarom sometime. The parents complained to the police, an investigation was launched, and the journalist presented the story as a sinister seduction, a brainwashing episode that was aborted to save the children. He insidiously implied that the violinist, who wasn't much older than the teens (referred to as "children" in the article) had homosexual designs.[24]

Mass Suicide at Mandarom

Another rumor predicted a mass suicide among the monks at Mandarom.[25] Two headlines, "French worry about Cosmic Christ" and "French officials are worried that another violent disaster may be in the making", are examples of how this rumor was taken up by the media. Between 1993 and 2000 the media carried many stories about how the Aumistes were planning a collective suicide.[26] The stories would begin by describing the OTS mass suicides in all their horror, and then announce, "Bourdin has come under public scrutiny as the man who reportedly exercises total control over his followers."

Several news reports tried to cram Mandarom into the OTS mould. Some claimed that OTS leader Luc Jouret "had contact" with the Knights of the Golden Lotus. The real story behind these rumours, according to V. Ekta, a former monk at Mandarom, is that in 1992 Luc Jouret came to St André, near Castellane, and directed a series of faxes and phone calls to His Holiness, seeking permission to attend the first ceremony of the building of the Pyramid Temple that was to take place on 20 August 1992. Permission was not granted, however, and Jouret was not on the list of guests (although he might well have been among the 1,200-odd summer visitors that toured Mandarom).

A second wave of suicide rumors circulated after the death of Hamsah Manarah in 1998. The police reinforced their surveillance over the Holy City for at least two weeks after his demise, and insisted on overseeing the group's meetings and

---

[24] François Koch, "Le violoniste recrutait des enfants pour le Mandarom", *L'Express* (20 February 1997).

[25] Suicide is explicitly forbidden in Aumisme (as in most religious traditions).

[26] "Un suicide collectif n'est pas exclu au Mandarom, selon d'anciennes adepts", *Le Provencale* (3 December 1995).

memorial services. When the Aumistes objected to these intrusions, the police explained, "there is a rumor that you may commit suicide, like the Solar Temple".[27]

The Aumistes tried to counter this rumor by putting a disclaimer on their website, "We will not commit suicide!", and cited the relevant passages from Hamsah Manarah's books. Dr Amory held a press conference on 8 January 1999 "to put an end to the rumor we were planning a mass suicide". She remarked, "I asked the media, 'Why do you say we are intending suicide? You can see it is against our religion.'" "Because we can sell newspapers!" one journalist replied frankly.

Rumors of Rape at Mandarom

In 1993 the first claims of rape and sexual misconduct laid against Mandarom's Messiah appeared in the French media.

A mysterious "Mme E" was interviewed in a 29 January 1993 article in *La Croix*. She claimed to be a former member who had been sexually exploited by Hamsah Manarah, and claimed he had solicited around a hundred women at Mandarom during his "*séances initiatiques*".

The Aumistes protested in a court document posted on their website that "Mme E" (they gave her real name) was merely a neighbor who had worked closely with Ferrato to oppose them.[28] Nevertheless, the theme of sexual misconduct at Mandarom resumed in a June 1993 television show, where journalist Bernard Nicolas interviewed "Mme E", her friend, and two unidentified young women (whose faces were in hidden in shadow). The Aumistes promptly unmasked them on their website as "Sylvie", the niece of "Mme E", and "Chloe", her friend.

After yet another stigmatizing TV talk show called *Mamies contre gourous* was aired, the Aumistes decided to stage a protest demonstration. They congregated on 22 December 1994 in front of the France 2 network offices, but all 120 of them were promptly arrested and the demonstration aborted.

On 24 January 1995, the day of the second (tax) raid on Mandarom, by 1 p.m. the journalist Bernard Nicolas appeared on TF1 with two fresh *soi-disant* victims –

---

[27] Interview with V. Ekta, April 2001.
[28] *Memoire en défense de Me A. Beraud dans le cadre de l'instruction menée contre l'Instructeur Spirituel de Mandarom* (unpublished manuscript), 1997.

the two Roncaglia sisters. Florence Roncaglia claimed she had been raped several times by the "Lord of Mandarom", first as a teen in 1984–1985, while her mother, a devout Aumiste, was staying in Mandarom. The sisters spoke in hushed tones of "Le Seigneur de Mandarom", their faces plunged in shadow.

Raids, Detentions and Detonations – Draconian Measures of Social Control

In the short history of Mandarom, one finds an extraordinary level of conflict – conflict that was one-sided, for the Aumistes, while they interpreted the conflict within their apocalyptic worldview, reacted with prudence, consistently resorting to legal measures of self-defense and protest. To a great extent this was due to the influence of Dr Christine Amory, whose spiritual name is Vedhyas Vishti. She is the administrative leader of Mandarom and President of the AVT. She also happens to be a geologist and researcher who was on the list of "100 Most Distinguished Frenchmen" in 2001. With her public relations team at Mandarom, and in consultation with its bishops, she has directed an effective self-defensive battle against the French media and UNADFI.

Mandarom was the target of three police and military raids. The pretext for the first raid, on 25 November 1994, was to inspect the temples and statues for violation of the civil planning code. No violations were found, however, and they left uneventfully.

The second raid was more dramatic. Its rationale was to investigate tax fraud. On 24 January 1995, 20 tax officials and 100 gendarmes stormed the monastery, while roads were blocked and helicopters hovered overhead. The police searched every room and seized documents and other items. No weapons were found. A simultaneous *perquisition* was conducted on the Paris apartment of Christine Amory.

The purpose of the third raid, launched on 12 June 1995, was to arrest Hamsah Manarah in response to allegations of rape that had been broadcast through the mass media since 1993. The journalist Bernard Nicolas, Robert Ferrato, and the UNADFI officials had all supported Florence Roncaglia's rape story. Together they contacted the gendarmerie at Var and filed a complaint. But because the police were slow to react, Florence decided to turn to the media. Her strategy succeeded, for it appeared that the sensational media reports finally spurred the police to launch a raid. Also, Roncaglia co-authored a 1995 book, *Mandarom: Une Victime Temoigne*, with the journalist Nicolas, who had become her boyfriend. In this she described her alleged rape, among other crimes allegedly occurring at Mandarom.[29]

The Aumistes claim that as a direct result of Roncaglia's testimony, Judge Yves Bonnet ordered the arrest of their Spiritual Master and 26 disciples on 12 June 1995. They complained that several of those arrested for complicity in the alleged rape had not even been members at the time.

The mass media made much of the rape story and the 12 June 1995 raid. A television crew arrived at 6 a.m. on that fateful morning, ready for action, and filmed the unique architecture and statuary – images that once again adorned every TV show, magazine, and newspaper in France. Bernard Nicolas, Florence Roncaglia's boyfriend and co-author, was poised with his camera crew as Hamsah Manarah was dragged out of his Lotus Temple in handcuffs and taken away by the gendarmes in a police car.[30]

The Delcourt couple reappeared in a talk show hosted by Mireille Dumas, which showed footage of Hamsah Manarah being arrested. They changed their story this time, complaining not only of separation from their granddaughter, but about the sexual abuse she had allegedly endured. The Aumistes sued them and won, and won again on appeal. No newspaper or TV show carried the story of the Aumistes' legal triumph.

The Magical Tattoos

Bourdin was released from prison after 18 days, on 30 June 1995. At his hearing, the Aumistes argued in their Lord's defence that Roncaglia was an "*ancienne prostituée*", hence an unreliable witness. Moreover, she did not know the exact dates or the places where she was allegedly raped. But, most importantly, she knew nothing about the magical tattoos that covered the torso of Hamsah Manarah.

---

[29] Florence Roncaglia and Bernard Nicolas, *Mandarom: Une Victime Temoigne* (Paris, 1995).

[30] *Memoire en defense de Me A. Beraud.*

Hamsah Manarah had demanded the right to question his accuser face to face in court. In this he was referring to an ancient code of law in France that goes back to the Middle Ages. When he asked Florence if she had seen his naked body at the time of the alleged rape, she replied, "Yes." Then he asked her if she had noticed any distinguishing marks on his body at the time. She said, "No, it was normal like any other man." Then Hamsah Manarah slowly stood up in the court room and cast off the coverings of his upper body – revealing garish, writhing tattoos of arcane symbols that covered every inch of his chest, belly, back, and shoulders. The court was stunned. There was a long silence. Roncaglia's credibility was now seriously in question, and Hamsah Manarah was soon released on bail. *Paris Match* commented: "Bourdin may not have been guilty of the rape of young girls, but he was certainly guilty of having raped a mountain."[31]

After his release was ordered, the prosecution launched an appeal, and on 13 September 1995 the Court of Appeal of Aix en Provence requested a million francs bail. Hamsah Manarah was never actually tried, and the rape charges were never formally resolved, so he lived for the rest of his life under an unpleasant miasma of suspicion. His rights of free movement and travel were curtailed, and he was kept under close surveillance. It is perhaps significant that the rape charges were filed just one day before the statute of limitations on the building of the Pyramid Temple was to expire. This timely raid had delayed the decision of the *Conseil d'État* regarding the Aumistes' appeal of the December 1994 decision to cancel the permit for the Temple by the Court of Appeals in Lyon.

The Death of Hamsah Manarah

On 19 March 1998 Gilbert Bourdin died of diabetes in the hospital at Grasse. Under French law, Bourdin, as a French citizen, was eligible for burial at Mandarom, but on 24 March 1998 the Mayor of Castellane and the Prefect of the Alpes de Haute-Provence denied permission for burial there, on the grounds that it posed a "threat to the public order".

The disciples then applied to bury their Master's body at the nearby town of Grasse, since Hamsah Manarah had made it clear he did not want to be buried

---

[31] Quoted in Introvigne, "Holy Mountains," p. 26.

in either of the two cemeteries near Mandarom, Castellane or La Baume. But permission for burial in Grasse was denied by the prefect Jean-Pierre Leleux. At that point, the Aumistes' funeral procession turned towards the Castellane cemetery.

But the mayor of Castellane had organized around 200 local citizens in a march to protest against the burial, so the funeral procession of Aumistes headed home towards Mandarom. When they neared the road leading up the mountain, outside the town of Castellane, they encountered a police blockade and a swarm of journalists. The event was eagerly televised, and M. Delcourt stood weeping for his absent granddaughter in front of the cameras.

Finally, on 6 April 1998 this ambiguous situation was resolved. An "Operation Omega" was launched, whereby 120 policemen seized the body and escorted it to an abandoned graveyard that was used as an ossuary, where the remains of Hamsah Manarah were "forcibly buried" (in the words of an Aumiste nun). The site was within a military zone which restricts access to civilians, and the grave was unmarked and covered with 700 pounds of reinforced concrete so that it could not be dug up again by devotees or by enemies.

For the Aumistes, their spiritual master's funeral required a long ceremony lasting several days, but the authorities interfered with the process. When the weeping monks and nuns finally returned to Mandarom after their distressing week of ordeals (the constant turning away of the funeral cortège and the ignominious disposal of their Master's body) and began to conduct their memorial service, the police kept them under close surveillance. Once, the police burst into the room, disrupting an important ritual, and threatened to arrest them for "planning a mass suicide".[32]

In January 2000, two years after Bourdin's death, two women, Florence Roncaglia and Francine Grad, were awarded damages from the Victim's Compensation Commission – despite the fact that Bourdin had never gone to trial for his alleged rapes.

---

[32] Interview with V. Ekta.

The Destruction of the Statue of the Cosmoplanetary Messiah

Since 1993, the French authorities had repeatedly challenged the validity of the building permit of the Statue of the Cosmoplanetary Messiah. The Aumistes claim that a building permit was issued on 11 July 1990, and that in 1992 they also received a certificate of compliance that reaffirmed the permit's validity.

On 30 August 1990, Robert Ferrato filed a request before the Tribunal de Grande Instance in Digne, on behalf of the Association for the Protection of the Lakes and Sites of the Verdon, that the statue be dismantled. A long-drawn-out legal battle ensued. An investigation was opened by the judges Yves Bonnet and Bernard Frery. They concluded that all the constructions had legal permits, except for the statue of the Cosmoplanetary Messiah. The President of the Association of the Knights of the Golden Lotus was ordered to pay fines and to dismantle the statue.

In June 2001, the prefect of Les Alpes de Haute-Provence asked for authorization to invade Mandarom and proceed with the demolition. On 6 July 2001 the tribunal authorized this action. On 17 August 2001 the Aumistes applied for an extension at the court of appeal. The hearing was rescheduled for 10 September, but the prefect did not wait. On 5 September 2001 the prefect paid a surprise visit, invading the monastery with 200 French army soldiers. They arrived at 6 a.m. accompanied by journalists, and during the next 48 hours the whole world watched the preparations for the detonation. The following morning at 5:20 a.m. the statue exploded and toppled down the side of the mountain. The face of the Cosmoplanetary Messiah, which bore an obvious resemblance to Hamsah Manarah, fell to the ground intact, so the army pulverized it with a shovel.

According to an Aumiste bishop, the statue was "a crucial pillar … in the world's invisible architecture. Its destruction represents a choice by humanity against the Light of the Golden Age, heralding great destruction and cataclysms in the coming years!"[33]

An Aumiste nun who witnessed the event at first hand said, "The statue of our Master had a symbolic role of utmost importance for Aumistes. It symbolized the preservation of world peace and the spiritual evolution of humanity and the

---

[33] Interview with an Aumiste, Jean-Marc Jacot, at Mandarom, May 2002.

unity of all religions." She compared the event to the destruction of the Bamiyan Buddhas in Afghanistan by the Taliban in the same year.

The Pyramid Temple

The Aumistes are still struggling to obtain a permit to construct their final Pyramid Temple, the last temple that is needed in order to usher in the Golden Age. The media have followed their battle for the temple closely: "Mandarom: les Aumistes résistent" (*France Soir*, 22 November 2000); "Mandarom: la secte demande un nouveau permis de constriure" (*La Marseillaise*, 2 February 2000).

This failure to construct the pyramid poses a serious impediment to the Aumistes' millennial expectations. In 2000 they responded by dissolving the Cultural Association of the Pyramid Temple and the Knights of the Golden Lotus. They then formed the new "Association of the Triumphant Vajra" to replace these former associations, and were thus able to reapply for permission. As V. Vishti, the administrative leader of Aumisme, explained:

> We have 100 years to succeed in ushering in the Golden Age. The first ten years (1990–2000) is the age of judgment, then 100 years of transition (2000–2100) then 2100–3100, 1,000 years of confirmation of the Golden Age. But we must build the Pyramid Temple as soon as possible. If not there will be a disaster (although there is no specific date). We just applied for a building permit for the fifth time.[34]

Aumisme's Legal Response to Persecution

When I visited Mandarom in June 2001, Dr Amory showed me three large cupboards filled with news reports, legal documents, and *droit de réponse* letters, all carefully catalogued and dated. The Aumistes have been vigilant in monitoring the news for defamatory articles and radio or TV shows. They found "several hundred" in 1995, a hundred in 1996, and fifty in 1997. They have defended

---

[34] Interview with Dr. Christine Amory, February 27, 2006.

their faith through a vigorous campaign of sending out letters of protest. Since 1998 they have sent fewer letters because they can broadcast their protests more effectively via the internet.[35]

This bureaucratic response eventually met with some success. The media finally realized it was counterproductive and expensive to defame Mandarom, and the Aumistes' deviant status ended when they won recognition as a *culte*.

Conclusion

After reviewing the Aumiste's controversial history, one might ask, "What are the roots of the pervasive hostility towards Mandarom that is reflected in France's media reports?"

There appears to be nothing particularly threatening or harmful in the Aumiste religion itself. Its message is one of peace, higher consciousness, tolerance of diversity, and the unity of all faiths. The monks and nuns living at Mandarom are tranquil vegetarians, celibate and physically fit (they practice yoga daily) – and they are all adults. They are multiracial, their head administrator is a woman, they do not hoard weapons or reject orthodox medicine. So what caused the conflict?

There were several factors. First, Mandarom was situated in a country where the public display of religious symbols is strictly taboo in accordance with the law of 1905. Thus, it is perhaps not surprising that Mandarom's blatantly religious architecture, the monks' liturgical vestments and its elaborate rituals (chanting, prayer wheels, incense, mandalas, drums) affronted France's secular sensibilities. One might see the opposition on the part of the French authorities towards Mandarom as a reaction to the group's flagrant display of alien religious symbols, or as a "gut response" aesthetic revulsion to Mandarom's pious folk art.

But another answer lies in the modus operandi of the media itself. The media, commercially driven to sell entertaining stories, exploited the public's xenophobia regarding *les sectes*, and assisted anticult activists in creating a strong climate of intolerance. Then all the journalists had to do was to sit back and document the spectacular battle that ensued, as the Aumistes fought through legal means to defend their faith and rights as citizens of *La République*. Journalists pride

---

[35] *Circulaire Mandarom Shambalasalem*, January 2001.

themselves on being objective reporters of controversy, "just doing their job". But there is ample evidence that journalists were active participants in, and even at times instigators of, the conflict. Thus Mandarom's troubles were at times caused by, and certainly shaped by, the biased, exaggerated, and blatantly mendacious news reports that fueled national prejudice and public misunderstanding – reports that pressured the local authorities and police to exert disciplinary control over a "*secte dangereuse*".

The Future of Mandarom

At its peak the Aumiste religion numbered 50 resident monks and nuns at Mandarom, and had around 2,000 members throughout the rest of France. Today, in 2007, only four hundred Knights of the Vajra Triumphant are left in France, I was told.[36]

According to Aumistes I interviewed, there were two waves of defection. The first occurred in the wake of the OTS mass suicides in 1994 and the appearance of the Guyard Commission's list of *sectes* in 1996. Around eight hundred left initially, discouraged by job losses and constant *perquisitions*. The second wave of defections occurred right after the death of the founder. "In March 1998, after the death of Our Master, around five hundred left, because they wanted to be with a living master", an Aumist explained.[37]

Today, the future of Aumisme is uncertain. While the Chevaliers (most of them retired or senior citizens) continue to enact their elaborate rituals at Mandarom, to find solace, ethical guidance, and mystical inspiration in the teachings of Hamsah Manarah, it remains to be seen whether or not a new generation will continue the tradition. Dr. Amory summed up Mandarom's decade of intense persecution as follows:

---

[36] Dr Amory claimed that "after the destruction of the statue, no one leaves. Today we have around five hundred, 10 are bishops, 129 are priests, and the rest are members who go to the centroms and around ten thousand fidels who attend our collective prayer. Only around ten full-time monastics live today at Mandarom. There are around a thousand associate members outside France, associated with the centroms in Africa, Quebec, USA, Germany, Italy, Belgium, Switzerland." (Interview with Dr Amory in Paris, 7 October 2007.)

[37] Interview with Christine Amory in Paris, 7 October 2007.

It was very hard on us – because we have the feeling they are out to destroy our Master. First they attack his honor by accusing him of rape. Then they attack his body by arresting him and holding him in prison for over two weeks. Then, when he dies they refuse to let him be buried in a tomb. Then they try to destroy his mission by opposing the Pyramid Temple and detonating the statue. Then they expect Mandarom will disappear ... But now they are surprised, because we are still here!

Chapter 3

Henpecked to Heaven? My Life in a Brahma Kumaris Retreat Center

Neville Hodgkinson

Life took a fateful turn for me in July 1994, when I joined a 20-strong group of spiritual aspirants running a newly opened retreat center a few miles south of Oxford, in the UK. I was aged 50, and over the previous 25 years had lived, worked, and raised a family in London. My marriage had finished some six years previously but I had continued in full-time, high-profile journalism, my profession for 30 years. The move to the retreat center was to become probably the biggest challenge I have faced.

Life in community is a house of mirrors, relentlessly reflecting your character, and in particular your weaknesses. It has been immensely demanding at times. The transition from the heart of affairs in London to a fledgling spiritual community in rural Oxfordshire was quite extreme and there have been occasions when I longed for a return to normal life. But I am still there, and enormously glad that I stayed. I have learned so much – not in the sense of information, but of an inner strength that brings joy by virtue of one's being, rather than from what one does or knows.

The retreat center is thriving. The number of residents has grown to more than 30 and the house, a stately home built in the mid eighteenth century, now hosts about 15,000 guests a year. Many are visitors attending one-day retreats, open days (the house is set in 55 acres of parkland), or evening classes in meditation, positive thinking, stress management and the like, but we also have residential retreats throughout the year with up to 100 guests at a time.

All services, including cooking, cleaning, administration, maintenance of the house and gardens, and teaching, are provided by volunteers. This makes it possible to use contributions to maximum effect and the house is kept in first-class condition. The gardens, a jungle when we arrived, are also now in good shape, and in 2012 more than 4,000 people visited during two successive open afternoons which we called "Peace in the Park". English Heritage, the body responsible for protecting and promoting England's historic environment, seems happy both with the transformation of the property and the rich use to which it is being put.

Those of us who have now shared this life together over a long period feel a substantial sense of attainment. Most of us have been through tough times but, like army buddies who have seen action together, we have developed a strong sense of camaraderie and unity.

Women Hold the Leading Roles

The retreat center is run by the Brahma Kumaris World Spiritual University (BKs), an international spiritual training organization that may be unique in being headed by women. The founder was a man, a jeweler named Lekhraj Kirpalani, but it was part of his inspiration from the beginning that women should hold the leading roles. I have been a regular student with this group since 1981, and have greatly appreciated the feminine quality of the leadership, in which love and cooperation are valued more highly than individualistic goals. Although men have played increasingly central roles as the organization has expanded, women are still kept to the fore as the main teachers, and ultimate arbiters of key decisions.

This gender bias is believed to offer particular opportunities for spiritual advancement in the communal setting. The idea is that it helps women to overcome any culturally acquired timidity as they rise to the challenges and responsibilities of leadership, whilst men are assisted in the development of humility. That is the theory, and to a considerable extent it does become practical. Certainly, timidity is not a characteristic of most of the women I have encountered within the organization as it operates today. Humility does seem to be quite a long time coming among most brothers, including me, but we are all definitely moving in the right direction.

Kirpalani came from Hyderabad in the Sindh province of northern India (part of Pakistan after the partition of India). He had a successful jewelry business, based in Kolkata. In the mid 1930s, when he was in his fifties, he experienced a series of visions in which he foresaw that a golden age for humanity was approaching, but that it would be preceded by a period of upheaval and destruction. He experienced his own eternal, spiritual identity very powerfully, and became convinced that he was being called to start a movement for global spiritual renewal, to ease the passage of the human family through the calamities that lay ahead. Understanding and experience of the higher self, the soul, would free us of the suffering linked to body-consciousness – our over-identification with the physical dimension. It would also enable us to help restore the pure consciousness needed to bring about an age of truth, in which the positive qualities intrinsic to our humanity would be fully expressed.

Kirpalani sold his business, left behind his worldly identity, and took on the name Prajapita (World Father) Brahma, or Brahma Baba. His understanding was that like the heroic Arjuna of the *Mahabharata*, India's most famous scripture, he was being led into a mighty battle through which God would restore order and righteousness in human affairs. The battle was an internal one, involving a shift of consciousness, but it would culminate in the disappearance of this entire old world in order to make way for a fresh start for humanity.

This body of knowledge emerged and took shape in the 1930s and 1940s. During this founding period Brahma Baba, his immediate worldly family, and around 400 women, with a handful of men in support, went into 14 years of isolation. The millenarian character of the teachings, along with an insistence that God was asking these daughters and mothers to remain unmarried or become celibate, even within marriage, challenged the authority of fathers and husbands, and of community and religious leaders.

An enormous row blew up and, persecuted and ostracized, the group moved in 1939 from Hyderabad to Karachi, where they established what was, in effect, a closed order. Brahma Baba gave his entire wealth in trust to the movement and a few other families did the same, making it possible for their total focus to be on freeing the spirit – practicing soul-consciousness, and regaining spiritual strength through dying completely to their former lives and relationships. They felt they were living in the lap of God. Local Moslem politicians recognized the purity of the movement and helped them find space to continue in safety, despite efforts by the Hindu leaders to have them closed down.

In 1950, with resources running low, the community moved to Mt Abu, Rajasthan, and from there began to carry the teachings across India. Thousands responded, despite continuing controversies, and today the organization has around one million regular students and is held in high regard within India. Madhuban ("Forest of Honey"), the Mt Abu headquarters, has grown enormously in the 30 years since I first visited it and now hosts gatherings of up to 25,000 at a time. The teachings, described as a form of Raja Yoga, have been adapted to make them more accessible to people leading regular lives and most practitioners now undertake the spiritual journey *in situ*, staying with their families and jobs.

Recreating Intensity of Early Days

Retreat centers, however, have played a prominent part in the movement's work outside India and provide an opportunity to experience some of the intensity of the early days. They have been the particular inspiration of Dadi ("Elder Sister") Janki, one of the founding sisters, who came to England in 1974, a few years after Brahma Baba died, to share the teachings within the UK and across the globe. She has overseen the expansion of the organization into 130 countries. She has been based back in India since 2007, when – at the age of 91 – she became the overall administrative head.

The Oxford facility, known as the Global Retreat Centre, opened in the summer of 1993. I was invited to join at that time but was caught up in a big journalistic controversy, which meant that my departure from the newspaper was delayed by a year. When I finally arrived, in July 1994, I soon found that a kind of civil war was going on. A middle-aged couple who had been given the keys of the house when it was first acquired had overseen its renovation over a six-month period, working with a few other western volunteers as well as professional contractors. But then came the arrival of what that first group called "the white sari brigade" – a group of Indian sisters, the toughest of whom soon made it plain that they saw themselves as the spiritual authorities and intended to take charge. What's more, they had the ear of Dadi Janki, the real authority.

The war was quite short-lived, but there were casualties. Some left the retreat center immediately; others limped on for a while, then moved to other roles within the organization; others quit the Brahma Kumaris altogether.

Looking back, I consider it great good fortune that I missed that first year, as it might have been too much for me. As it was, I had a huge shock on joining the retreat center family in July 1994, because of the state of relationships there. At that point, I had already been practicing for nearly 14 years the meditation and spiritual study taught by the BKs. But for half that time I had still been with my wife and children, and for the other half, with the children grown up and my marriage ended, I had lived alone in a flat in central London, putting most of my energy into journalism. My exposure to the BK community had been mainly confined to formal class settings. Despite having found joy in the teachings and in exploring relationships with my new-found extended family, my understanding was limited, and tended to be theoretical rather than practical.

Hence my amazement at the power struggles, slanging matches, insecurities, tears, recriminations and exhaustion that I found at the retreat center. Sometimes these were quite funny, as tough, pint-sized sisters faced down brawny brothers, the brothers responding to their defeat with self-effacing humor. But it did seem to me at times as if almost everyone was slightly mad, compared with the world I had come from.

The insecurity caused most of us to behave badly. I remember acutely the fear I used to feel in passing the reception desk of the main building, as I was liable to be asked – usually just as I thought I had gone by safely – where I was going. I felt as though I was in a prison. One day, unjustly accused by the "receptionist from hell" of some misdemeanor, I exploded in anger, telling her that she should get her act together. This happened in front of some guests. Later I received a note from the young woman involved, telling me that she hated me, and that I was old enough to be the one who should have his act together.

That must have been about 15 or 16 years ago. The sister survived those difficult times, and is today a yogi of strength and maturity, a pillar of the retreat center who helps many others through her kindness, honesty, and perceptiveness.

Another early story engraved in my memory took place one winter's evening, when I was sitting in a classroom with a visitor. I had forgotten to ask for the room to be heated, the required procedure. There was a two-bar electric fire, so I switched on one of the bars and we sat huddled around it. After an hour, a brother with responsibility for heating looked into the room. He asked me who had given me permission to use the fire. The next day, both bars were removed.

Understanding and Appreciating Men

Despite incidents like that, community life has greatly increased my appreciation of men. In childhood, I grew up with two sisters and a rather distant father, and although I attended a boys' school and had one or two close friends, always felt it somewhat of a struggle to understand and relate to masculinity. That sense of mystery has now gone. I have found that generally men are more fun than women, more ready for adventure, and more ready to challenge authority (although that might be specific to this woman-led organization). Women do tend to be sweeter, gentler, more considerate and homely, and less ego-based. But I have found to my surprise that men really are much softer than they try to put out. In fact it's my experience that brothers with the biggest bodies are even more likely to dissolve into tears of hurt or frustration than those who are weaker physically. It all goes to show that under the skin, male or female, big or small, white or black or brown, we share a common humanity and common needs.

Another gift I have received is an understanding of the joys of football. Somehow, this passed me by in my schooldays, when I tended towards lone activities such as distance running. I found that I loved learning to play with my spiritual brothers. Although I was next to useless, it was hugely entertaining to join in. Volleyball was another novel experience for me. Sport can be a great way of learning about one another's specialities. It also offers quick-fire tests of emotional and spiritual capacities, such as cooperation, team spirit, and equanimity in success or failure – the ability to move on regardless. Nowadays, football games are less frequent and I never join them because, in my late sixties, injuries tend to be slow to heal. But I am pleased to have learned more about a game that plays such an important part in the lives of so many.

I also found it reassuring to discover that even after quite hard knocks, the body does not break easily. I was shoulder-charged in one of the first games I played, and it took six months for a cracked rib to heal completely. But that was the worst injury I received and it seemed a small price to pay for the fun we had.

Once, the sister in charge of the retreat center – known by some as the Commander – had threatened to ban football because injuries were taking too big a toll, putting brothers out of action so that they could not fulfill their duties for a while. I had nevertheless joined a game, and was trying to tackle a young player from behind when he threw his head back, hitting me on the forehead above an eye and briefly knocking me out. I was fine, but the big concern was that if I developed a black eye, the ban might be implemented. That night I skulked in the background, but by the next morning had a huge shiner. In our morning class, I sat towards the back but the Commander suddenly appeared to be trying to stifle a fit of laughter. Eventually she burst out, "Neville's got a black eye!"

Despite good times, the tensions present during the early days of the retreat center tested Dadi Janki beyond the limits of her patience and tolerance. I remember complaining to her on one of her visits that she was making matters worse by berating the community over its failings, even though these were apparent to all of us – often, I am sorry to say, including our guests. She has learned, too, and today gives much more carrot than stick in her leadership style.

Mostly, however, the way she steered us through those troubled early days was exemplary, which I think is why we survived and thrived. She never lost sight of her vision that each one of us had the truth of our original, peaceful nature within us, however distorted it might have become by the selfishness and ignorance associated with body-consciousness. She held fast to the idea that one day, as our spiritual consciousness grew stronger, we would become a "mini-Madhuban", an oasis of peace in a troubled world. Gradually, that vision has taken practical form.

Early Feelings of Disempowerment

Compared with the self-determining life I had led previously, I felt immensely disempowered in my early years in the community. This was partly because a year before joining the retreat center I had "surrendered" most of my wealth to the organization. I had decided that I wanted and needed to pursue the journey of spiritual improvement more wholeheartedly than I had managed up to that point. But my head was in front of my heart in this regard. It would take some years before I would realize that true surrender requires a much deeper form of renunciation. In fact, I have learned that for some, true surrender can take place without the need for any change in physical circumstances.

Feelings of loss also arose because the move to Oxford finally put a physical distance between me and my ex-wife, with whom I had remained on good terms after our separation and divorce and who was still important to me internally. It was now being brought home to me that my family days, which I had treasured, really were over.

But the most immediate source of my frustration was that whereas just about everyone else seemed to have some area of authority – whether it was in the reception, servery, kitchen, administration, teaching, heating, cleaning, maintenance, gardens, etc. – I had no well-defined role. Hence, although everyone else – sisters especially – seemed to boss me around, I had no one to whom I could return the favor.

I had an office, where I could pursue various forms of study and writing, producing a few books, and from which I would gradually become more and more involved in BK matters worldwide. I did also try to maintain certain journalistic involvements, though fate was to make me increasingly isolated in this regard as well, with eventual almost total loss of my professional identity.

But as far as the life of the community was concerned, I felt for years something of an odd-man-out. I did occasional mopping and washing up, sat at the reception desk, and tried to make myself useful in the garden. None of these roles felt right for me, even though for others they have brought about great advancement spiritually, as well as being of obvious practical value. We have a large wood-burning stove in one of the main rooms, and in the winter months it is my job to look after that, bringing in the logs and cleaning out the ashes. This is a job for which I volunteered myself, as a condition from the head of cleaning for installing the stove, as she was worried that it would create extra work for her team. But when after several years I was awarded my first official household appointment, in charge of cleaning the men's public toilets, I lasted less than three months in the role.

Looking back, I think the lesson from this sense of isolation has been that I was stubbornly resisting the loss of the everyday features of family life. As it has now evolved, my role includes participating in a wide range of the spiritual university's activities globally. My professional background equips me for this, but it took time before my spiritual stage had become strong enough for me to stop fretting about what I had lost, and start to make the most of the new opportunities that have opened up.

Dadi Janki was relentless in refusing to allow us to complain about others, no matter how justified the complaints might be. If we went to her in an angry or upset state, she would insist that we put ourselves right rather than point the finger at others. Probably because of feeling so disempowered, this policy was agonizing for me at times. The habit of blaming others for our suffering runs very deep. Eventually I realized that whenever I am reacting strongly to another, it is because their behavior mirrors some weakness that still needs to be addressed in me. This is a deep spiritual principle which, once grasped, brings a remarkable change of trajectory in life, in which our character really does start to improve.

One other demanding aspect of my relationship with Dadi Janki in particular has been her repeated call to me to "think less". This comes hard to intellectually oriented Europeans who have seen the horrible consequences of blind obedience to authority perhaps more than any other people over the past century. Gradually, however, I have understood that there is a way of being in which much more wisdom and understanding becomes available to us when we quieten our thoughts, than when we habitually worry at problems.

Celibacy Contributes to Atmosphere of Peace

Today, we really do have a strong community at Oxford, men and women from a wide range of nationalities and backgrounds living together with love and respect. We find happiness in contributing, in our varied ways, to an atmosphere of peace within which our guests can be refreshed, and take away some spiritual skills that will help them in everyday life. Of course, we are all still human, in the sense that we continue to irritate or upset each other on occasions. But the atmosphere is immeasurably improved and guests frequently comment on its almost tangible positive quality. Sometimes they say they feel it even as they drive towards the house from the main road.

Another main factor contributing to this success is the avoidance of physical intimacy. Sex lust is considered the biggest enemy of our ability to maintain awareness of our spiritual identity. It is not just the intensity of the physical impulse, but the way it can give rise to a complex of other thoughts and feelings. These include strong personal attachments, for example, as well as tendencies towards trying to manipulate others, either through being excessively controlling, or through dependency and "people-pleasing". Such tendencies interfere directly and immediately with the aim to become a constant "yogi", a soul linked in love with the Supreme. The deep peace intrinsic to this divine relationship is the central, healing, empowering and – at its best – blissful experience within the spiritual journey.

So, as a group of men and women of all ages, living under one roof, we have found it practical to live with certain precautions against igniting emotional dependency or sexual desire. When dining, for example, the resident brothers sit in one area and the sisters in another, although there is also a "neutral" area which can be of mixed sex if necessary. When we have a houseful of BK guests, we have separate dining rooms for the brothers and sisters. For regular guests, who are not BKs, no such requirement is made, though we do point out that abstinence from sex is one of the disciplines of the house and ask visitors to bear this in mind in their dress and behavior.

My own experience, from the start of my spiritual journey, has been that this discipline is a most beautiful one. It facilitates an ease and lightness in relationships that I value enormously, enabling us to live with a kind of sweet simplicity. It frees us from the "games" that so often otherwise color relationships between the sexes.

I have learned that the sex drive is not a necessity, like eating. Rather, it is a habit, which I now see as a kind of substitute for the happiness that comes with knowing the truth about our eternal spiritual identity. The sexual impulse fades when we become free of the over-identification with the body and limited personality, and experience instead the joy of knowing the higher self in relationship with God. I believe now that one reason why sex seems so important in many people's lives is that it can give a taste of self-transcendence, but this is fleeting and insignificant compared with the experience of union with the divine.

Conversely, the impulse can return when the thought complexes associated with body-consciousness reassert themselves, such as an inflated sense of self-importance, or the anger or unhappiness that can come when the ego takes repeated knocks. At such times, the temptation to indulge in sexual arousal as a means of temporary escape or comfort can re-emerge. When such tendencies fire up, I have learned that guilt only makes matters worse. Rather, the requirement is to identify the emotional need that these old longings signal, and find a spiritual solution.

Finding Spiritual Solutions

Much of the body of knowledge with which the spiritual university works is aimed at guarding against such tendencies, and providing solutions. Learning to inculcate spiritual self-respect, for example, helps to counter the distortions in our perception and behavior created by the narrow sense of self, the hungry ego. When we truly understand and experience ourselves as souls (units of consciousness, in the more scientific language that some theorists use) distinct from the body and the roles we play on the stage of the world, and that in this eternal, timeless sense we really are one family under God, we automatically fill with a power of truth that acts like a force field protecting against negative, selfish impulses, whether from within ourselves or others.

We learn that whilst it is in the nature of the physical world to be in a state of constant flux, souls have an identity that transcends time and space. When we over-identify with our physical selves, we suffer repeatedly, as circumstances change. This suffering is not a natural and necessary part of life, but a consequence of our "fallen" state of awareness. Through renewed understanding and experience of our original spiritual identity, we free ourselves of the unhappiness and neediness that have become so widespread and become more accepting of that which "comes to pass".

We regain the freedom and strength to be still internally, and in that stillness we know the Source from which we understand ourselves to have originated. When we direct our thoughts and feelings repeatedly towards God in this way, we fill with such peace as to enable us to see more clearly what is going on around us, and how we can best help.

I have gradually understood and accepted that as well as bringing about this life-enhancing change of outlook, the teachings may offer a more accurate description of reality than the determinedly materialistic scientific world view to which I used to subscribe. Has this faith developed because the teachings have helped my own life so much? Are the ideas a kind of scaffolding, supporting the building of a new structure of thought and feeling, but liable to fall away once the new building is in place?

Frontier thinking in science suggests there is more to it than that. A case is emerging in the fields of theoretical physics, biology, and even psychology that turns upside down the conventional view of mind as an outcome of eons of evolutionary development. The new thinking argues instead that mind is primary, the ground of everything that is. An informational, purposive, non-material matrix, of which the individual soul forms a part, provides a template that gives rise to the material world and the drama of our existence within it. In a sense, the spiritual dimension is more real than the material world.

I can say with certainty that year by year, more and more of the materialistic beliefs once dear to me have fallen away, to be replaced by what I believe to be a deeper understanding. This shift has been accompanied by a big reduction in tension, and a huge increase in peace, happiness, and love. But not all those with whom I have shared the journey have had the same experience. Some have loved the knowledge deeply for a while, only to conclude, sometimes after many years, that they had been deluded.

Retreat Centers Established in Several Countries

In India, the BKs have grown rapidly over recent years and now have more than eight thousand centers across the country, staffed by an unpaid army of highly trained meditation teachers, almost all of them women. Service also takes place on a huge scale through a variety of specialized wings, offering programs in moral and spiritual values to different professional groups. The movement is now socially respectable in India. Honorary doctorates have been awarded to founding sisters. A postage stamp commemorating Brahma Baba's life and achievements was released in 1994, marking the 25th anniversary of his death.

Internationally, the number of regular students remains relatively small – probably a total of about 15,000 – even though there is now a presence in 130 countries. But through the lectures and courses offered globally, and through the retreat centers now established in several countries, the spiritual university's social impact is much greater than the number of regular BKs would suggest, with hundreds of thousands receiving benefit. BKs also contribute actively to the work of the United Nations, as a non-governmental organization affiliated to the Department of Public Information and in general consultative status with the Economic and Social Council.

Some controversies remain. The core teachings are still radical, insisting that we are at a turning point within a repeating cycle of time in which the need is to detach, internally, from this tired old world. Paradoxically, this detachment makes it easier to live with love rather than ego, selfishness, and greed. But whilst seeking to support others spiritually, and to fulfill family and social responsibilities, the goal is not to sustain this present world. Rather, it is to restore in ourselves, through the power of remembrance of God, the pure consciousness that is a prerequisite for a return to a golden age of humanity, of heaven on earth. This is an uncompromising aim. As described above, it can prove profoundly challenging for as long as our consciousness remains bound to mundane values, and the identities inherent in our limited roles. Constant vigilance is needed to ensure that one's intellect is holding the wider picture, and that one's mind stays linked in loving relationship with the Supreme.

Sometimes, when the power of this relationship has been deeply experienced but then fades, it is as though mundane ways of thinking return and reassert themselves with a vengeance – literally. Having tasted the sublime, and then lost it, there can be bitterness and anger, and a temptation to blame. My experience is that this can happen to almost anyone on this spiritual journey. Some are lucky enough to come through such dark patches. Others move away and get on with their lives in a different way. Still others remain stuck in criticism and regrets.

It is not that the institution is above criticism – far from it. It is made up of people who as a group are, to my mind, exceptionally well-intentioned, but all are learning. When the teachings were first brought to countries outside India, some sisters thought westerners were filled with arrogance and must be made to follow strict disciplines if they were ever to accept the ideas and practices, and make progress. The sisters may not have realized that though the arrogance is there, it hides great insecurity.

Although I value enormously the shift in understanding and outlook that has taken place in me, I believe now that our first need is for a reminder of our highest potential in terms of kindness and wisdom – an education for the heart, as Dadi Janki puts it. At their best, that is what the Brahma Kumaris provide.

Chapter 4

Realizing the Guru's Intention: Hungry Humans and Awkward Animals in a New Kadampa Tradition Community[1]

Carol McQuire

Mexico City, 1994

I had been praying to find a spiritual path. I'd spent 18 years as a professional musician in Mexico but life had become complicated and painful; my relationship was breaking down and as I had a young child it was difficult to work. On the desk of a friend in her "eco-house" on a mountain was *Joyful Path of Good Fortune*,[2] by Geshe Kelsang Gyatso, a Tibetan monk who had started to teach Tibetan Buddhism in England in 1977, open on a page that reflected thoughts I'd had that week. I bought a copy for myself as soon as I could; reading it I knew I had found the teachings I craved – they seemed deeply familiar. And my friend studied this book with an *English* Buddhist monk! I sent the monk a message, my cultural and spiritual yearnings united and he appeared in a Mexican *plaza* as arranged, telling me how to cope with too many beggar boys requesting money, saying that giving was an intention and not necessarily a physical action.

"If you want more teachings," he said, "organize them." I did. I knew where this monk could perform and where to advertise. Many people came and he was grateful.

---

[1] The New Kadampa Tradition – International Kadampa Buddhist Union (NKT–IKBU) will be shortened to NKT and Geshe Kelsang Gyatso, its founder, will be called Geshe-la or Gyatso.

[2] Geshe Kelsang Gyatso, *Joyful Path of Good Fortune* (London, 1990).

"First you put the Dharma into your life, then you put your life into the Dharma!" That's how he phrased it, this beautiful English monk who answered all my questions week by week, and was so polite when he stayed in my house after teaching. I'd fallen in love with Dharma; this ethical and compassionate philosophy of Buddhism seemed both complex and coherent. Through the Dharma I loved the monk; he brought community and focus into my fragile life and gave me an active role in my own future. Hauled in by the attractions of Tantric teachings and spiritual friendship, practicing the moral discipline he taught calmed my mind. I had needed this. And the enlightenment he promised I would attain was the ultimate in mental stability; no attachment, anger or ignorance, only bliss, for the benefit of all. I soon received a Tantric empowerment in Mexico; the sacred blessings and instructions of Avalokiteshvara, the Buddha of compassion. I learnt to "self-generate" or imagine myself as this Buddha, a way of "realizing" or bringing that blissful Buddha-nature into my conscious experience.

In those early months I remember staring at an aerial photo of Manjushri Centre, the mother center of the NKT, such an enormous mock Victorian castle in Cumbria, England, that I thought *What am I doing? This could be a cult...*, but I swamped that voice with the joy I felt from the practices. I'd "checked out" Geshe Kelsang Gyatso with the well-known owner of the biggest spiritual bookshop in Mexico City. "Reliable and orthodox," he'd said.

I was heartened to meet other students of Tibetan Buddhism in Mexico, but after mentioning me to their Tibetan Lamas they wouldn't talk to me again. I was shocked. The English monk explained a little; the Dalai Lama appeared to be an "enemy" who was unjustly isolating the NKT from other Buddhists. It was 1995, before the internet, and I did not understand the conflicts at the heart of this Buddhist world; Geshe-la's spiritual guide, Trijang Rinpoche, had been the Dalai Lama's Junior Tutor, but by 1996 Geshe-la would be expelled from his monastery, Sera-Je, by 15 prestigious Lamas, a fact rarely mentioned within the NKT.

Within five months of meeting the monk I separated from my partner. The money the monk offered me to stay and run an NKT centre in Mexico City couldn't meet my family's needs. I would survive better as a single parent in Britain; there were NKT residential centers in the UK and Geshe-la, the only Spiritual Guide in the NKT, was teaching Highest Yoga Tantra at Manjushri Centre that summer. I felt it was an extraordinary opportunity I did not want to miss.

NKT "Highest Yoga Tantra", the empowerments and practices of *Heruka* and *Vajrayogini*, were seen as the "fast path to enlightenment". I was told the commitments could not be explained beforehand but these were meditations that even celibate NKT monks and nuns could engage in. I returned to the UK in 1995 to live near my parents, took those empowerments and happily dedicated myself to promoting the NKT's "pure Dharma" of Je Tsongkhapa, the fourteenth-century monk seen by Geshe-la as the source of the NKT's "essential practices" of Guru Yoga and devotion to Dorje Shugden in the daily *Heart Jewel* prayers. Je Tsongkhapa himself did not practice Shugden.

The Shugden ritual crept into my NKT life slowly. I did not practice it in Mexico but in 1997, enthused by the deep sense of injustice expressed by all the NKT teachers I knew and with free transport provided from my NKT centre, I attended a pro-Shugden/anti-Dalai Lama demonstration in London. The NKT became, slowly, less Tibetan; all the prayers were translated into English and "Western" music composed. I was sad; in 1996 I'd learnt how to play the Tibetan trumpet for the Shugden *Tsog* pujas, extensive chanted prayers during which we'd offered food and music. No money was ever collected for Tibetan causes. The reason for the Tibetan Lamas in Mexico advising their students not to talk to me was that they, and the Dalai Lama, considered "Shugden", the being prayed to in this daily "protector practice" of the NKT, personally and culturally damaging, detrimental to a unified Tibet and the mental stability of the practitioner.

Five months of intense retreat in a quiet house in a Surrey village during 1998 convinced me that the methods of meditation that Geshe-la taught were invaluable and extraordinary; my personality had changed profoundly and irrevocably. I wanted to live in an NKT residential community in Britain to deepen my practice and find support like that I had received from the Sangha, the NKT Buddhist community, in Mexico. I stopped training as a counselor and from 1998 to 2006 I lived within or very near an NKT centre with my children, depending entirely on British government social security benefits. I joined the Teacher Training Programme (TTP) and then, to fulfill my intention to promote these teachings for the rest of my life, requested ordination, scrawled on a slip of paper as, simply, the last on a list of study questions I'd sent my Resident Teacher, the teacher assigned by Geshe-la to my local NKT centre. Weeks passed. When I asked again he was in a hurry to leave for Italy and apologized for not having time to talk.

He told me to "send an email to Manjushri Centre" to ask. Three weeks later, with only two weeks left to find ordination robes to wear as well as gifts and money for Geshe-la, I was given permission to ordain. I was told that my path to enlightenment would be even faster as, being ordained, I could concentrate on helping others. The only prerequisite was having the desire to ordain and my only preparation was the NKT monk from Mexico giving me a short whispered "transmission" of the commitments at an NKT Summer Festival, with a suggestion to keep these for a year "as if" I were ordained. I had done so, content. Ordaining, I would promise to abandon killing, stealing, sexual activity, lying, and taking intoxicants, and would promise to practice contentment, reduce my desire for worldly pleasures, abandon engaging in meaningless activities, maintain the commitments of refuge (to Buddha, Dharma, and Sangha), and practice the three trainings of pure moral discipline, concentration, and wisdom. For the rest of my life.

Entering the Guru's Mandala – 29 July 1999, Cumbria, UK

A vision of perfection draws me on: our method is "Sutra and Tantra", "Lamrim, Lojong, and Mahamudra"; my goal is enlightenment. The path I follow is that of Venerable Geshe Kelsang Gyatso Rinpoche and the whole world is Geshe-la's *mandala*, his sacred Buddha world we enter to make offerings and be blessed, and he is the monk who has taken the Dharma from Tibetan culture and given that complete path to bliss to us – non-Tibetans, "westerners". I will not fail; I will become a good nun. I feel it is an opportunity that no one else can give me; I do not have to find sponsorship, leave my daughter and live in a Tibetan nunnery. Geshe-la's kindness brought the Dharma to me so I, now, will join my life to his path – Kadampa ordination. My daughter and her godmother will wait for me outside the New Kadampa Tradition's first World Peace Temple, recently opened at Manjushri Mahayana Buddhist Centre, the New Kadampa Tradition's "spiritual home" near Ulverston in the Lake District of northern Britain.

I am the last to arrive, my excuse childcare. I quickly choose a meditation cushion in the back row on the right next to some future monks but am told that future nuns are to sit on the left. I had not seen any sexual distinctions in the NKT before; I had trusted that, but I step over to the other side and sit on the only empty cushion I can see. It's in the front row, almost at the center, just below Geshe-la's throne. No way back, no way out; previously ordained Sangha, the third Buddhist "Jewel" after the Buddha and the Dharma, many of them Resident Teachers from all round the world, are seated on the Temple chairs behind me, watching. I am no longer sitting behind thousands of people, whispering to my child to be quiet during the main teachings. This is the ceremony where my inner refuge will take on an outer shape; I will become one of them, an ordained person on the fast and only path ...

We are told to stand as Geshe-la is arriving. He prostrates alone three times towards the shrine and we prostrate to him as soon as he is seated on his throne. Then we sit and he gives us the ordination talk, preparing us for a new mind, a new name, and the new "physical aspect" of a shaved head and Tibetan robes identical to his own. Mine are too large for me; they were left behind at my center by monks who had "run away" to lay life again, but I know I will never give up on this pure tradition. I already know those commitments, just 10, and I also know that, by relying on my Highest Yoga Tantra practice, I can keep them; sexual energies are transformed into "energy for meditation". No more need for sexual intimacy. *No more babies ...* Reverting to habit, I wrap my *zen*, the long rectangular sheet of dark red compassion, round both my shoulders like a Mexican *rebozo*,[3] not off one shoulder as it should be, and listen to the teaching that only the soon-to-be-ordained and the ordained can hear as no one else is allowed in the Temple. During the ordination I take notes – I do not want to forget any of the words; all my life has led to this precious ceremony. Ordaining, I will become one of Geshe-la's "Fortunate Ones" ...

Soon Geshe-la speaks of keeping our ordination through to future lives. I glance around; no one moves, nobody looks upset. *Are they all such realized beings they know this already? Have they been told?* I suddenly feel alone. I am prepared for no killing, stealing, lying, sexual conduct, or intoxication. I am prepared to commit to my training, to refuge, and to promoting the tradition, but only for this life. *Not for them all!* The vows expand indefinitely; my mind follows and I fall into a space where I am terrified of breaking my promises, even before I have taken them.

---

[3] The *rebozo* is used to wrap babies and young children in. They can sleep and breastfeed unnoticed.

I am not prepared for this ... My ordination Master continues and insists that if we have powerful realizations we can carry our ordination into future lives ...

We are told to prostrate again to him, to Geshe-la. *Is this my test, my training – he knows I can do this? It feels far too big ... I did not know ...* A senior teacher had said that Geshe-la would only push us as far as he knows we can go ...

We prostrate together in a line, in time, and it is a majestic sweep of color, shape, and sound, a Buddhist wave. Dropping swiftly to the floor you can hear a gentle wind in these wings of cloth, but if you fall too fast your robes will slip. This is new for us. Someone gets out of sync but we try to stay together, sixteen Sangha, almost ordained, heads shaved except for one small tuft of hair which Geshe-la will cut off each of us in turn. But I cannot prostrate towards him – there is a small yellow bee lying on the floor directly between myself and my Geshe, my preceptor. I pray to the bee to move but it writhes in the same place. If I prostrate on top of it I can kill it so I prostrate to the left, towards the shrine behind our Guru. *What is most important, my compassion or my respect?*

My second prostration is to the right, towards the monks and Geshe-la's sister, an elderly nun. *Perhaps this bee is an emanation of my spiritual guide to see what I will do?* I will not fail. I pray again. The bee wobbles, and stays. Is it hurt? We wear no shoes but monks, and some nuns, have large and heavy feet. *Surely someone else will notice it? Or should I pick it up and walk out?*

Again I prostrate, the third, the last, at an angle completely out of line with the others. *Where is my refuge if my compassion stops me prostrating to my Guru, to the person who is giving me ordination?* I pray that Geshe-la knows what I am doing. *And if I can't promise to be a nun in my future lives, then it means I have attachment to having a relationship in a future life.* I must let go of that mind ... *I must practice contentment ...*

I stand up, have my hair cut, sit down again and wait for the envelope with my new name. I want a Sanskrit name, not a Tibetan one. But I have told no one; it is just a thought.

I was the only person to get a Sanskrit name at that ordination ceremony. The envelopes were given out according to where you were seated, apparently at random. *But he'd known, hadn't he?* He knew that name was the one I wanted; Kelsang Shraddha, Fortunate One of Great Faith. I'd been mentally naked, now I was clothed. "Faith" is a mind that does not see faults in a virtuous object.

That was the NKT definition I had learnt. Not to see faults in the Buddha, Dharma, and Sangha of the NKT world. That was the view I was told to develop, construct, like my identity – for days I felt like no one. I had to look at my Festival Pass, a card hung on a string around my neck with a tiny NKT logo on it, to see my name, to make my "new imputation" firm. *I am one of Geshe-la's nuns. I am Shraddha, Shraddha, Kelsang Shraddha ... From nothing, I will become someone ... forever ...*

When we stood up at the end, I was beside Geshe-la. I looked at his face but he did not smile or appear to see me; he seemed tiny, immoveable, and distant. I fled to the back of the group and my face barely shows in the photographs. Only later, wearing the wisdom robe, the golden *chogyu*, seemingly identical to the Dalai Lama's and one of the highest robes of the Tibetan tradition, did I realize I had forgotten the tiny bee ... Did that matter? I would follow one tradition purely! Faith, compassion, wisdom – surely "faith" was the most important? It was my name.

NKT Ordination:
Traditionally Breaking a Tradition and Teaching it With Shugden

Even though we were ordained and he was considered our only "Root Guru", we were not generally given access to Geshe-la for "spiritual advice" – in 12 years I never talked to him personally – and he would only give public teachings a few days each year. He told us that his books would "function as a spiritual guide" instead; we had to rely on our Resident Teacher, the NKT study programs he or she gave, and our practice. I saw a gradual increase in security precautions and secrecy. Geshe-la spent all winter months "at a secret location" in the US, but he would directly oversee the purchase of land or buildings for each new NKT Temple.

The preoccupations of earning a living and saving for old age were regarded as mundane and irrelevant; we needed to become Resident Teachers of new centers to receive sponsorship. There was no other NKT support. After my center room rents went up, the rate set by the Resident Teacher, I was so poor that I once had to cook the rice from my *mandala* kit, picking out all the precious stones before I could boil it for my daughter. The *mandala* offering represented creating the universe in a pure form as an offering to the Buddhas; a set of metal plates and rings, rice and precious stones was repeatedly built up into a small cake-like palace then tipped out on a cloth spread on the floor whilst chanting prayers. It was a practice of giving.

When Geshe-la said that we did "not need to receive full ordination in a separate ritual ceremony" as we would "naturally become a Gelong" (a fully ordained monk)[4] by developing our practice, I did not know what this meant. He said that our moral discipline was not based on external behavior or "rules", the hundreds of vows of the "Lesser Vehicle Hinayana" practitioners that the Tibetan ordained follow, but on intention; our function was to increase others' "faith", to enlighten everyone. Therefore, we could handle money, live with ordained of the opposite sex and lay people in the NKT centers and, like myself, also live with our children if we already had them.

As there were no formal instructions, and guidelines for our behavior weren't clearly defined, each Resident Teacher developed his or her own way of "disciplining" monks and nuns at their centers, and at mine this could be harsh. As to the non-ordained we had to "reflect the purity of the Guru", "harmony", and "contentment" and there was an ethos to be "more professional than the professionals" (even though we had no specific training for our center jobs); we had "Sangha meetings" where our "performance" would be analyzed. Admonitions and tears were frequent. It was accepted that ordained Sangha could easily get upset; cold coffee or a ripped robe could suddenly provoke irritability. So, as compensation for the stress of "giving up everything" and trying to be "humble" monks and nuns like Geshe-la, the ordained were given the better rooms in the center. This did not apply to me as I had children.

Unlike in the Tibetan tradition, there was no ceremony for disrobing, no "clean break". Those who disrobed had to stay away for a year and could never teach in the NKT again. Leaving was seen as shameful and a person who left would rarely be mentioned. It was said that disrobing would make our "bad karma" ripen as "hellish" experiences. We were told we were following a "special, new" ordination

---

[4] In the Tibetan tradition, full male ordination requires a ceremony. Full female ordination (Gelong-ma) is not given as yet in any Tibetan tradition. This "issue" is sidestepped as the NKT commitments are the same for both sexes.

that "nobody has done before" but even though our ordination was different, we looked like Tibetan monks and nuns.

I was told the robes "tend to lend authority to ordained teachers" and soon after my ordination I began teaching. The first time I taught, enthusiastic, I heard voices in my head during the teaching saying *Who do you think you are?* and criticizing me for teaching when I knew nothing! Upset, I stopped teaching even though Geshe-la said that teachers who get "discouraged" are "foolish". A year later, my *Heart Jewel* practice was stronger so I began again. Teaching was considered our main practice for "promoting the tradition", a "heart commitment" of Shugden practice, along with regarding Shugden as inseparable from our Tantric practice deity and our Guru. We needed to become "qualified spiritual guides" as soon as possible; one NKT teacher would be "more important" to Geshe-la than "the hundred [students] who become Buddhas".[5] Being qualified didn't mean passing our exams, that wasn't necessary; it meant "relying on the Guru" through *Heart Jewel* and then teaching others the NKT texts. The *Heart Jewel* Guru Yoga and Shugden practice was recited at every NKT center in the world every day and by every NKT teacher before teaching. NKT study books were edited versions of selected texts from the Gelug school with commentaries by Geshe-la, many of them common to all Tibetan Buddhist traditions.

One function of a Buddha, we were told, was to teach Dharma, the path to enlightenment. Geshe-la told us that whether a teacher "is a real Buddha or not depends upon the student's faith and view, not on the actual qualifications of the teacher", and this applied to any NKT teacher, including Resident Teachers, and whether we were listening or teaching. Students would "meet Geshe-la" through us. I was told we needed "to project that we are fully qualified teachers. This is not a sham because we are holding the Guru at our heart". During the meditations of *Heart Jewel* you could "download" the "wisdom minds" of different Buddhas to your own mind at your spiritual "heart" in the center of your body. For me, Geshe-la's "wisdom mind" was the most present; Geshe-la "appearing as" Guru Je Tsongkhapa would give me all the Buddhas' wisdom. In the second half of *Heart Jewel* practice, "Wisdom Buddha Geshe-la", "appearing as" Shugden, would reinforce those "blessings" and "protect" them. I was told Geshe-la would

---

[5] Geshe Kelsang Gyatso, "Training as a Qualified Dharma Teacher", in Susan Mumm (ed.), *Religion Today: A Reader* (London and Aldershot, 2002), p. 30.

"always remember" me and "never let go", but I had to remember him at the time of my death to gain a good rebirth. I knew nuns who would "write" and "talk" to Geshe-la daily even though they rarely, if ever, met him.

Requests were made in *Heart Jewel* to prevent obstacles to the expansion of the tradition; the "success" of our teaching meant new students and new venues. In 2011 the NKT claimed to have "1,100 Kadampa centres and branches" in 40 countries around the world. As well as at the centers and in "branches" (rented rooms in towns), NKT teachers taught at schools, universities, health services, hospitals, prisons, and chaplaincies, and "Kadampa Communications" continuously promoted the NKT on the internet. It was our commitment to distribute publicity.

Historically, "Shugden" was a practice dedicated to an "external" being who "comes into" an oracle.[6] I attended a ritual at my center, unknown to the general public, around 1997, when Kuten Lama, Gyatso's uncle, was "possessed"; he "became" the Shugden oracle and gave advice to senior NKT teachers, but he did not teach Dharma. For me, "downloading the Guru's blessings" worked; I loved teaching. My nerves were intense as I had suffered from memory loss in public all my life, but straight after *Heart Jewel*, which I sometimes did several times before teaching, I could become relaxed, confident, and articulate for hours; it did feel as if Geshe-la was talking "through" me as I'd often speak with beautiful phrases and make spontaneous hand gestures like the "teaching *mudras*", hand gestures representing enlightened states of mind I'd seen in Tibetan paintings. I heard and led meditations using the low and slow "NKT" voice which I identified later, during training in hypnotherapy, as that used to create hypnotic states in clients. I have not heard it used in any traditional Tibetan Buddhist context. We were not allowed to "mix traditions" as this would "cause sectarianism"; we would be asked to stop teaching if we referred to texts other than Gyatso's books or if we weren't "happy" teaching. "Ordinary" society was based only on greed and selfishness; our "Kadampa society" wasn't, but we had to be careful with newcomers – they could read other books and see other teachers, but if one of us went to see another teacher then this would "destroy our function as NKT teachers". We were not to talk about the protests against the Dalai Lama as this could discourage new students. Or explain our ordination vows. We should never talk to the press or to

---

[6] As "sacramental, deliberate deity possession". Jean La Fontaine, *The Devil's Children* (Farnham, 2009), p. 182.

academic researchers. Only senior teachers could do this, by appointment, so what was said could be "authorized".

Soon I had a sequence of answers for every query without "thinking" about it; I "spoke" Geshe-la's words of wisdom and was told I would "receive protection, blessings, and special care continually" from Dorje Shugden. In this way I would become "extraordinary" as I had an "extraordinary goal" in which "ordinary rules don't apply"; words from a teaching I had pinned to my bedroom wall as inspiration. However, I still searched for my "inner Guru". In a hotel bedroom in New York, at an International NKT Festival, I was invited to "work for the center" as Bookings Manager by an impressive group of ordained teachers. A few years later I was asked to be "Deputy Admin Director" and look after my center for the benefit of all. Community life was complicated and had to be "managed" properly, prioritizing "harmony" for roughly 30 residents and the wider community. I was moving up the hierarchy.

Living With the Rats

I yearned for more teachings and answers to my questions. As Dharma realizations depended on my "merit" which would increase the more I "worked for the Guru", I knew I needed to work more. I was already dealing with the rats. The rat-catcher said we had very few, but left alive these could become hundreds. All the rice was removed from our offering bowls in the bedrooms and the main meditation rooms or *Gompas*, all edibles were packed in tins, but still they'd come, those brown rat urban dwellers. "My" admin office (we weren't encouraged to call anything our own) was in the basement where I could relax from the public side of the "mission"; Geshe-la would hold up the example of Christian missionaries. I felt on call 24/7, my admin, teaching, and center retreat and study schedule was relentless, but the "office" rat didn't disturb me. It made no demands; it would run the edge of the room behind the desks and office equipment. There was always Geshe-la's photograph, quotes reminding us that we had work to do, boards on the walls listing places to teach, numbers attending. Little was in order; the priority was receiving the money, increasing attendance at classes, and sending teachers all over our area of England, creating new branches, then new centers under ours as the "mother" center. If I hid here (as long as there were no "complaints", I could do my jobs however I wished), answering emails, creating Excel files for all the course bookings, then with me was the rat, fast, furred, a rustle like a whisper of something alive and responsive. This rat wasn't one I wanted to kill, even though I was responsible for "cleaning up" the center. After a detailed discussion on methods of killing, the Resident Teacher had decided to use poison but that meant we had to search for the smell of freshly dead rats and take out the rotting corpses ...

Another dead rat was under the lounge, in the social area, there was the smell; probably a mother, as we'd heard tiny hunger cries in the weeks before. Perhaps it was the warmth that drew them as the lounge was the only room that was constantly heated. The men didn't think I could move it; they usually did the maintenance whilst I did office work, but they showed me what to do. *Empowered by my Guru's blessings I can do anything ...* I needed merit; I wanted a challenge.

One floorboard was pulled up. The space was tiny. I had to put my head and arm down into the gap and stretch along with the broom handle until it reached the bloated body then pull it towards me as fast as I could without piercing the flesh or it would explode and force us to pull up all the floorboards and be blamed for the cost and inconvenience. The *Gompas* had thick luxurious carpets and elaborate, expensively decorated shrines. But the lounge wasn't a *Gompa*! Money should not be spent on the social areas, for residents. The rat had to stay whole.

That stench, putrid and fetid, corrupt, held as a mark of hell; there is nothing like the smell of a rotting rat corpse, poked and rolled, exploding with tiny pockets of gas as it nears you. It stayed almost like a physical presence on my tongue for days. I was breathing shallow and telling everyone else to go away. I moved the rat into a black bag. We were undertakers clearing up corpses.

Oh, the outrage that killing should happen here, where the kind Buddhists live! Mother sentient beings do not deserve this! The law – we could be shut down as a public building if we did not kill them. But "all the restaurants in town have rats", said the residents who used to be Animal Rights activists and gave this up to be Buddhist practitioners in a community. Rats have community. They'd appear according to karma, we'd say. We gossiped in the lounge. Buddhist texts say "bad smells" are connected to moral discipline; breaking it "smells" bad. Dead rats smell very, very bad.

The rat-catcher had found rat routes – they got inside the building via the drainage, ran under the lounge and up into the Resident Teacher's private flat, less frequently to the other residents' single rooms. The Resident Teacher told me he was feeding the rats the offerings from his shrine! Whilst below we had to prod the rotting carcasses of the mothers …

I liked my rat and wished it well, but I didn't *feed* it.

Who were these rats? Were they impelled by karma to run a conveyor belt of pleasure up to the attic and out into the Resident Teacher's feast above? The best offerings were there, unpacked – the best plates, the best fleshy fruit and imported chocolate, the best bottles of non-alcoholic fizzy drinks, pungent cheese, and perfumed toiletries. These were offerings to show respect and consideration for the teacher and a creation of merit for the giver. The Resident Teacher had to eat from each plate that was offered during the ceremonies. *Tsog* offerings were a banquet, color-matched and decorated. If you got fatter whilst you were ordained you didn't have to get new clothes, you just loosened your robes …

In the *Gompa*, fresh offerings to Shugden of alcohol, tea, cake, milk, and curds were made each day as in every NKT center all over the world, as well as water bowl offerings to the Buddhas and a cup of tea for Gyatso next to the teachers' throne. The alcohol and meat offerings for the Tantric *Tsog* were in tiny egg-cup-shaped bowls placed on a beautiful box. But at my center in the early days the box they were on contained the measuring mechanism and weights a previous resident had used for selling drugs. It was like that – what appeared was what mattered. And more than that, it seemed that what "appeared" was what things were. And if things were their "appearances", what things used to be or what "ordinary people" would think they were became unimportant and was often seen as mistaken. We had to "keep the center going"; that was the priority, and if that meant creating an illusion, or even killing, then so be it. Whatever it took.

Fear and Fitting the Dharma into "Sectarianism"

My Resident Teacher had sat down on a sofa in the lounge and given me advice after my ordination.

"Pray not to be a mother in your next life," he'd started. *Obvious if I was supposed to stay ordained!* But I asked him why not.

"You could be more useful to Geshe-la if you weren't a mother ..." I gulped. I needed to be *more* useful?

"How?"

"For instance, you could travel, be a Resident Teacher. And don't you think there are aspects of behavior that are suitable for a parent to follow but unsuitable for an ordained person?"

I couldn't think of anything, except perhaps killing the lice on my daughter's head, but what difference to killing the rats? I had blessed the lice with mantras, connected them to Geshe-la. To future lives with Dharma. And there were already Resident Teachers who were nuns and mothers ...

I became determined to show that Dharma practice and ordination were compatible with motherhood. I organized entertainment and child care at NKT Summer Festivals and "Dharma for Kids" and "Parent and Baby" meditations at my center. But instead of reconciliation, I increasingly developed fear. I feared "outsiders" who did not understand the purity of the NKT and "insiders" who could "destroy the Tradition". This was not a lonely paranoia; in 2008, the NKT published a list of "enemies" on the internet – specific individuals blamed for harming the "pure Dharma"[7] – and an author was threatened successfully with libel in 2010.[8] Unlike many residents who simply wished to "live a quiet life" in a community, I wanted more Dharma. However, I always feared criticizing Geshe-la; I thought that without him my life would be meaningless and painful. But I felt that what I thought was Dharma, based on moral discipline, wasn't sufficiently respected by some NKT teachers. And the teachers were "his", Geshe-la's. Unsupervised.

---

[7] http://www.newkadampatruth.org/behind-the-lies (accessed 17 August 2012).
[8] http://www.wisdom-books.com/ProductDetail.asp?PID=22023 (accessed 17 August 2012). Libel documents – copies are with INFORM, London School of Economics.

I was exhausted – I hadn't had much time to sleep for years – but I began waking up many times each night with anxiety, unable to cope with the contradictions between what I was trying to do and what I was "allowed" to do, between what I saw and what I was "supposed" to see. Soon, needing to talk to someone I trusted, I "disturbed the harmony of the community" by raising serious concerns about my center with a senior monk in the NKT. No longer deserving of the "Guru's kindness", I was told to stop teaching and admin work immediately, not to talk to anyone and to leave the center as soon as possible. However, I "should continue studying on the Teacher Training Programme" and could "perhaps teach again" if I "behaved properly". I was told later by that same Resident Teacher that I had "needed the shock" of becoming homeless to destroy my pride.

I left the center and the Teacher Training Programme in 2006, but stayed ordained. After it became known that the then current, ordained Deputy Spiritual Director of the NKT had allegedly engaged in sexual misconduct with nuns I had my last conversation with an NKT nun who was a Resident Teacher and a friend. She told me that, unlike ourselves, Geshe-la's "special disciples" who had sex with their students wouldn't go to hell. We discussed what Geshe-la meant by telling us we couldn't get enlightened if we disrobed as that contradicted the idea of Buddha-nature; that every sentient being, possessing a mind, can get enlightened.

On asking, I had been told at Manjushri Centre that I was only allowed to study at the center I'd been made to leave, but I could no longer see my local teacher "as a Buddha" or even as a legitimate teacher either on or off the throne. I told my nun friend how I felt and she asked me what was I going to do if I couldn't study Dharma?

"Do you mean to say," I replied, "that you don't think it's possible to get enlightened at the feet of any other teacher in the world?"

We stared at each other in silence. I knew I would not see her again.

I could no longer support any NKT teachers or practices. I had nowhere to send people who took refuge in me as a robed nun on the street. I found out that my ordination name, practices, and robes were tied to the NKT and could not be transferred. My daughter, having left the center, did not want to leave the town she'd grown up in, and as a mother I would not leave my child to "retrain" as a nun. I felt forced to disrobe because of my own integrity and distraught with that inevitable decision. Even when Tibetan Lamas and Geshes assured me I could still get enlightened as a lay person I did not believe them.

In 2008 I emailed kadampa.org with my decision to disrobe. I received no answer except the confirmation of receipt I had asked for. I symbolically drank alcohol but it still did not feel as if I had broken the hold of my promises to Gyatso. My "Buddha-nature" felt lost as if it only had Gyatso's name on it. I stopped every spiritual practice so that his influence would wane, but his name mantra still "said itself" and I could "hear" NKT teachings continuously. My symbolic world collapsed, slowly folding in as I tried to find out who I was without the "Shugden Guru" or Dharma to guide me. I no longer knew how to live or earn my living, and "ordinary life" seemed meaningless. I did not fit anywhere. I felt I was neither a nun nor a lay person. I was a hungry ghost floating in the *bardo*, the "in-between" of leaving the NKT, transitional and uncertain. I was diagnosed with "complex trauma". My identity had become so tied to the hook of the NKT that it took me four years to realize I was not a bad person.

The NKT did provide "spiritual homes", Temples and "Vajra (Tantric) brothers and sisters", but exactly what spiritual path was I following as an NKT practitioner? The plentiful supply of Dharma teachings available elsewhere had been hidden from view by my NKT ethos of the "pure tradition". Attending Tibetan Buddhist groups I was astonished and shocked to find out that every person who so wished could talk one-to-one with Tibetan teachers who had decades of Geshe training and retreat experience. Each time I asked I received astute, personal, and careful advice which I was not obliged to follow. The contrast with NKT practice upset me. My questions had not been "intellectual pride"; they were necessary for a deeper practice. I had spent 12 years of my life dedicated to a path that led to my exhaustion and stress. Even though I had had concerns and buried them I was not prepared for the shock of finding out that my NKT ordination, in which I had believed so much, could arguably not even be called a "Buddhist ordination" as, according to fully ordained monks and nuns, it did not correspond to any given by Je Tsongkhapa[9] or Buddha Shakyamuni,[10]

---

[9] These are very specific instructions for behavior and for "overcoming" faults. See Je Tsongkhapa and Geshe Graham Woodhouse, *The Essence of the Vinaya Ocean and The Namtse Dengma Getsul Training* (Dharamsala, 2009).

[10] Graham Woodhouse (trans.), *Direct Instructions from Shakyamuni Buddha: A Gelong's Training in Brief*, His Holiness XIVth Dalai Lama (Dharamsala, 2009).

but only to the pre-ordination vows of the Tibetan tradition.[11] We did not study the traditional Tibetan Vinaya, the monastic teachings; there we would have seen that all Tibetan and other Buddhist ordinations cannot be taken into future lives. And that disrobing is not dishonorable; it is an allowed choice and does not necessitate exclusion from the Buddhist community. Ten NKT "promises" contrasted to 364 vows for fully ordained Buddhist nuns. I remembered that I was told that Gyatso did not train at Tantric College and, on his own admission, did not receive a formal Geshe degree. I felt so deeply betrayed, so naive; I had taken my ordination and disrobing so seriously but there had been no need to do so.

Sadly, I found it difficult to follow the instructions of any spiritual guide; I became overwhelmed with distrust, frightened of what these teachers might feel a right to demand from me in return. But, contradictorily and mistakenly, I also regarded an organization as insufficient if it did not demand profound and prompt commitment. It has taken me years to unthread "Dharma" from "NKT Dharma" and find a path to my Buddha-nature separate from my commitment to Gyatso. It is a painful and profound psychological journey I do not wish on anyone.

I did find "very special", "extraordinary experiences" through meditation during my first years in the NKT, but I did not find "a pure happiness that will never let you down" or feel closer to the enlightenment in this one lifetime that the NKT claimed to offer. My faith in the NKT was created through this illusion of quick results and based on my yearning to practice. My insecurities whilst in the NKT were valid; I was not a "Dharma teacher" even though I tried, with Guru Yoga and Shugden practice, to be a good one. My teachers were westerners new to Buddhism. How could it have been possible to become a "Dharma teacher" so quickly, responsible for the spiritual welfare of others, even if Gyatso himself had trained me? Tied to the desire to "keep my vows", I feel I, and the "Dharma" I studied, were pushed into the box of an organization in expansion. What reason was there for the Guru's "intention" of creating a "World Peace Temple in every city" if Gyatso and NKT Dharma were not "the source of all goodness and happiness" for all living beings? But how could they be? That was a question Gyatso's students, including myself, did not ask or answer.

Meditation practices are not superficial. Traditional Tibetan texts tell you to check out a person for up to 12 years before taking them as your teacher, but, as a

---

[11] See Geshe Tekchok, *Monastic Rites* (London, 1985), p. 9.

westerner unused to Asian traditions, how could I have known the need for this? I now understand Buddhist "faith" to be a trust based on the completely verifiable qualities of what is trusted, but I did not have "un-mistaken knowledge" of Gyatso as a trustworthy teacher and his NKT as a reliable refuge based on personal contact and long experience of following personal advice. I had simply convinced myself they were trustworthy and worked unceasingly for the NKT, unpaid, thinking this, as I was told, a privilege and a path to enlightenment. Without experienced spiritual advice I lost my meditation practice and my quietening mind. The NKT was the instrument of the "Guru's intention". I could not "realize" it; instead I realized that for me it was questionable.

I can only relate my experiences. What brought me to the telling was the similarity of my story to that of many others and the concern this provoked. The finer details require more explanation but this will suffice as a general "insider's" introduction to the life and practices of what was my "NKT world".

Chapter 5

Tamera, a Model for the Future

Leila Dregger

What does the future of humankind look like? Can we imagine a world in which humans live in peace with each other and with nature? Is a different life really possible? Current global development is not encouraging. To be able to imagine a different world with a positive future, we need places where we create such a world in real life – at first on a small scale. This is the most basic purpose of a model.

Tamera is developing such a model for the future.

Why is Tamera a Model?

Let us journey to the far south-west of Europe: to Southern Portugal. We leave the Atlantic coast, with its scenic cliffs and dunes behind us, and travel the dusty road inland. It is quiet here. Occasionally we pass through the villages typical of this country, with their carefully whitewashed houses. Cork oaks and eucalyptus trees shimmer in the heat upon the low hills. Sheep and goats graze between old farmhouses. Those familiar with the Alentejo know that this view will change little over the next few hundred kilometers.

But now the road rises gently, curving to the left, and suddenly a different world lies before us. A lake glitters in the sunlight. The terraces by its shore are green and abundant with vegetables, fruit trees, and sunflowers. We see the curved shapes of tents, gleaming solar installations and an assembly hall. And we see people of different colors and cultures, working and sitting together, talking and reading. We have arrived: this is the Future-Workshop Tamera.

About 200 people are working, studying, and living here, building a model for the future. With its Testfield for a SolarVillage, its experiment to heal the land by creating a water landscape, and its internationally networked peace education program, Tamera is a highly complex center for living futurology.

"The Silicon Valley of Peace" was one name given to Tamera by journalists. Others chose "Paradise under Construction". And it really is under construction. Many things are still unfinished, improvized, pioneer-style, and visitors are asked to bring good shoes because of the bad roads. Undeveloped areas of the site, covered with blackberries and rock roses, are a reminder of the time before the project was founded.

At the same time, one senses paradise everywhere. One feels the unusual, the utopian, the orientation towards joy and contact with all that lives, the courage for the unconventional and the longing for what is to come. The goal is as high as everyday life is consciously simple and the material facilities basic: Tamera was founded to develop suggestions for solutions to global issues.

Evolution as a Role Model

Aurelio Peccei may have imagined something like this. The Nobel laureate and co-founder of the Club of Rome was already saying in the 1970s that research settlements should be developed worldwide to solve the basic problems of humankind.

Peccei believed that the future of humankind would not be decided at a desk, but rather demanded decentralized models. The problems of these times are too complex and too interlinked to be solved in isolation from each other by specialists, no matter how well educated and equipped they might be. The problems require deeper changes than can be envisioned from within the current systems of economy and science, as it is these very systems which have led to the current crisis. In the interest of the whole of humankind and all co-creatures, different and novel paths must be found.

When faced with a large challenge, evolution also works experimentally with models. For example, the transition of the original water-bound inhabitants of this planet to land-dwelling beings: a seemingly insoluble problem 400 million years ago. How could they survive on land? How would they breathe and move? It seemed impossible. But evolution created the essentials, as life wanted to expand, overcome borders, and create something new. So nature started its creative work. Innumerable beaches, riverbeds, and lake shores became laboratories of the future. Solutions were developed, tested, abandoned, corrected, and tested again, until *IT* worked. Once the first beings had primitive lungs instead of gills, and rudimentary feet instead of fins, everything changed. Suddenly the system contained new information about the solution. It spread rapidly – in the timescale of evolution. All over the Earth, on the ocean shores and in fresh water, amphibians developed.

All leaps of evolution have taken place based on this principle. It is the principle of frontier-crossing and field-building. Biologists cannot yet say with certainty how the information spreads so quickly, but as soon as the solution is found in one part of the system, it is accessible in the whole, because the Earth and all that lives are one wholeFrom the processes of evolution, Lynn Margulis has concluded that (as John Briggs and F. David Peat have paraphrased her thinking) "If we are to survive the ecological and social crisis we have caused, we may be forced into dramatically new kinds of cooperative ventures."[1]

The community undertakings considered necessary by Lynn Margulis are taking place all over the world. Outside of the huge central laboratories, universities, and cities, researchers of the future are applying their developments practically in places like Tamera.

The Power of Models

What is a model? A model is a part of the whole which is big enough to represent all significant aspects, and small enough that one can quickly notice mistakes, correct them, and continue in new directions. A model can be used as a feedback system in which the effects of actions which are too complex to analyze in the whole system can be tracked and corrected. The more varied the composition of the model and the greater the ability of its members to reflect and communicate, the better the questions of the whole can be perceived and answered.

Tamera is on its way to becoming such a model for the future. Problems and challenges which arise are perceived as issues of humankind. The questions for the experiment, to be solved on the large as well as the small scale, develop in everyday life:

---

[1] John Briggs and F. David Peat, *Turbulent Mirror: An Illustrated Guide to Chaos Theory and the Science of Wholeness* (New York, 1989), p. 166.

What makes communities ecologically and socially sustainable? How can people live together in such a way that rather than developing competition and aggression, they find joy in each others' company and develop the ability to solve conflicts without violence? How can the abundance of energy from the sun be used sustainably without destroying nature or polluting the environment? How can we deal with water in such a way that every being has enough to drink, and the land regains its fertility? How can enough healthy food be grown, even on impoverished land, without exploiting nature, animals, or other humans? What kind of architecture supports community and the solar age? How can this be accessible and easily built in the poorer regions of the world? How can the economy be managed within a society so that instead of creating painful separation between poor and rich, it creates balance and lively exchange? How can children be raised in freedom and security? How can young people use their enormous power and intelligence in a meaningful way? How can the difficulties in the contact between the genders be dissolved, and how can lastingly fulfilling love relationships be developed? How do we end the pain and the exploitation of animals? How can we appreciate the sacred aspect of life free from dogma, and which kinds of ritual or prayer are appropriate in a modern multicultural society? How does a community communicate effectively? How does trust arise? And how does real grassroots democracy come about?

In a comprehensive model, such questions, and many more, are connected with each other and are solved by perceiving the whole, as it was specifically the fragmentation of life into separate areas which led the whole system into the state it is in today.

> "The crisis inside of us and the crisis in the environment are two parts of the same whole and can only be solved from that perspective." (Dieter Duhm, founder of Tamera)

Since industrialization took hold, centralization and specialization have separated important aspects of life from each other. Production has been separated from consumption, theory from practice, the human being from nature, and especially humans from each other. Actions which used to take place naturally in an organically functioning community, which lived from self-organization, mutual support, and common sense, now need specialists. Ever-new efforts to treat isolated symptoms have led to ever-new problems, producing a chain of reactive solutions which could never have a lasting effect.

A comprehensive model which reconnects separated areas with each other activates the little-researched powers of self-organization, synergy, and the resilience of biotopes. These powers are needed to lift the whole system to a higher level of order. A living model which succeeds in making it possible for all beings to live together in a healing way will generate a field which adds this information of success to the overall organism, and has the potential to influence the whole in a healing direction.

Tamera Today

A walk through Tamera today takes one through cascades of lakes and ponds, on the shores of which grow the permaculture gardens used for both teaching and food supply. In the coming years the water landscape will be expanded and completed, so that the trees on the hills will also be able to grow again and return to health. The summer kitchen of the Testfield for a SolarVillage demonstrates techniques for cooking with solar energy and biogas, electricity generation, food preservation, and water pumping. Almost all of the systems were built in our own workshops. In the research greenhouse, new technologies are tested which are intended to free settlements of the future from dependence on centralized energy supply systems. On the building sites, simple traditional construction techniques are combined with modern architectural concepts. Participants of the peace-education programs study in seminar rooms and the auditorium. Theatre and music groups rehearse for their performances on the stages of the *Aonda* and the *Aula*. The participants of the Youth School for Global Learning are being taught by young adults who were themselves students here a few years ago.

Men and women from different countries and cultures are working together, supporting the development of the new systems. They contribute their knowledge and experience and gain insights which they will use for the creation of autonomous settlements in their home countries. They benefit from the presence of international experts in the various research areas. The joy of experimentation is as important as the finished solutions.

The most important aspect in all of this is the coming together. People who previously learned to perceive each other as enemies, for example those from Israel and Palestine, are working here hand-in-hand. Common work towards a higher goal, more important for the people of both "sides" than the conflict, leaves no space for hostility. Compassion, responsibility for the whole, and mutual support are the basic ethical guidelines for living together in Tamera.

In addition to specialist knowledge, participants bring back home the joy of experimentation, greater self-esteem and experience of community. Research, education, and participation unite in all areas – ecology, technology, social competence, and political networking. Through this combination, a worldwide network of different groups and initiatives has developed, all connected with Tamera to bring its knowledge to their projects, or to create new projects based on similar principles. Young people love to invest their whole power and joy into such a planetary perspective.

Let us now take a look at the world. We direct our glance not towards today's densely populated areas, but to the places where new centers for peace are developing. If we look closely, we discover the signs of a global renaissance. Gentle yet unstoppable, a powerful movement is forming – a movement for reconnection with nature and reconciliation with each other in the certainty of a different future; a movement for a free Earth.

The children of the future will be able to build on the knowledge and experience of these centers. If one day our survival depends on choosing new ways; if the breakdown of large economic and supply systems comes close; if whole landscapes become uninhabitable or social unrest threatens a peaceful way of living together, then these centers will be catalysts for a new beginning.

In this way Tamera wants to put itself into service for the world.

Two Examples of Tamera's Projects

From the different projects Tamera has realized or has been working on so far – the Global Campus Initiative, Youth School for Global Learning, Animal Project, Politicyl Ashram, Love School, Publishing House Meiga, Place of the Children, Institute for Global Peace Work – I will describe the work on two major research fields which play a crucial role worldwide: Tamera's work on water, food, and energy.

Water Retention Landscapes as a Local Solution for a Global Problem

> When I walk through Tamera today, I can already see the first glimpses of our vision taking shape: a landscape flourishing in its vitality, an abundant diversity of flora and fauna, a well-designed interplay of elements, a living space radiating health, a land whose abundance can nourish all of its inhabitants. (Silke Paulick, Coordinator of the Ecology Team in Tamera)

A model settlement of the future should be well integrated into healthy natural surroundings. For this we need to interact and communicate well with our co-creatures. Ecology is the outer expression of a human settlement. It encompasses contact between humans, animals, plants, and natural elements. A decisive aspect of a healthy ecology is water. Tamera is developing a model project for natural water management and the natural regeneration of damaged landscapes – for Southern Europe and worldwide.

Since 2007, Tamera has been building a water landscape in conjunction with the Austrian hill-farmer and permaculture specialist Sepp Holzer. This water landscape will serve as a model that shows how severely damaged landscapes can be restored to their original, healthy, natural state. In place of the dusty road which was here a couple of years ago, there are now lakes, pools, and retention ponds. Where there were gardens which were too wet in the spring and too dry in the summer, there is now an abundance of fruit and vegetables growing on the lakeside terraces throughout the year. And this is only the beginning. A complete water landscape is planned, including more than ten retention ponds for rainwater.

By then it will imbue the soil with sufficient water to enable forest growth. Many visitors are already coming to see the current state of the permaculture water landscape. Specialists in water engineering, professors, and conservationists from the whole of Portugal and further afield are following the developments attentively. Many of them see this as a viable recipe for the prevention of desertification.

How Desertification Can Be Prevented

"No, a water landscape is not the same as a reservoir. It is precisely the opposite. The water is not taken out of the earth body and collected centrally, but instead retained in a decentralized way so that the earth body can recharge with water." Sepp Holzer has answered this question many times. The resolute hill-farmer has gained the title "The Rebel Farmer" by insisting on his unusual methods. Success has proved him right. Starting with his own farm in the Austrian Alps, he has restored huge areas to their natural vitality in Scotland, Russia, Spain, South America, and, in recent years, Portugal. "The drought in this country is no natural catastrophe," he says, "it is the result of wrong agricultural techniques. Mismanagement of water, deforestation, overgrazing, and monocultures lead to desertification."

When the Austrian is driving through the Alentejo, there are many things that he can hardly bear:

> What I see here, hurts. The landscape has been destroyed and the soil and the plants are exposed to the sun and wind. No animal feels well here. And as a farmer I would also feel totally lost here. The soil has been washed away as a result of overgrazing, and only inferior grasses still grow. The farmers give up, the children go to the cities, and the most beautiful farms fall into ruin. The land falls into the hands of speculators and is finally abandoned completely. But Portugal could be a rich country if people relearn how to read the book of nature.

Holzer knows an alternative. He has designed and implemented it many times, in many places. Water is always at the core of his work. Where there is rain only at specific times of the year, the landowner has to learn to keep it on the land.

Not in giant reservoirs, but on the contrary across many decentralized retention ponds, following the pattern of nature. "Water is capital. Someone who works the land and lets the winter rain flow away is letting his wealth disappear unnoticed."

After his first visit to Tamera in March 2007, Holzer drafted a plan: a model project for the natural regeneration of the landscape, for large-scale production of healthy food and for natural reforestation. An edible landscape with retention ponds, pools, and lakes was to be created, in which wild animals too would find food and protection.

Four years later, the lakeside terraces and raised beds supply the co-workers and guests of the Peace Research Center with healthy food. Tamera gardener Silke Klüver: "We are now harvesting more fruit and vegetables around the shores than we were previously able to harvest in the entire former garden. And the summer interruption in the growing season is no longer necessary." The many visitors have the feeling that the lakes have always been there.

With its varied microclimate, the water landscape offers a new living space for wild animals and plants. The original flora and fauna return to the region: otters have been sighted, water birds use the new living spaces, turtles and other amphibious animals find a home.

The permaculture teacher and peace activist Starhawk, from the USA, was impressed during her visit: "Only someone who lives in a summer-dry climate can imagine the churning mixture of inspiration and sheer envy that filled me while walking the paths that meander between the beautiful series of lakes and ponds."

Bernd Müller: "Imagine that one thousand landowners in the Alentejo decided to build such water landscapes. Not only nature would recover. Also many people would find a new economic basis for their lives. The Alentejo would be revitalized."

Tamera is developing a model for regional food self-sufficiency: in cooperation with neighbors, organic farms and small-scale producers of the Alentejo, a supply network for regionally produced food is developing. The farmers produce to order, so that their income is secured independently from market fluctuations; the surplus is sold. In this way communities and villages can become more economically independent.

Freedom From Complicity

Almost all products from the supermarket are part of a system under which animals or humans suffer. Everything bought there makes one an accomplice of this system, yet even though it is difficult to step out of this, Tamera as a community is deciding more and more to refrain from buying these products. This means that wherever possible, if not produced in Tamera's own garden, food is bought from regional farmers, organic agriculture, or ecological fair-trade sources. In compassion to animals and as an expression of non-violence, Tamera has adopted a vegetarian, mainly vegan, diet, usually not using cheese, eggs, or milk. The cooks aim to prepare food in such a way that nothing is missing. Only biodegradable toiletries are used in Tamera. A resident: "It is not about refraining from pleasure. It is about building a life in which one knows more and more what one is doing, without having to close one's heart."

Testfield for a SolarVillage:
From the Illusion of Scarcity to the Reality of Abundance

The transition into a solar age will be easier if the appropriate technologies have already been developed at some places to the point where they are ready for use in the field. It is for this purpose that Tamera founded the Testfield for a SolarVillage: a prototype for the testing of decentralized solar energy systems under the everyday conditions of a village of about fifty people. The results will be used to build a solar village which is autonomous in energy and food, as a research and education site of the Global Campus. At its technological core are the inventions of the physicist and inventor Jürgen Kleinwächter.

> Every moment the sun radiates onto the Earth fifteen thousand times more energy than the entire energy needs of humankind. The energy of the sun is abundant: we only need to develop the appropriate technology to use it. My dream is that Tamera becomes a 'free-lab' where inventors enter an inspired space where they can learn from and support each other and implement and test their inventions. (Paul Gisler, Leader of the Solar Technology Research Group in Tamera)

A greenhouse is reflected in a clear lake. Within and in front of the lake there are solar energy systems of various shapes and sizes, forming an inspirational technology park. A machine with a large flywheel pulses like a giant heart. In an open kitchen, people are preparing lunch, cooking using neither gas nor electricity. Here in the heart of Tamera, a mini utopia of decentralized solar energy has been created – the Testfield for a SolarVillage – which arose from the wish to build a living example to show how a small village of fifty inhabitants can achieve the goal of energy self-sufficiency.

This is not a very distant future. In cooperation with Jürgen Kleinwächter, and led by Paul Gisler, the technology team is continuously developing the inventions and optimizing them through everyday use. Sometimes they experience setbacks, but they do not let this stop them. They are guided by the knowledge that energy exists in abundance. Developing an appropriate technology to make this energy accessible for all humans without monopolization and power struggles is real peacework. In Jürgen Kleinwächter the technology team has found a solar-age visionary as a cooperation partner.

The centerpiece of his inventions is the machine which now stands gleaming in the sun: a low-temperature Stirling engine, in this case the "SunPulse Water". The large solar-driven water pump is in demonstration, running the fountain in the middle of the village plaza. It could become an alternative for the millions of agricultural water pumps which use vast quantities of electricity and fuel. The engine transforms the temperature differences between the heat of the sun and the cool of the shade directly into mechanical energy, without any of the intermediate efficiency losses of electrical generation, transmission, and consumption.

The cooking equipment for the summer kitchen is also solar powered, in this case by hot plant-oil which is heated in the energy greenhouse and stored in a special tank. The oil provides heat not only for cooking day and night, or for disinfection, but can also be used to generate electricity, drive mechanical tools, or run cooling equipment. It is, in simple terms, the core of a completely new energy concept for a village.

Its main component is again a low-temperature Stirling engine, a machine with a large flywheel, the "SunPulse Hot Oil". It transforms the temperature differences between the hot oil and cold water into electrical, mechanical, or thermal energy.

"So far, the system generates 1.5 kW of electrical energy," explains Paul Gisler, "which, together with Jürgen Kleinwächter, we intend to increase considerably."

The Testfield, which was opened in October 2009, is already an attractor for other inventors and inventions. It is intended as a place where pioneering researchers can test novel developments, away from the mainstream and with the supportive human conditions of Tamera. The connection with the research areas of ecology and social sustainability provide interesting possibilities and answers to important questions.

Kleinwächter does not want to compete with mega-projects like the giant solar plants in the Sahara. "Instead of energy monopolies, we aim for regional autonomy in energy and food supply. In this way the land can be cared for, and workplaces can be created so that life can return to the villages," he said, speaking to the TV crews who came to report on the opening of the Testfield. About the young people who want to come from many countries to learn in the Testfield, he says: "It is our dream that the world's first solar university arises here."

Earth, Straw and Grass: The Rediscovery of Ecological Building Materials

Providing space for 400 people and with walls eight meters high, the Aula, Tamera's auditorium, is the largest straw bale/adobe building in the Iberian Peninsula. Despite its impressive size, its green roof and the earth-coloured walls blend harmoniously into the landscape.

Visitors who enter are amazed by its grandeur. The timber construction and harmonious proportions give a feeling of magnitude. "Almost like a cathedral" is often heard. The Aula consists of a wooden construction stacked with straw bales and plastered inside and out with clay. On the outer walls the clay was mixed with lime as protection from the rain. Grass and herbs grow on the roof.

The History of Tamera – How it all Started

The founding of Tamera in 1995 was one of many steps on the path towards the model for the future which is now becoming visible. The first steps began in May 1978 in Germany.

In May 1978, three people met in Germany to exchange their thoughts about the situation of the world: the theologian Sabine Lichtenfels, the sociologist Dr. Dieter Duhm, and the physicist Charly Rainer Ehrenpreis. A plan developed from these talks: to create an interdisciplinary research and education project; an alternative university for the renewal and reconnection of natural science and the humanities.

Dieter Duhm was born in 1942 in Berlin, in the middle of the Second World War. He experienced violence during the nights of bombing in Berlin, on the refugee trail to Southern Germany and then at his new home at Lake Constance. He was not yet six years old when local boys took him one day, undressed him, bound him to a lamppost and covered him with tar. He had not done anything: his only crime was being "a stranger". They needed somebody against whom they could direct their anger and the homelessness of their souls. He had already received his first lessons on the character of fascism at an early age.

He was 14 when he heard of the concentration camps for the first time. At first he fought with all of his inner power against this realization, trying to convince himself that the victims were criminals or that adults somehow do not feel pain so clearly. Then he started to ask his parents and their friends about it. His hope was to find some comfort, something to ease the horror. But the more he investigated, the more he had to let go of this hope. There was no comfort. Auschwitz was reality, or at least an ineradicable part of it. One last hope remained. To say that it *had been* reality, but now it is not any more. This hope, too, disappeared. Years later he became one of the leaders of the German Left in the Student Movement of 1968. Together with his companions he fought against imperialism and the Vietnam war. He saw the pictures of Vietnamese women with their breasts hacked off, and people burned in napalm. He knew that this was the integral dark side of Western morals and culture.

At that time, he wrote:

> Why was it so far impossible to establish an ideal human society? Because it is not only the outer conditions which are at fault, but particularly inner structures and patterns of thinking. It is impossible to form a free society from people who are structured by authoritarianism. It is not possible to erect a non-violent society when the impulses of hate and violence within are suppressed but not dissolved. A revolution that has not taken place inside cannot succeed outside. This is what we learn from history.

Dieter Duhm could no longer reintegrate himself into bourgeois society. He refused several offers of professorships. In the face of global violence he could not simply return to everyday life. He withdrew to an isolated farm in Lower Bavaria, Southern Germany, to find time to think. His hermitage became a *geistig* futurological workshop. He worked with diverse sources – Nietzsche, Hegel, and Van Gogh, Rudolf Steiner, Jesus, Lao Tse, Wilhelm Reich, Prentice Mulford, and Teilhard de Chardin. Slowly the fragments of knowledge started to unite and form a new picture. A new *geistig* pattern appeared from the insights of biology and cybernetics, psychoanalysis and mathematics, art, history, and theology. A vision appeared: It is possible. This is how peace could develop. From this vision he formulated a political concept. Its starting point is the place where wars develop each and every day: in the human interactions of daily life between man and woman, children and adults, individuals and society, and between humans and nature. A change must be created here. A paradigm shift must take place not only in words but in reality, in actual-life praxis.

He started to bring the idea into reality. When he later founded the first community experiment together with Sabine Lichtenfels and Charly Rainer Ehrenpreis, he suffered setbacks and had to face societal resistance, slander, and hostility, through which he deepened, corrected, and extended his concept and started anew. Long years of work passed without visible success. But his belief grew in the inner pattern of life which he later came to name as the "Sacred Matrix". Even though he had long before turned away from Christianity and all other religions, an ever-louder prayer for support and guidance was growing within him. He did not know to whom he prayed. *IT* prayed itself. He found a way to a faith based not on adopted dogmas, but on compassion, research, and experience.

He particularly believed in the human being; in the human ability to be truthful and the human power of insight.

The Founding of the Project

Together with the physicist and musician Charly Rainer Ehrenpreis, Dieter Duhm traveled through Germany looking for suitable cooperation partners, until they visited the theology student Sabine Lichtenfels in 1978. She and Rainer Ehrenpreis had been friends since their teenage years and had been inspired by the thought of founding an artists' colony.

Sabine Lichtenfels was born in 1954 into a family of artists. Her quest was love:

> I have practically always been in love, for as long as I can remember. I wanted to know how it is possible to be truthful in love. I saw how isolated people were from each other in our Western culture. It had to be possible to love more than one person without the automatic fear of loss, jealousy and separation.

She followed the turbulent paths that arose from this, experienced the happiness of great love; motherhood, marriage, jealousy, and divorce. All the "normal" events of a woman's life. She surprised her atheist family by studying theology as she loved Jesus the revolutionary.

For a long time she was tortured by the feeling that anything she could do for the world would be a drop in the ocean. One can help at one place, but injustice continues at another. She wanted to discover a new way for people to live together in which peace could be learned.

She did not accept the principle of "either/or": either political work, or fulfillment as a woman. She felt that outer revolution had to be accompanied by inner revolution and she could not believe in the implementation of a just social system if it did not include an inner revolution in love. Love and the political will to change the world should come together: "If we do not want war, we need a vision for peace."

The rapidly growing group started a first interdisciplinary research center on a farm in Southern Germany. Specialists in bionics, architecture, cymatics, information technology, and medicine came together. The first experiments started in the fields of vortex research, wastewater treatment, building techniques, and research into life energy.

But soon the group had to accept that good intentions and the best expert knowledge was not enough. What was happening in the team was the same as had happened in a thousand teams before. Conflicts started over details and developed the explosive potential to break apart the whole group. Was it possible that people who wanted peace on Earth were actually not able to live together peacefully amongst themselves?

What is this explosive potential? What is it at the deepest level of truth? And wouldn't it be worthwhile after so many failed projects and experiments to observe it more closely and make this the actual object of the research? Ultimately, the question was: "How does violence develop and how can it be ended lastingly and structurally, meaning within the global system?"

This deeper level seemed to be connected with those spheres so far considered private or intimate: love, sexuality, partnership, living together, God. What was needed was a research project that dealt particularly with these core issues. So they decided on a new social experiment. Knowing that they would be pioneers in this, the members of the community decided to make themselves – the way they lived together and also their most intimate questions – the subject of the research. Fifty people would stay together for three years. Nobody would step out.

Their research covered construction, food, economy, arts, the decision-making structures of a community, healing, gardening, contact with animals, water management, and dealing with mistakes, of which they made many. They learned to pray, and learned to be interested in each other. They learned that a single sentence spoken authentically could sometimes be worth more than an entire doctoral thesis.

This social experiment ran from 1983 to 1986. After three years the group had built a profound base of knowledge about building stable communities, effective communitarian forms of communication, and the social conditions necessary for truthful and lasting love.

Dieter Duhm formulated the "Political Theory" in which he explains, based on scientific insights and many experiences, why and how a small inner shift in one part of the organism can influence the Earth as a whole; in other words, why and how local peacework can have a global effect. This is the theoretical basis for the strategy of initiating a global movement of autonomous models.

As a result of this social experiment, the group had developed generalizable community knowledge which now provided the basis for starting a comprehensive global peace research project together with global cooperation partners and specialists in various areas.

At that time this was almost impossible in Germany. Many of the results of the group's experiments had led to conflicts with the mores of society. The project was attacked by factions of the Church and media. It seemed to become more and more difficult to find a free space within German society where wide-ranging research could be possible.

After this social experiment the participants started several projects: the ZEGG (*Zentrum für experimentelle Gesellschaftsgestaltung*) seminar center close to Berlin, the dolphin research boat *Kairos*, and several ecological undertakings and cultural meeting places in cities. Parallel to this, Sabine Lichtenfels was running desert camps in various countries. Her idea was to create a space where people could concentrate on the essential things in life; to find in Creation and simplicity a new beginning. In these special surroundings, questions of global survival gained a new existential significance. One of the desert camps took place in the dune-landscape of the Alentejo, where the group came to know and love Portugal. The country made its way onto the shortlist of locations where a permanent research project could be built.

An Eagle Wants to Land

The group chose Monte do Cerro, a 134-hectare site with the shape of an eagle landing. The shepherd who showed them Monte do Cerro told them of good water and led them to a spring surrounded by a palm tree, a fig tree, and a rose. In ancient legends, such places are the home of the Goddess. Even today, when there are several water sources on the land, this spring retains a special meaning. It is said that its water is especially pure and healing.

Sabine Lichtenfels named the project that she wished to build here "Tamera". Later she came to know that the name in old Egyptian means "at the original source".

Thanks to the generosity of private donors, the site was bought in 1995 without any starting capital and without public support.

Tamera was not first explored by construction workers or electricians, nor by ecologists and gardeners, but by artists. They started to perceive the site and its character through the medium of painting. In the first weeks paintings developed: paintings of cork oaks, toads, rolling hills, bleached summer landscapes, and other manifestations of the Goddess – love declarations to the Alentejo.

Once a small group had created the infrastructure, work started on building a core community. Workshops, studios, networking offices, seminar rooms, and accommodation were built, gardens were planted, and reforestation started; all from private funds and donations. Then the group started to weave a global network of peace initiatives, inventors, and researchers and to lay the groundwork for cooperation. Experiments in energy research and ecology were part of the project from the very beginning. In the first year there was already a so-called "Summer University" with more than 100 visitors from many different countries. Soon the first education programs and conferences started.

Generation Shift and Going Global

Since 2000, Dieter Duhm and Sabine Lichtenfels had been offering peace education programs for young people. From these programs, a group of young people who had become deeply acquainted with the peacework philosophies of Tamera came together to take on responsibility. Today they are the new generation of leaders. They organize the peace education, teach today's youth, and work on the creation of the Global Campus. It is a generation shift that has succeeded, thanks to the experienced elders of the project who fully support the young generation with their knowledge.

2005 was the year of the first Grace-Pilgrimage through Israel and Palestine, and the year in which the friendship and close cooperation began between Tamera and the Peace Village San José de Apartadó in Colombia. Since the first visit in early 2005 not a year has passed without mutual visits, periods of education, or actions to support and help. The world came closer. What had been abstract news from far-away lands became true compassion. The people who suffer and die as a consequence of globalization had become friends, not statistics.

All involved realized that they had to work on the establishment of local models for the future for a globalization of peace.

Tamera had been in long preparation for the 1 May 2006 opening of the Monte Cerro Peace Education program. Peace groups and communities worldwide had been informed and a first provisional infrastructure for 200 students had been built. Since then, several peace education training modules have taken place each year and have expanded to become part of the Global Campus.

2008 saw the first education modules of the Global Campus held outside Tamera. In April, Sabine Lichtenfels and Benjamin von Mendelssohn led a seminar at the Tent of Nations, near Bethlehem in Palestine. Then in October of the same year they led, together with Padre Javier Giraldo, a pilgrimage and peace seminar in the peace village San José de Apartadó, Colombia. The program emphasized the training and skills needed to make a peace village autonomous: culturally and socially, and in medicine, energy supply, food preservation, and drinking water management.

Conclusion: Tamera as a School for the Global Community

Tamera today has become an education place, a training site, and a retreat place for peace workers from all over the world – embedded in the experience of community. The experience of the founders and the revolutionary will of the young generation, along with the need of people from crisis areas, gave the ingredients for this "School for another Future" in the frame of the "Global Campus".

The basic ethical guidelines of Tamera are studied and practised every day, in every single situation: truth, responsible participation in the community, and mutual support. They have become the guidelines for the cooperation with our emerging partner organizations like the Peace Village San José de Apartadó in Colombia; the Favela da Paz in Sao Paulo, Brazil; the Holy Land Trust in Bethlehem, Palestine; and many others.

In this way a global community awakens. May our work and that of our friends and partners serve the world and help to make the great shift towards a global peace society.

Chapter 6

Spirituality in the Camphill Villages

Jan Martin Bang

Camphill Villages, a Short History

During the 1930s a group of intellectuals began meeting regularly in Vienna. They were inspired by Anthroposophy, the teachings of Rudolf Steiner, and how these could be put into practice in the fields of health and education. They were joined by Dr. Karl König, Viennese by birth, originally Jewish, but in his teens he stopped attending the local synagogue and began attending a Catholic Church. Later he became deeply inspired by Anthroposophy. As the political situation became more threatening, they decided they had to move. After the *Anschluss* in 1938, when Nazi Germany invaded Austria, they dispersed throughout Europe. Many of them came together again at Kirkton Manse in rural Aberdeenshire in Scotland in the beginning of 1939, where they found an already very well-established and connected British anthroposophical network.

They opened a curative educational institute and began taking in children with special needs. When the Second World War started some months later, the group was registered as enemy aliens, the married men were interned on the Isle of Man and the single men were transported to Canada. The women carried on working with the children and a larger house was found, and they moved there to Camphill House on 1 June 1940. When the men returned the community then comprised some 30 people of whom just less than half were children with special needs. The group saw themselves as political refugees working with social refugees.

During the 1940s the community grew and, by taking over other houses and estates, created a movement. During the next few decades the Camphill network expanded and developed, reaching out to England, Ireland, Germany, Holland, Norway, South Africa, and the United States. In the early 1950s, König began to think about village communities, where adults with special needs could live together with co-workers in extended family situations. This was first put into practice at the Botton Estate in 1955, and the first Camphill Village as we know it today was established. Botton created a model which has been the basis for Camphill for over half a century. The village now contains well over 300 residents in four clusters spread throughout a valley leading up to the North York Moors in northern England.

Throughout the world today there are more than 100 Camphill Communities in over 20 countries. They are organized into seven regions, and a number of magazines and newsletters keep information flowing between them. There is a strong element of internationalism, and regular meetings are held within the regions. There is a good deal of internal movement of co-workers and residents from one community to another. In addition to the communities that are formal members of Camphill, there are many similar communities and institutions, also inspired by Anthroposophy and working with people with special needs.

Camphill Villages, What are They?

Within Camphill villages most people live in large extended families, co-workers (both long-term people with their families, and young temporary volunteers) and villagers (adults with special needs), sharing their lives, their meals, their living rooms, and bathrooms. There may be as many as fifteen people or more gathered round the dining table three times a day. Each house has its own budget, and is run more or less autonomously by a team of responsible co-workers. In the morning and the afternoon everyone goes to work, in a variety of workplaces. A typical Camphill village might have a farm, extensive vegetable gardens, a bakery, a weavery, herb growing and drying, and a large forest for timber and firewood. All farming and gardening is done biodynamically, that is farming with a full cosmic consciousness, aware of the rhythms of the seasons, the earth, the moon, the sun, and the planets, and of cooperation with the spirit world. Biodynamic farming uses no artificial chemicals or fertilizers.

Other villages have workshops which produce pottery, candles, dolls, or wooden toys. It is possible to eat meals in Camphill houses where the table and chairs came from the carpentry shop, the tablecloth from the weavery, the plates and cups from the pottery, the candles (which are lit at every meal) from the candle shop, and virtually all the food could be produced by the village: bread, milk products, jams, vegetables, herb teas, honey, and meat. This self sufficiency is not an end in itself, but rather a way of ensuring that each person is employed doing something that is useful to the village. In many cases in mainstream society, people with special needs are peripheralized and "looked after", and so denied an active and useful role. In the world of Camphill, every person has something to contribute, and feels self-worth even when fetching the milk or laying the table.

In addition to the work branches, there are the houses to be run; washing, cooking, and cleaning. This is considered work, just as important as production, and the occupation of "housewife", "house mother", or "homemaker" is as vital to the well-being of the community as any other profession. Everyone has a workplace, and contributes something useful to the running of the village, according to his or her capability. Within this sphere no money changes hands, and work is seen to be something that is freely given within the fellowship, recognizing that some people have higher capabilities than others. In recent years, more and more Camphill communities are experiencing a need to employ people for specific tasks, introducing a new group of salaried employees. However, Camphill still strives to create fellowship in the economic life, and a flexible equality in the social sphere.

The farms and gardens in Camphill villages are usually biodynamic, producing food of the highest quality while nurturing both soil and wildlife. Generally, the organic waste from the kitchens is composted, usually by a village compost set-up. Horse transport is quite common, being very efficient and low cost at a village scale. Villages in England have pioneered waste water treatment using ponds, reedbeds, and "Flow Form" water cascades. These are now standard in the Norwegian villages, and throughout Camphill worldwide. Buildings, both communal halls and chapels, and the large residential houses, are largely constructed out of natural materials, and avoid the use of poisons and plastics as much as possible. However, there is still much to be done in the raising of consciousness, and in building, transport, recycling, and energy use.

Bible Evening

One of the things that creates a special atmosphere within Camphill is the gathering held on Saturday evenings called the Bible Evening. Originally this was for co-workers without the children or residents with special needs. Later this gathering was held less formally in households in the villages, and everyone was made welcome, and in some places it came to be called the Bible Supper. Today the more formal Bible Evening, for co-workers only, has virtually disappeared, and has given its name to the less formal household gathering, but even this is now becoming less widely practiced.

For the less formal Bible Evening, or Bible Supper, everyone from the household meets in the living room dressed in their best clothes and sits in silence around a lit candle for ten to fifteen minutes. Some of the younger co-workers sit cross legged with closed eyes and in deep concentration. Older co-workers tell me that they picture to themselves co-workers who have passed away, bringing them back for their support and help for the present. Personally I go around the room, making myself aware of each person present, and picture their spiritual qualities. I then picture the spiritual quality of the household, a symbol of our little house community present at that place and in that time.

The founder of the Camphill communities, Karl König, called this part spiritual recollection. This sets the scene, creating an atmosphere quite different from other household gatherings. It is not often that we sit in silence together. It can be a powerful tool for reflection, and for togetherness. By being together in silence, we invite everyone in. Silence can speak louder than words.

At a signal, someone who has agreed to do this beforehand gets up, lights the candle at the dining table, extinguishes the one in the sitting room, and invites everyone to the table.

A simple meal has been prepared beforehand; rolls with a variety of spreads, often with sprigs of salad or a dash of mayonnaise. Juice made from our own berries or fruit is already poured into glasses. There is a tablecloth, and next to the candle a vase of flowers, a crystal, and a piece of driftwood. These represent important things. The crystal is a mystery from the mineral world, something very basic to our physical existence. The driftwood is a reminder of the plant world, the organic element upon our table, as is the living flower. The candle is something alive, it has an archetypal quality, bringing us back tens of thousands of years. For most of our existence as human beings upon this planet we have gathered around the fire in the evening to talk, to partake in rituals, to sit in silence.

Before we bless the food we recite a short verse:

> Let the peace of Christ rest upon everything we see,
> Upon the food we are about to eat,
> Upon my body which comes from the earth,
> Upon my soul which comes from the spiritual world.
> Bless the food!

Other verses may be read instead of this one. As we eat we try to focus the conversation on the events of the last week. Personally, I favor small groups for these gatherings, so that we can easily have one conversation round the table. More than eight or ten people tend to split up into two or three individual conversations.

"How was your week?"

"Can you remember something special from this week?"

"What happened this week?"

We try to remember birthdays, changes in our work, new people, others leaving or traveling. I expand from those present to what happened in the village. Was there a festival? Some special event? What happened in the country, in the world? Often there is someone at the table who listens to the news or reads newspapers. We try to go through the week, winding it up, putting it away, the good times with the hard times. It's important to allow people to say what they think, and not make value judgments. What is important to one person may not resonate with everyone else; it's completely subjective.

König considered this part of the Bible Evening to be spiritual reflection. We concentrate on what has happened since we last sat together and make sure each individual around the table is included by asking questions.

When we have finished the food, we clear away the plates and glasses, hand out Bibles to those who want them, and read the verses selected for that week. Every year, someone within the wider Camphill Community network takes it upon themselves to select readings for every week, and this gets circulated to every village. Mostly they are from one of the four Gospels, but occasionally something from an Epistle or the Revelation of St John appears. I usually stick to the designated readings, but if the passage is too obscure or difficult for me, I choose something else. Most Bibles have cross-referencing notes, and the first thing I do is to check any Old Testament references. These often open up new readings which may be easier to deal with. Whatever the text, we read it, and then use the text as a starting point for a conversation. It could be a phrase, a word, the story we just read, or whatever is suggested to us by the reading. Again, the challenge is to get everyone involved, asking questions, telling anecdotes, eliciting comments.

König suggests that this part of the evening can be used to gain spiritual insight. This need not be the exclusive domain of intelligent co-workers. In fact, I see the over-intellectualization of the conversation as a dangerous pitfall. For me, it's vitally important that villagers, people with special needs, be encouraged to participate as much as possible. Images and stories are much more powerful tools to use than intellectual ideas. Pictures speak louder than clever thoughts.

Eventually it's time to finish, the Bibles are closed, and a verse is said, always the same, and often several of the villagers join in.

> The stars spake once to man.
> It is World-destiny
> That they are silent now.
> To be aware of the silence
> Can become pain for earthly Man.

> But in the deepening silence
> There grows and ripens
> What Man speaks to the Stars.
> To be aware of the speaking
> Can become strength for Spirit-Man.

This is the traditional Camphill Bible Evening. There can be variations, we can choose different texts and different verses, and sometimes young co-workers arrange for completely different activities: going to the cinema, taking a walk, teaming up with another house, or painting together.

Anthroposophy – The Inspiration

The group that established itself at Camphill House in 1940 was attempting to put the ideals of Anthroposophy into practice. This is a spiritual science based on the books and lectures given by Rudolf Steiner from about 1900 until his death in 1925. Anthroposophy proposes the physical world as a development and outgrowth of the spiritual world, and presents a scientific method of analyzing this spiritual world. Anthroposophy was in turn inspired by Theosophy, eastern mysticism and the traditions of Gnosticism, the Rosicrucians, the alchemists, and the worldview expressed by Johann Wolfgang von Goethe.

Steiner's lectures and books had encouraged people in many professions to develop their fields according to the anthroposophical worldview. The most well-known today are probably the Steiner Waldorf schools in the educational field and biodynamic agriculture. These concern themselves with the soul development of the child, and the spiritual aspects of soil and plant growth respectively. In addition, a great deal of work has been done in the fields of architecture, art, music, dance, health through anthroposophical medicine and therapies, health products such as Weleda and Wala, nutrition, and such technical developments as waste water treatment and food quality analysis. The Camphill network specializes in curative education and social therapy, both directly inspired by the lectures and writings of Rudolf Steiner.

Anthroposophy is based on two Greek words which mean the study of or the wisdom about human beings. It recognizes each individual's humanity, not just as a product of biology and environment, but as a productive and creative spiritual creature. It places humanity in the center, regardless of sex, culture, religion, or other grouping.

Anthroposophy regards the earth as a living organism and that humanity has a responsibility to care for it. Because of this, Anthroposophy encourages the creation of humane social structures which find their expression in kindergartens and schools throughout the world, biodynamic farms, anthroposophical medical practice, curative education, ethical banking, and many other initiatives.

Anthroposophy regards art, science, and religion to be of equal value in our understanding of reality. It tries to combine these three aspects into a holistic perspective. Every individual can develop the means to be in touch with the spiritual world through meditative practices. Anthroposophy tries to develop independent thinking and avoids dogmatism and sectarianism.

Steiner had his own thoughts about community, and how the evolution of human consciousness had moved from community based on blood ties and tradition, through the fragmentation of pursuing individual freedom, and into a new and transcendent form of universal community, this time out of free choice.

> The evolution of individuality is such that the human being passes out of a condition in which he is part of the community, subservient to it and dependent on it, through the processes whereby the ego emancipates itself from the community, and thence into a condition in which the independent ego either goes off on its own, or recreates human community out of its own.[1]

Steiner connects the freedom of the individual with the impulse to create community:

---

[1] Quoted in Christopher Boughton Hudd, *Rudolf Steiner, Economist* (Canterbury, 1996).

> This is an important characteristic of spiritual life: it has its springs in freedom, in the individual initiative of the single human being, and yet it draws men together, and forms communities out of what they have in common.[2]

The Camphill Movement is a community-building initiative composed of many individuals working together. Each individual brings a unique contribution, and together these individuals create the character of Camphill life. This in turn reflects back onto the individual in a feedback loop, reinforcing the Camphill impulse. Anthroposophy is embedded in this process and contributes to the social renewal which is such an important feature of the Camphill ideals.

Spirituality in Camphill

The celebration of the Bible Evening was originally undertaken by those who entered into what König established as the Camphill Community. While the Camphill Movement includes all who live and work within the schools and villages comprising the Camphill network, Camphill Community is a much smaller and distinct group within the Camphill Movement. This is a group of core co-workers, who commit themselves to spiritual self-development with regular study meetings, and a strong connection to the Christian Community, the church established by anthroposophically inspired religious people, with its own structure of priests and rituals. The Camphill Community has a clear membership process, regular local, regional, and international meetings, but very few archives, no real statutes as such, and no financial or legal existence. To quote from a letter written after a recent international meeting: "We do not want to give a report as this could fix what is living and fluid." Members of Camphill Community keep the spiritual aspect of community alive by being aware of it, studying it, and letting it permeate the outer, everyday work they carry out in their community.

For the members of Camphill Community, it is important to gain an insight into one's own personal situation. The founders of Camphill met powerful spiritual forces, and paid a great deal of attention to their inner lives. There was always a danger that the outer life would dominate, and that the inner schooling

---

[2] Rudolf Steiner, *The Inner Aspect of the Social Question* (London, 1974).

would be overshadowed. What happens around an individual is the result of that person's inner life. The events of our daily lives are mirrors of internal events. Today, Camphill Community is an international network combining esoteric inner work with external social strivings.

Christianity in Camphill

Count Nicolaus Ludwig von Zinzendorf (1700–1760), the early leader of the Moravian Church, and regarded by Karl König as one of the ideological and spiritual guiding stars of Camphill, wrote in his day that "there is no Christianity without Community". König turned this around to say that "there is no Community without Christianity". This might be disturbing to all those people who live communally in thriving, healthy communities, but don't adhere to any Christian faith. However, König develops his idea in a more flexible way:

> For the Camphill Movement, Christianity is an indispensable part of its life and work; it works out of Christianity, not for Christianity. Just as the Movement is not an anthroposophical group or society, it is equally little a Christian sect or congregation. Those who work in and for the Movement are entirely free to be members of any Christian church as well as of any group or society if they so wish.[3]

This was written decades after Steiner welded Anthroposophy firmly to the Christian impulse. He wrote in his book about the festivals:

> If you accept the spirit of Anthroposophia in reality, then you will find that it opens up the human ear, the human heart and the whole soul of man for the Mystery of Christ. The whole destiny of Anthroposophia intends to be the destiny of Christianity.[4]

---

[3] Karl König, *The Camphill Movement* (Whitby, 1993).
[4] Rudolf Steiner, *The Festivals and Their Meaning* (London, 1981).

From its beginning, Camphill has been inspired by the Christian ideals articulated by Rudolf Steiner and on the acceptance of the spiritual uniqueness of each human being, regardless of disability or religious or racial background. Christian ideals, practices, and attitudes lie at the heart of Camphill's cultural, religious, and spiritual life.

Even though many of the founders, the youth group that met in Vienna in the 1930s, were Jewish or atheist, there were a number of Christian influences which became important for them. They studied and performed the Oberufer Christmas plays, which gave them a good deal of comfort during the chaotic days in Vienna just before the *Anschluss*. These Christmas plays were a cycle of medieval mystery plays from the village Oberufer in the vicinity of Bratislava. König was strongly influenced by the Herrnhutter communities of the Moravian Church. His wife Tilla came from the Gnadenfrei Moravian community in Silesia (today Poland). The importance of this last influence is reinforced by König regarding Zinzendorf as one of the guiding stars of the Camphill Movement, together with Robert Owen (1771–1858) and Amos Comenius (1592–1670).

Another strong influence was embedded in their study of Anthroposophy. Steiner regarded the Christ impulse as fundamental to understanding how humanity is evolving and developing. The Crucifixion and Resurrection of Christ is the leverage point for humanity, often referred to by Steiner as "The Golgotha Event". The founders of Camphill combined study sessions with Bible Evenings, Christian Community services and the celebration of festivals such as Christmas, Easter, St John's and Michaelmas throughout the year. This Christian calendar gave Camphill inspiration, hope, and the strength to establish new communities on several continents.

This is a Christianity which focuses on a universal Christ figure rather than on the human Jesus. This elevates the Christ to a cosmic spiritual force relevant to all cultures and traditions. Love and respect for each individual is fundamental, as is the urge to carry out good actions, "loving your neighbor as yourself". When practiced in the context of Camphill village life this becomes a universal code of behavior, rooted in Christianity, but no doubt not much different from Buddhist, Islamic, or any other religion's code of behavior.

For its first 70 years, these Christian ideals gave Camphill its special character, defining it as a movement, and giving it an identity. But Camphill lives in the world, and the world around it is changing, is regaining the sense of the spiritual, not only going back to embrace the traditional established religions, but reaching out to a more universal spiritual awareness. In this process, established religious practices are often lumped together with the older ways of thought and action, and become less attractive. So the Bible Evening is increasingly neglected, services and festivals are not celebrated, study groups are less well attended, and Camphill Community meetings are no longer held regularly.

Universal Values in Camphill

Since the time of Steiner and of König, albeit from small beginnings but gaining ground throughout the 1970s and 1980s, there has emerged in the world a new idea of major world religions having a respectful dialogue, accepting each others' differences and likenesses, listening and trying to understand each other without attempting any kind of missionary activity. The spread of inter-faith dialogue is a departure in human consciousness that gives an enormous sense of hope for the future.

Today, in the twenty-first century, an increasing number of people are not satisfied with what they perceive as old and restrictive forms of regulated religion. This may be one of the reasons co-workers hesitate to engage with the traditional religious life of Camphill, such as the Christian Community services and the Bible Evenings. They are often more interested in a spirituality that respects differences of understanding, that is open to diversity, and which recognizes the universal spiritual reality in all religions and cultures. The question "What is Camphill?" is an ongoing debate, and as society struggles to emerge from centuries of thought dominated by a hierarchical and dogmatic worldview, there is no doubt that Camphill reflects that struggle within itself.

Interestingly enough, the traditional Camphill forms of spiritual life are often stronger in the pioneering communities, while well-established villages experience the weakening of familiar forms of services and the Bible Evening. It may be that a truly mature community has the flexibility to experiment with new forms, while pioneering groups need the strong structures which carried the earlier Camphill communities through their formative years.

With new initiatives emerging in Vietnam, Pakistan, and India, embedded in Buddhist, Islamic, and Hindu cultures, a new debate is emerging within the Camphill Movement. One school of thought regards the original Christian framework as an integral and necessary part of the Camphill definition. Others take a more universal approach, and as long as the spiritual essence of every individual is safeguarded will happily welcome new initiatives into the Camphill fold. The interesting irony of this particular debate revolves around the ideas of karma and reincarnation, ideas which Steiner elaborated on with much detail, and which are more at home within the Hindu and Buddhist cultures than the Western European Christian tradition. Acceptance of a more universalist approach does not necessarily imply that the essence of Christian tradition would disappear, rather that there would emerge an openness to what other cultures and religions have to offer the spiritual life within the community.

Such a change would take time, thought, and reflection to emerge within Camphill, but would constitute a growing strength and relevance to the movement. The fact that the Camphill form is seen to be manifesting itself in other cultural and religious matrices shows that it still has a part to play in a world that is inevitably becoming global.

Karl König's guiding star Zinzendorf is quoted as having said:

> Nature is full of different creatures of different inclinations, and it is the same in the spiritual world. We must learn to regard various ways of thinking as something beautiful. There are as many religious ideas as there are believing souls, so we cannot force everyone to measure up to the same yard stick. Only God, according to his infinite wisdom, knows how to deal with every soul.[5]

Zinzendorf was talking here about different Christian traditions, but it might equally apply to the many different religions rubbing shoulders in today's globalized world.

Rudolf Steiner formulated a similar idea in a slightly different way:

> Spiritual Science, when considering individual religions, does not look at outer rites and ceremonies, but at the way in which the age old universal core of

---

[5] Janet and Geoff Benge, *Count Zinzendorf* (Seattle, 1958).

wisdom is contained/manifest in it. The religions are so and so many channels which allow that which was once poured out evenly over the whole of humanity to shine out in single rays ... and if we really search this essence/kernel of truth in all religions than this leads to peace. No religion, when truly recognized in the light of spiritual science, wants to impose its own special ray of truth on another religion ... All nations and religions on earth can belong to Buddha, the great teacher of the highest truth. And all nations and religions on earth can belong to Christ, the divine power of the highest truth. And this mutual understanding means peace on earth. And this peace, this is the soul of the new world.[6]

Addressing universal human spiritual forms can create a dialogue which crosses cultural boundaries. The individual needs to link up with others, linking up beyond individual initiatives, linking together whole communities and whole movements. Margarete van den Brink sees organizations as passing through seven stages of development, the ultimate one summed up as follows:

In Phase 7, the organisation aims in particular at the contribution it wants to make to the development of the greater whole. Here again we see that spiritual development in people always continues. While the emphasis on the development of awareness lay on the personal in Phase 5 and on relationships with others in Phase 6, we see that awareness and effort of organisations in Phase 7 are aimed at care for, and further development of, the greater whole of which we are part: society, mankind, nature, the earth, the world, the cosmos.[7]

Camphill as a Spiritual Organism

All communities are, at heart, spiritual creations. They are held together by a web of relationships that spring from the spirit. The material forms, the buildings, the fields, the technology, and the economy are all dependent upon these subtle

---

[6] Quoted by Angelika Monteux in Jan Martin Bang (ed.), *A Portrait of Camphill* (Edinburgh, 2010).
[7] Margarete van den Brink, *Transforming People and Organisations* (Forest Row, 2004).

relationships between the individuals that make up that community. If these relationships fall apart the community will also fall apart. We can keep community artificially alive, the buildings can still stand, the fields can still be cultivated, and people can seem to go about their daily tasks. But without that subtle web of relationships that builds community, the spirit of community will cease to function.

In Camphill there are two parallel impulses. One consists of working with people who need help, based upon meeting people and recognizing that they have physical, psychological, and spiritual aspects, each contributing to create the unique individual that we come face to face with. This can be considered an "inner" work, and co-workers are encouraged to spend time studying, both on their own and in groups.

The other impulse consists of creating an alternative society, based upon the idea of threefolding. This idea was presented by Rudolf Steiner in lectures during the last part of the First World War and the years that followed. He traced how the three great ideals of the French Revolution – Fraternity, Equality, and Liberty – had been corrupted by the rise of nationalism and the development of the centralized nation state. Threefolding was presented by Steiner as a way of rebuilding Europe after the disaster of the First World War, but his ideas did not gain credence and remained largely dormant until taken up by Karl König in building up the Camphill communities in the 1940s and 1950s. König based his thoughts on his study of the development of European society over the preceding centuries. In England, he saw the industrial revolution as the modernization of economic life, leading to demands for fraternity, the development of trade unionism, and labor party politics. In France under the French Revolution he saw a change in the legal life leading to demands for equality, and in Middle Europe (later unified to become Germany) changes in the spiritual life leading to demands for liberty. König further traced how a failure to integrate these three ideas led to the insanity of Nazism, fascism, and state communism after Steiner's death.

We worship and philosophize, educate, create music and art in the *spiritual sphere*. Here we need our freedom to develop ourselves.

We decide amongst ourselves, regulate our lives together, in the *sphere of laws* and rights, and here we need to regard ourselves as equals, with equal rights.

We work, produce, buy, and sell in the *economic sphere*, and need the fellowship (brotherhood and sisterhood) of looking after each other, not necessarily as equals, for clearly, some have more capacity and some have greater needs.

These three spheres are always with us; they are not determinants of how we should or might behave, but an attempt to make sense of our everyday lives and how we come together as human beings.

There are a few other community movements which combine these two impulses of working with people who have special needs and creating an alternative society, but Camphill is by far the largest and most widely spread. This combination has given Camphill the strength and motivation which has enabled it to spread to over 20 countries and kept it alive and healthy for 70 years.

Many communities are focused around some higher ideal of improving society or encouraging greater environmental awareness. This may be a collective task that the individual can, to a certain extent, lose him or herself in.

Many new ideas are introduced into the social realm through community, and live on after the community phase of the idea is over. The communal manifestation of these ideas is often an initial "ephemeral" period in the life of the idea. We can see this in Christianity, Seventh-Day Adventists, Baptists, Mormons, Robert Owen, and Fourier, all of whom introduced new ideas that went through a communal phase which faded away, leaving just the ideas to establish themselves throughout society. Communal living could be seen as a vehicle rather than a destination, and the widely viewed failure of communities to last beyond a few decades may be a completely misleading interpretation. The whole idea of measuring the success or failure of community should be directed at how much the idea behind the communal impulse penetrates the wider society. It would be fitting to enquire whether this idea is relevant to Camphill, a movement that is now 70 years old, including communities in over 20 countries spanning several continents.

A hint of this idea can be found in a book by Friedrich Glasl, writing about corporate development:

> I am convinced that the social forms which will occupy us intensively over the next decades already exist in embryonic form.[8]

---

[8] Friedrich Glasl, *The Enterprise of the Future* (Stroud, 1994).

The Future of Camphill

In 2003, Michael and Jane Luxford, two seasoned Camphill co-workers, published the results of several years visiting Camphill communities around the world. Their conclusion was:

> In 50 years very few Camphill places may remain; but by then there will be new ways of working together out of an impulse through which you learn to practice the reality of empathy. In the future our present working and thinking will be useless, but through Camphill life we will have learnt something about human love, human discipline and human involvement.[9]

Whether few or many Camphill communities will still be functioning 50 years from now may be unimportant. What is certain is that the ideas and practices that have been developed within the Camphill network will be found as the seeds of the social forms of the future. In this way the spirit of Camphill will live on, regardless of the physical form.

---

[9] Michael and Jane Luxford, *A Sense for Community* (Whitby, 2003).

Chapter 7

The Farm

Albert Bates

What is the essence of a religious view? It might not always be called religious, and that can confound an inquiry. In numerous public appearances over 40 years, Stephen Gaskin was frequently asked to describe the religion of The Farm spiritual community, which he founded in 1971. "Free thinkers" was his usual reply.

In the countercultural blossoming of the late 1960s, Stephen, as everyone has always called him, began teaching an experimental course at San Francisco State College. He outgrew that venue, and what became known as the Monday Night Class also outgrew the Gallery Lounge, the Straight Theater, the Glide Memorial Church, and eventually filled a concert hall on the coast with as many as 2,000 free spirits once every week. After three years of the class, Stephen left on a bus tour of colleges, churches, and seminaries that crossed the United States. More than 80 school buses followed in the now-famous "Caravan". The 320 inhabitants of those buses became the core group that landed in Summertown, Tennessee, and founded The Farm in 1971. *The Wall Street Journal* would later call The Farm "the General Motors of American Communes".

What can be said of The Farm is that its spiritual philosophy was neither uniform nor unique. Stephen often remarked that The Farm was the largest Jewish congregation, the largest Buddhist Sangha, the largest Hindu ashram, and the largest collection of Catholics in southern middle Tennessee. All of these faiths, and others, were drawn into The Farm, and seldom were any of those faiths completely abandoned by those who were brought up in them. The Farm's "religion" was really a unifying philosophy: that all who believed in something greater than themselves – "Big Mind" as Stephen put it in Monday Night Class – held an inherent truth that could be proven simply by the feel and fit of it.

To try to get inside that philosophy, I interviewed Stephen Gaskin on 12 September 2011. He was 76 years old and we met in a bedroom "office" that had once been a salvaged army tent, but was now framed, roofed, and insulated. He had been living there for 38 years and the room was filled with mementos from the lives of Stephen and his wife, Ina May Gaskin. Stephen is the author of over a dozen books, a father, grandfather, teacher, musician, and political activist (he was a Green Party presidential candidate in 2000 on a platform that included campaign finance reform, universal health care, and decriminalization of marijuana). He went to prison in 1974 on a one-to-three year sentence for marijuana possession following a raid at The Farm that turned up more than a thousand cannabis plants being privately cultivated by Farm residents contrary to his express wishes. Stephen became the first Right Livelihood Award laureate in 1980 for his work in establishing The Farm and Plenty International – its emergency relief and sustainable development organization now active on six continents. Ina May received the Right Livelihood Award in 2011 for her work in restoring the practice of midwifery to a respected profession.

Through several decades of regular sermons at the Farm and from speaking tours abroad, Stephen produced a substantial body of spiritual teaching, much of it published by the community's Book Publishing Company. For all of that, Stephen Gaskin does not call himself religious but rather, according to Wikipedia, "a self-proclaimed professional hippy".

My own history follows Stephen's from the time I was 25 years old. I arrived at The Farm in 1972 as a law school graduate who was in the midst of hiking the Appalachian Trail and had stopped by for a visit. After a brief taste, I never left. Attracted by the power of the teachings and the beauty of The Farm community, I chose to become a "Farmie". For my first seven years there, I abandoned my legal career for one of horse trainer and plowman, brick mason, flour miller, and solar engineer. Only when the battle over nuclear power arrived at our doorstep did I feel compelled to return to the practice of law. In 1978 I opened a small public interest firm at The Farm, called The Natural Rights Center. When Tennessee passed a law retroactively disenfranchising felons, I brought litigation on Stephen's behalf that carried to the State Supreme Court where we not only restored his right to vote but also restored the franchise to more than 250,000 convicts. Many cases, political intrigues, and books ensued from my choice to resume a career as a lawyer, but I retired a second time in 1995 to pursue my abiding interest in broader alternatives, the legal system included. I guess you could say I was more of a carrot than a stick person. I became a founding director of the Global Ecovillage Network and for 10 years traveled the world looking at efforts underway to alter the way humans relate to our planet and its ecosystems. I found myself writing, doing public speaking, and developing useful approaches to cultural transition, on the ground and in actual practice. In 2005, I retired again and now just teach and write about what I've learned, and I try to guide a younger generation towards real sustainability in all its dimensions.

We begin the interview speaking of the beginnings of Stephen's "coming out" as a home-spun, hippy public speaker in the late 1960s in the Haight-Ashbury district of San Francisco.

***

Stephen: I guess you want me to start back at Monday Night Class.

Albert: Well, for you, the religious experiment experience began earlier, so I guess I'd like to take it back to an earlier point in your life. You started with attitudes that you held in the Marine Corps – agnostic, atheist, whatever – and at some point it switched to "I am going to follow God, I am going to follow God, I am not coming back" in the words of the peyote prayer. So what was that change?

Stephen: Well, one of the main things about it is, what my concept of God is. And my concept of God has become the absolute all totality of everything. So, you can't do anything that isn't God, because that's all there is to do. So, the question to me in that case is, are you good people? And I don't consider myself a religious person except in those terms. And I don't follow any culture or religion or anything like that. I've read deeply a whole lot of them, but if you want to pass out the praise and blame, right now our culture's down on Islam, but nothing Islam ever did holds a candle to the Spanish Inquisition.

Albert: Or Christianity in general.

Stephen: Yeah.

Albert: That's the place that John Lennon was singing about when he said, "And no religion too". Some of your thing, as I understand it, since the beginning, has been to keep from getting institutionalized.

Stephen: Yeah, that's why I never really tried real hard to do Monday Night Class at The Farm. And now I'm trying not to do Sunday services anymore. I don't mind talking to people and stuff but I'm not starting a religion. The only reason we did our meetings on Sunday was that that was when the stores were closed. It was an open day of the week that way. I don't want to be considered a preacher. Preachers bug me.

Albert: (laughs).

Stephen: I don't want to be considered a preacher but I figure if anyone has a question they want to ask me they're welcome to.

Albert: So who do you think your greatest influences in retrospect were, at this point in your life? I can think of Aldous Huxley, Suzuki Roshi, but whom do you think of?

Stephen: So, I went to go see Aldous Huxley and he was a smart, good dude. I really loved him a lot and he's my idea of how a guy who's blessed with being born smart can pay his taxes by doing good.

Albert: Being someone with an AA, BA, and MA, I take it you don't have a lot of truck with academic credentials?

Stephen: Everyone knows what bullshit is. My grandmother used to say, MS means "more of the same". And PhD means "piled higher and deeper". Been reading the Farmlist lately and a few other distinctions come to mind. There's bullshit, which is true by accident or design. There is horseshit, which is very regulation-tight and strict, and then chickenshit, which is irrelevant and petty. And then I would add one to the list, which is the straight poop.

Albert: So whom did you get the straight poop from?

Stephen: I was a voluminous reader from the time I was a kid. My father got me started reading when I was four. I was getting in trouble in the first grade because I couldn't stay with the reading circle. I was reading ahead in the book. I got to the point where I realized that nothing I encountered in school was a higher grade of information than what my reading was providing for me.

I was always going to a new school. My father had asthma and so we moved a lot and it took me to school in different places; we were moving all the time. In Denver I had an English teacher who knew I couldn't produce the parts of speech if asked, but she could give me any twisted, messed up sentence and I could make a perfect, perfectly correct, sentence in seconds. Which is from reading all the time. The structures of the language are ingrained in my thought processes.

So LSD got me thinking in terms of God. I never had previously thought in terms of God. I got to a place where acid and native religious structures seem to come together. As much as you could call me a Christian you could call a Peyote Catholic (laughs).

Albert: It seems you do have an extraordinary gift with words, and it's likely that that formed early.

Stephen: And when I was 10, I walked to school every day alongside the barbed wire fence that ran along the perimeter of the German POW complex. Some of the prisoners were trustees and spoke English. And I could talk to them through the wire. So I was having conversations with prisoners of war when I was 10. One prisoner told me he was a perfect physical specimen, an Aryan in full blood, and he had his special card. Which meant that any tall, perfectly blonde, well-endowed German woman had to put out for him to make the master race. Well, he had a problem with this. His girlfriend was short, dark, and Jewish. So what he did was, he surrendered to the first American GI he saw. So everything I learned about World War II, I learned through him.

But then as I studied more and more, it was outside the norm, and when I started doing Monday Night Class that also started off like a research thing. We were all relating our psychedelic experiences to see what we could pull together and what our knowledge was. I was having to read constantly to do my homework, to be able to speak knowledgeably about all the directions of religion and philosophy that kept coming up. So I had a really intensive care of that discussion.

Albert: Yes, I remember that; at Monday Night Class you are talking about Hermes, Kaballah, Transmission of Mind, and various other arcane teachings. You were a regular walking Wikipedia.

Stephen: (laughs) Yeah. Yeah. And then it got to where it stopped being theoretical. It wasn't just theoretical anymore. One of those was around the time of Kent State. About a hundred hardcore political guys showed up Monday night and said, "got to get guns and get arms 'cause they're killing us".

Albert: That was the night you got dosed with acid.

Stephen: I'm having that argument, and a little girl gave me some candy that was loaded with acid. Then I'm on a lot of acid having an argument. So it was 2,000 people and I told them, I've been dosed with this acid and I'd like to go out onto the beach now. And the consensus was "You are going to stay here and come to a resolution of the argument before you can leave." And without thinking much about it I said, "Man I been coming in here to say, love and peace, and you guys been saying 'yeah yeah' and I say love and peace, and you guys say 'yeah yeah' and I say love and peace, and you guys say ..." And the whole audience said, "Yeah yeah". And I said thank you I'm going out to the beach with my acid now.

Albert: A lesson I took from that particular Monday Night Class also, was that you got to a certain point under the gun from all these folks at you and you're tripping and you said at that point you "just got to jettison the baggage", meaning anything you had planned for, anything you had going on, had to be set aside, and you needed to just be in the moment.

Stephen: Yeah, and in a way it was one of my best trips, because it came to such a crackerjack resolution.

Albert: Is there anything about your spiritual beliefs that you consider original to you, as opposed to derived from someone else's teaching?

Stephen: Well, I think that the thing about my definition of God comes from Catholic credo among other places.

Albert: "Catholic" is all of it together.

Stephen: Yeah. And it was that if God has all knowledge and is everywhere at once, well, I thought, well that which has all knowledge and is everything and everywhere at once is the totality of the manifestation; that's the universe, the whole thing. Well, once you look at it like that, it's sort of obvious. What else? So for me, the idea that God is a separate entity from his creation who reaches into that creation and does things, is inconsistent.

Albert: So it seemed to me that Buddhism had a certain kind of draw, whether it's the presence of the Zen Center at Tassajara or whatever, it was that Buddhism seems to encompass what you were feeling.

Stephen: Well it wasn't Buddhism, but a specific school of Zen, because Zen cuts itself off from much of Buddhism.

Albert: Okay, let's be specific. Would you say it was the Soto school, as a particular path of Zen?

Stephen: Yes! I would get that particular about it. I have a picture of Suzuki Roshi right up there (points) on the shelf, next to Ina May's picture of an Alabama granny midwife.

Albert: So could you explain that a little bit? What is it about the Soto school of Zen that distinguishes it?

Stephen: One of the things is there's no such thing as the sudden school and the gradual school. If you're in the gradual school, you're just slow in the sudden school.

Albert: (laughs)

Stephen: The reason there can be a sudden school is because it's so simple. There is only one and you are part of that one. And if you're honest in how you deal with that one, you fit in. And I don't really have any special claim. There are smart guys that I really like, but putting Saint in front of somebody's name doesn't really do anything. I was not canonized, I was satirized (in "St. Stephen", a Grateful Dead song).

Albert: Meditation is a big piece of Soto school. Meditation was also something we did here at The Farm and you did at Monday Night Class and the Caravan. How do you feel about that practice and how has your practice evolved over time?

Stephen: I pretty much take any quiet place or moment. I pretty much take any fruitful moment as it comes by. I don't take any special time or place for it. I don't have a position to sit in or anything. But when it gets to a certain place, I stop and pay attention. And attention is the real gold standard. Pay attention to what's going on, and to other people, integrate all of it together and it gives you a nice worldview.

Albert: I think, sitting enough, you can get to a nice state where you can be in a sitting frame of mind just walking around the world. You can't help, actually, but lapse back into it from time to time.

Stephen: Yeah! That's how I feel. I don't mind anyone who wants to have a meditation any time. That's fine with me, go for it. Actually, it doesn't have anything to do with me, it has to do with you, in your head.

Albert: Okay, and then, the association with plants and how that changed you, warped you, as you began to experiment.

Stephen: Well, I didn't smoke pot when I was young and, you know? I didn't smoke until I was in the Marine Corps. And that one is mostly famous for coming home and eating everything in the refrigerator (laughs).

Albert: Has it changed?

Stephen: I have basically been very short rations on reefer for several years. I just don't smoke very much very often. I wouldn't tell anyone they have to stop smoking, or stop alcohol. I don't miss it.

The most reefer experience I had was actually in Belize. There was a guy there, Mr John Scorn from Scorns Bay, who said "smoke dope and don't hope", and I was at his house one time when the police came to raiding and were suddenly there at his door and he says to them, "What I don't understand is, how is it that old white lady in England can send you out here to hassle me, your brother, and what would make you do that?"

The air was completely full of aromatic smoke and that was wafting outside. So the guy who was in charge said, "Well look, we can't get this door open, so we're going to have to go back to the station and get some tools to come back and open the door." And it was a screen door! (laughs) So they went back to the station and got their tools and came back and by then John Scorn had cleaned up his house and they did a thorough search and didn't find anything.

Albert: That's what they told the white lady back in England.

Stephen: Yeah. Well, the Prime Minister at that time, Mr. George Price, had John Scorn busted and sent to psychiatrists to candle his head for a while. And he came back from that with a letter saying not only was he sane but he was a very original and creative personality. And so he took that letter and painted it on a four-by-eight piece of plywood and put it out front of his house and put a sign next to it that said "Mr. George Price: here's the papers about my sanity. So where is yours now?"

Albert: When you first started seeing yourself the center of the crowd what did you think? Did you think you could handle that? Did you think yourself worthy of that?

Stephen: I went to Suzuki Roshi and said I have this class, and I have a couple hundred people coming. I wonder if I can be your student? And he said, don't be silly, I have my own problems. I have this monastery to take care of. I have enough to do.

He thought for a while and then said, "What will you tell them?" I said I didn't have anything but I can start up a discussion and I can handle stuff. "What will you tell them about acid?" he said.

I said, "Acid has something valuable, but it's also dangerous for people who are too young or not strong and it should be used very carefully, not thrown around or taken lightly." And he said you should probably teach the class. And that's the closest thing I've ever had to having my ticket punched.

Albert: That's also the message of, well it's raining everywhere, best take care of business wherever you are.

Steven: Really. Well that's it, it's raining everywhere, don't bother walking any faster. But I'm grateful I was able to study all those religions and stuff but I also ran into a whole lot of fakes and not everyone cut me as much slack as Suzuki. Sufi Sam [Samuel Lewis, an American Sufi teacher in the 1960s] confronted me outside Monday Night Class one night and said "Cut it out with the Hitler shit, Steve." He thought I was on a power trip.

I never wanted to be a guru. I say the way you can tell a guru is, he's guru-vy.

Albert: So Monday night began more or less as an open forum where you started off with a small group.

Stephen: I went to Belize with Margaret [Margaret Nofziger, Gaskin's second wife, before he married Ina May] and when we came back I went to the fellow who ran the Open University at San Francisco State and asked if I could give a class. He's the one who gave me Monday night. Started with about 12 people that first year. Then I moved out to the Gallery Lounge (a few dozen people), then the Straight Theater (a few hundred), then Glide Memorial Church (several hundred), and finally the Family Dog (one to two thousand people). Chet Helms let me do the original Family Dog but lost the lease on that and he got a place out on the coast for the new Family Dog, a skating rink on the Great Highway. And that was where the group of religious scholars found me. I was the only hippy who would talk to them and they wanted to talk to hippies about religion. And they finally said, well, we need you to come speak at our places around the country, about 1,000 different places where they all came from.

Albert: I have spoken with some of those academics who were there. That was an annual meeting of the American Academy of Religion in San Francisco, and Gordon Melton, Bob Rosenthal, and many other scholars who have since written about you or The Farm were there. Bob Rosenthal told me that they had spoken with Alan Watts, too, and then they came down and saw you at Monday Night Class and that's what set up the tour.

Stephen: Yeah, they had me come to 42 states. The acid and Jesus question was one I had to answer at every place. So when it came time to edit the Caravan book I had to edit that out a lot, like 41 times.

Albert: What got you started dropping the bells and the fringe and getting into wearing white?

Stephen: Well, Ina May made me a really beautiful new white shirt so I wore that when I gigged to show off that shirt.

Albert: But it wasn't anything special? Didn't have any special significance about purity?

Stephen: No.

Albert: Acid is an amplifier and it amplifies your character and whatever you got going on. I guess I wonder, what did it amplify for you?

Stephen: I was a very skinny puny kid and I got bullied a lot. I never was the kind could put on weight. I guess you could say my weapon was the jawbone of an ass.

Albert: Were you influenced by the beat scene, Alan Watts, Gary Snyder, Kerouac?

Stephen: I never met Kerouac but I met the other guys and I was part of that scene.

Albert: Earlier I asked if there was something particular that was original to you in your teachings and it occurs to me that there was something that I think was pretty original, which is the concept of telepathy. And maybe it comes out of your readings in science fiction or the paranormal or something else but I think you are the only one associating that with religion.

Stephen: Yeah, I definitely read that in the science fiction books, and I used to think wouldn't that be neat, but when I started taking acid I saw it for real and called it for what it was. And to me that explains a lot of kinds of enlightenment, and transmission of mind, and so forth.

Albert: Can you distinguish telepathy from body language, or auras, or just sending signals?

Stephen: Well, I have really good vision, but there's something much deeper than that, which I call mind to mind.
    When I first met TC Carroll, our County Sheriff here, I said to him this is a pretty rough county with moonshiners, KKK, and all, and you got to be our sheriff, too. And then later when he was part of the bust that came and arrested us, he was carrying an M16 carbine. And I thought to myself, we're a bit outgunned for hippies. And when I thought that it was as if I'd said it out loud because he turned around and waved the carbine and said, you may not be afraid of these rattlesnakes around here but I am (laughs). And when he arrested me and locked me up in his jail he cooked vegetarian food for me, and later on he married me and Ina May.

Albert: I developed a litmus test back when I was in college, to see if I was still tripping, or needed to, and the test was just to stare at a tree and let my vision go loose and stare at it long enough to see if I could just melt it (both laugh). And there's a thing there, about widening out your vision, and just letting the world wash over you so you get a deeper sense and pick up more signals. But you're not talking about that?

Stephen: I like to be right down on the ground and in the front row so I can see people's faces. I like reading faces. But the mind to mind kind, that's flashes. And Ina May and I have that and I can feel her and feel her mind really strong and know exactly what she's thinking. And what she's experiencing.

Albert: Well, I know that when I'm speaking to an audience, I can pick out a face in the crowd, and sometimes I can see they are not in agreement with what I'm saying, like they're frowning or looking at me suspiciously. And so I'll back up the conversation and direct it their way to explain what I mean and see if I can get some understanding. And I'll know we have that if they brighten up and start giving me back their good will.

Stephen: Oh yeah, and I really like that part of speaking with a group, and the thing about Monday Night Class was to have that many minds trying to do the same thing, and the amazing thing was we could do it, a lot. And I felt I was among friends and could talk freely. And there was this code that I had to obey to get to do that. I could not stand up to talk, I could not be on stage, I had a small band-riser that I sat on. I couldn't stand on it or walk across it, I always had to walk around it.

Albert: What do you think was your intention? I mean you had to go back week after week after week. You had to come back with a sense that you intended something.

Stephen: They made me study. I was reading everything I could find from all religions. Everything I could find in English. And I became like an amplified mind. And I would know pretty quickly that was happening if I was getting off.

Albert: So it was like Homo Gestalt?

Stephen: Yeah Homo Gestalt, who was that who wrote that?

Albert: Robert A. Heinlein, in *More Than Human*.

Stephen: *More Than Human*. I was a big science fiction reader and I particularly liked mind stuff.

Albert: And that was the intention of The Farm was it? To create a space where it was safe to trip? And by that I mean to extend your mind out.

Stephen: Yeah, so when we got back to the San Francisco scene on the Caravan, it was hard drugs, speed and heroin, and robberies. Couldn't deal grass without getting robbed. We knew from being on the road we'd seen that we're a pretty potent thing together. And people came to The Farm and they'd say how is it you got this thing going, how was it you got to be the leader? And I said, well it wasn't like I came to a random group of people and battled my way to the top. This was a really smart bunch of people and I got this thing started when we talked to each other.

Albert: There is another piece that I think of when I think of the original elements of The Farm. It was the part about sorting it out and keeping the vibe clean, or mutual self-criticism, to use John Humphrey Noyes' term from Oneida community. Sitting around …

Stephen: Well, that all came out of the pot circle.

Albert: And Fritz Lang and Esalen and Gestalt therapy? That was about the same time.

Stephen: No, I didn't know about that. It was the pot circle. And I took the intimacy of a bunch of people sitting around and smoking pot and going to a good place and took it out to all of them, the whole larger group. I just amplified that to 2,000 people. And to do that, they had to want to.

Albert: Well, sometimes it was confrontational. Sometimes it was calling it like it was. As you saw it. Until everyone could see it.

Stephen: Yeah, yeah. And the person asking the question got to see if it got answered.

Albert: Some of the boot camp period of The Farm, and Monday Night Class, and the Caravan too, was this business of minding the vibes. And doing self-analysis as a group in a much more intimate way, because everyone was becoming a whole lot more dependent on each other.

Stephen: Yeah. Right.

Albert: I mean in Monday Night Class, people are only together for a short period of time and then everyone goes back to their apartments. At The Farm you're working together, you're eating together, you're bathing together, and everything's happening together. And so you really didn't have anything to hide, and it gets around to who gets on each other's nerves, and where's that coming from, and was it your upbringing, or is it something you're holding, and can you be nicer, and if not what can we do about that? And that is something that I don't see in a lot of places, and even a lot of intentional communities.

Stephen: Well, a lot of that is about getting psychedelic together. And the first time I ever hallucinated, real honest to God hallucination, wasn't on acid. It was Acapulco Gold.

Albert: Yeah, I've actually been pretty high on Acapulco Gold, too (they laugh).

Stephen: Well, doing Monday Night Class was a yoga for me, too. I had to come up and improve my standards all the time, to be able to carry that circuit load.

Albert: That's the place about jettisoning baggage. I understand that completely. And, you're human too. And so you get memory lapses, sidetracked, struggle, all that.

Stephen: Oh, I got memory lapses in Monday Night Class, and I would just say anybody remember what I was saying? And people put it right back on track.

I don't think I have any more memory lapses now than I had back in Monday Night Class, but I have more problems with balance lately.

I have been traveling with Ina May as she goes from place to place speaking about midwifery and turning it into something to respect instead of root out. Ina May is not against abortions. I'm not against abortions. Farm ladies made this a refuge for folks that needed to come here and didn't want an abortion and needed an alternative. Ina May fights for the right for women to do what they want with their bodies wherever she goes.

Albert: And its all really good karma, I mean, lots of live babies to be thankful for.

Stephen: Oh yeah. And there is this idea that I have been a champion of midwifery. I had backed up Ina May and the midwives as best I could, but I thought they were a "natural" school. Didn't have to build it. It's there – it has its own enlightenments.

Albert: So there's the birth end of the cycle, and traveling with Ina May to midwifery events you are getting a whole lot of that now, but there's also the other side of this cycle, which is the death end. As you get older, do you find yourself thinking more about that? What do you think happens at death?

Stephen: Well, I think you quit (both laugh), you know, and if you're lucky, your relationships helped the world out and will continue.

Albert: You live on in the lives of other people?

Stephen: Yeah.

Albert: That's what Bill Mollison says: "They are as dragons' teeth."

Stephen: Yeah. I don't expect any immortality or anything like that. I don't believe in it.

Albert: I've sat with a number of dying people at their bedsides and especially in the case of atomic veterans, and other clients I've had, radiation victims and the like, although I don't want to get superstitious about it, I felt like they empowered me. They empowered me to speak on their behalf. And I've always taken that very seriously, and tried to honor it.

Stephen: Yeah.

Albert: After you're gone, what would you say is your legacy?

Stephen: Mighty works will stand on their own for a few years but they'll fade into the background over time. I don't read my own books much (laughs).

Albert: Well, I think you've touched the lives of the great many people, down into a number of generations now.

Stephen: Every now and then some of those people who were little kids once and whom I was nice to, tell me they appreciate how nice I was to them. And I take that as an indication that I should spend as much time with younger people as possible. I talk duck talk with the little ones. But I also treat them as smart people. And they appreciate that.

Albert: Is there anything else we should say for a book on recent religious movements? You said you don't really consider yours a religion, and your religion is that it's all one anyway, and there's nothing outside of that. That doesn't really help much, for what they're trying to accomplish with this book.

Stephen: (laughs) I think we had a great planetary realization in those days. Some of it was rock 'n' roll and the ability put together crowds of the thousands in the same mind at the same time.

Albert: And some of it was really great people. I mean, I think of Peter Berg, and Emmett Grogan, and the Diggers and the Mime Troupe, and Alan Watts, Gary Snyder, Allen Ginsberg, some really fine minds and some of the ideas that were floating around San Francisco and filtered out through the artist movements, in the happenings and concerts and into the popular culture – really made a powerful change in a whole generation.

Stephen: We all cross-fertilized.

Albert: Exactly. It was like a seasonal flowering.

Stephen: And I think that, I feel grateful for having lived in a time of great realization like that. And, I didn't make it, but I'm one of the guys that made it. There are thousands of other ones, hundreds of thousands, millions. And I'm just so grateful to have got to see something like that.

Chapter 8

A Tradition of Innovation and the Innovation of Tradition: The Cultural Developments of the Twelve Tribes Community

Torang Asadi

Elbert Eugene and Marsha Spriggs started a Bible study group in the early 1970s in their living room. The couple opened a sandwich shop in Chattanooga, Tennessee, where they offered free meals, conversations about Jesus, and "the fruit of the spirit" to the needy. Their home was open to all and their household began to expand as they began to live communally in a larger residence known as the Vine House. The group attended the First Presbyterian Church until it closed for Super Bowl Sunday. Disenchanted with mainstream Christianity and, eventually, with society in general, Spriggs began to preach and formed the Vine Christian Community.[1] Expansion from Chattanooga began later, initially to Island Pond, Vermont, and then elsewhere.

As the group's theology evolved and matured, and as leaders gathered the young believers into communal households, members began to see similarities between their community and the First Church (the early Christian community) since they lived "a radical life of self-sacrificing love for one another" and "were distinctly different from the society around them".[2] Members began to believe

---

[1] *How It All Began*, A Twelve Tribes Freepaper, 3. Freepapers are self-published newsprint magazines used for evangelism.
[2] *The New Wineskin*, The Twelve Tribes: The Commonwealth of Israel Website. Available online at http://www.twelvetribes.org/about/beginnings, accessed October 24, 2011.

the group to be the "true Israel", while scripture, most specifically Acts 2 and 4, dictated the structure of the community. Consequently, members came to believe the group to be the kingdom, mentioned in Daniel 2: 44, that would shatter other kingdoms and stand forever. This theocratic kingdom is believed by members to be the one that, withdrawn from the outside world, will summon the Second Coming and be governed by Jesus (called Yahshua by the group).

The movement took the name Twelve Tribes (hereafter TT) because members came to believe that all twelve of the original tribes of Israel have been nonexistent for centuries; their spiritual descendents are not today's Jews and Christians, but the TT's newly configured communities, scattered across nine countries, that are preparing the world for the end times. The group attempts to mold its communal practices to biblical precepts. In bridging both testaments, the group has developed a syncretic Judeo-Christian theology that is embodied in its culture. Members take Hebrew names (Elbert and Marsha are now Yoneq and ha-emeq), enact Jewish rituals, and perform Israeli folk dances – all examples of an ideological and cultural syncretism that seems to serve as the group's theological and scriptural validation: the Twelve Tribes Community is the true Israel, one that both Jews and Christians have failed to be, and, affirming this status, the Bible in its entirety is the holy book.

Most new religious movements and utopian experiments are characterized by the radical, alternative ideas that serve as foundations for their development and appeal. The Twelve Tribes communities,[3] however, seem not to be characterized by new and different ideas so much as by a series of innovative syncretisms of traditional ideals that constitute what they call "a very distinct culture."[4] In other words, the TT, taken as a sum of its parts, is a radically new communal religious movement whose parts are, paradoxically, not new or radical, but are rather culturally "traditional" and theologically restorationist.

The culture of the Twelve Tribes Community helps attract aspirants and retain long-time members. Approximately 78 per cent[5] of the members I have interviewed claim that they were initially attracted to the culture of the group and not its

---

[3] I will use Community to refer to the group as a whole and communities when referring to the individual clans within each tribe.

[4] *A Brand New Culture*, A Twelve Tribes Freepaper, 4.

[5] I have noted 74 instances in which I specifically asked what initially attracted each member to the group. Fifty-eight of those members claimed that the culture is what

theology. Some, about 15 percent,[6] have even told me that they struggled with the theology at first, but were eventually able to accept it.[7] This is a surprisingly high percentage considering that members are decidedly religious and that TT theology permeates the community. The culture manifests the theology since every cultural practice is extracted from the Bible or somehow supports the theology. There are evidently multiple reasons why the TT is attractive to the many who aspire or adhere to the group. Some members, for example, reference forgiveness as the enduring appeal of the group:

> There's a mysterious element that sustains us and produces the motivating force in us to love ... That element is forgiveness ... It heals us of our hurtful ways and communicates love and oneness of heart and soul. This power isn't being communicated through conventional world religions.[8]

This chapter, while acknowledging the multitude of factors involved in the appeal of any group to diverse individuals, more specifically seeks to examine the culture of the TT in order to investigate its appeal, its development, and some of its eventual functions in the group.

The cultural ingenuity of the movement is based on practices, or (as members would call them) "traditions", that keep long-time members interested and engaged. Often, these cultural practices (such as the observance of Jewish rituals) are used to support the movement's theology, or the theology is used to validate cultural activity (such as the orchestration of weddings). Examining the TT's culture in this light accomplishes two things: (1) it provides insight into the development of the group's culture and the establishment of its innovative social structure, and (2) it allows for the study of identity production and authentication.

---

interested them, but only initially. Many claimed that the theology was either too complex for them to understand or that they wanted little to do with religion.

[6] Of the 74 members interviewed, 11 mentioned that it not only took them a while to start reading the Bible and other teachings, but that, initially, they would have preferred that the group not be religious. All 11, however, added that once they finally understood the theology, this all changed.

[7] Although I suspected that these comments were reactions to my inability to relate to the members' religiosity, I have abandoned that notion since very few were aware of my personal views prior to these interviews.

[8] Email communication with a member, 25 March 2012.

In the following, I will examine elements of the TT culture in two categories. First, newcomers are attracted to cultural elements that I categorize as familiar, ideal, and desired. Second, there are syncretic characteristics of the culture – its development of tradition, its theology-based cultural creativity, and its adoption of existing customs of the larger society – that continue to appeal to adherents. I categorize these elements as multicultural, communal, and symbolic. Finally, I will examine some of the consequential functions of the group's cultural activity in light of its identity formation and legitimation.

The Development of Culture and Social Structure

In developing a theory of recruitment, Rodney Stark and William Sims Bainbridge combine "deprivation", "ideological appeal", and "interpersonal bonds" as fundamental to a movement's appeal to aspirants. They conclude that "[r]ecruits must not only suffer relevant deprivations and be open to a radical group's ideological appeal; they must also be placed in a situation where they will develop social bonds with existing members of the group."[9] Introduced earlier by John Lofland and Rodney Stark,[10] the interpersonal bond component accounts for more than ideology; it recognizes sociality and "[s]ome minimal kind of ideological preparation or predisposition" and requires an acceptance of "the plausibility of an active supernatural".[11] In the case of the TT, I would reject the latter element as essential.

In some cases, religiosity or acceptance of a supernatural being was absent and members described themselves as either social or environmental seekers with no background or interest in religion. Two members I interviewed were discontented with their relationships in the world and one was searching for a way to save the earth and escape the corruption she saw in society. Eleven members claimed that religiosity was not a factor in their initial interest in joining. Hence, for the purposes of this research, I retain *deprivation*, *ideological appeal*, and *interpersonal bonds*

---

[9] William Sims Bainbridge and Rodney Stark, *The Future of Religion* (Berkeley and Los Angeles, 1985), p. 312.

[10] John Lofland and Rodney Stark, "Becoming a World-Saver: A Theory of Conversion to a Deviant Perspective", *American Sociological Review*, 30 (1965): pp. 862–875.

[11] Bainbridge and Stark, *The Future of Religion*, p. 311.

from Bainbridge and Stark's theory and add *cultural appeal* to a repertoire of elements that can be used to characterize TT recruits. By the latter I mean social, cultural, and structural conventions that are specific to the group, not widely practiced in society, and appealing to certain individuals.

Aspirants

Many new members find the TT an attractive alternative to the highly institutionalized and less personal mainstream religions. For many others, the appeal rests solidly on the group's culture. *Familiar* and *ideal* elements fuel this cultural appeal in the case of the TT. Familiar elements are ones that the aspirant already recognizes and values, and ideal ones are those that are commonly valued in society. For example, family values are not a foreign concept, even to those who lack them. *Desired* cultural elements speak to the deprivation that can be simultaneously specific to the recruit and felt by a majority in the larger society. For example, most recruits who struggle economically seek financial stability.

Most often, aspirants are initially exposed to a TT community at a Friday Night Celebration. These festive events mark the beginning of the Sabbath and are open to the public. TT members often encounter people through their businesses or at a farmers' market and invite the ones who express interest to Friday Night Celebrations, where the community gathers for singing, dancing, and enjoying a feast. Guests hear not only leaders, but also other members, and even children, speak out about what they have learned during the week, what obstacles they have overcome as a community, or what lessons they would like to remember when entering the Sabbath. All participants stand in a large circle and face each other, allowing no one to stand in a position of authority and inviting everyone to participate. Depending on the number of guests and their familiarity with the group – many guests visit multiple times and become regulars – elders briefly introduce the background and theology of the group. Afterwards, members introduce guests to the community and applaud them profusely. Singing and dancing follow.

TT communities compose their own music and write their own lyrics, since they reject music from "the world". The songs are composed to complement the Israeli folk dances and are tailored to reflect the movement's theology in simple language. Some songs, such as "Come as you are", are directed towards guests, asking them to leave their worldly desires behind and join "the Body" along with all their imperfections. These songs communicate a level of acceptance, asking guests to "come as you are. Leave your goals behind. Come, sing with me a new song of Love." Other songs are testimonies to the ideal life the Community lives, as demonstrated in "A Brand New Life":

> Yahweh gathered us together
> To live this brand new life,
> Where love will reign forever
> And what was lost will be restored.
>
> Our hearts have turned to live as one
> And this will bring an age of peace,
> Where there's no more pain and sorrow
> And death has lost its power.
>
> This is the hope we're living for.
> And we can all stay together
> To live this brand new life,
> Where love will reign forever.
> The love of God will fill the earth.

These lyrics attest to ideals that are familiar and widely desired, such as solidarity and togetherness, strong bonds in nuclear families, and an emphasis on loving one another and demonstrating a supposedly leaderless community where all are equal.

Members choreograph the dances in the form of Israeli folk dances or circle dances in which members hold hands. This form of dance symbolizes the group's existence "in unity like one big living body".[12] Although some dances can be very complex, members teach the simpler ones to the guests, who are invited to join in and dance with the adults and children. Members who visit often join the

---

[12] Michael's Testimony, *We Dance in a Circle*. The Twelve Tribes: The Commonwealth of Israel Website. Available online at http://www.twelvetribes.org/testimonies/we-dance-circle, accessed August 13, 2011.

dances without invitation; encouragement to participate never ceases. This sense of inclusion, togetherness, and equality is both an ideal and a desired element of the Community for aspirants.

Most of the above-mentioned elements (family values, solidarity, and sociability) are mirrored in the way supper is served. Families sit together and invite guests to eat with them. Interpersonal bonds have been shaped by this time through the assignment of members as potential "shepherds" to guests. For example, in every community I have visited, a single sister who is close to me in age has been responsible for keeping me company, informing me of "traditions", teaching me the dances, inviting me to supper, and introducing me to others. I have noticed that most guests are paired with members that are similar in age, marital status, social and educational status, or ethnicity and background; couples are paired with couples, families with those with the same aged children, and the educated with members who were considered successful by society's standards before joining. In this manner, interpersonal bonds are created based on commonalities and guests notice that people not too different from themselves have given up their lives to be in "the Body".

As guests are seated for dinner, a team responsible for supper serves the food, bread, and drink. Like busy servers, a select few check on the tables, tending to the needs of members and guests and clearing the dishes. Each Friday a different team is responsible for supper, while the rest of the community enjoys the feast. The day-to-day responsibilities in the community are divided the same way; one might work hard to serve lunch during the day, but another team of brothers and sisters serve supper and take care of the laundry.

Food is a source of pride for the TT. The food in the Community is wholesome, fresh, unique, and organic. Although the regular menu is simple, Friday Night meals are extravagant and festive. Ideally, fish and salad are served, but in many cases where fish is unavailable, another "special meal" is planned for the Celebration. Fresh, home-made bread is abundant and the supper team offers second servings to all. In fact, many guests are drawn to Friday Night Celebrations through the group's cafés and delis, which are extremely popular for their food.

Once guests become more familiar with the group outside of Friday Night Celebrations, they identify with the community's ability to meet their individual needs. For example, there are a number of poverty-stricken single mothers who have joined the group. It cannot be said that these women joined the group only because it provided food, shelter, and parenting help, but undoubtedly these benefits were attractive to them. Similarly, there are many members who mention overcoming addiction, abandoning suicidal thoughts, and finally gaining a sense of belonging when speaking about their past and joining the Community. Aspirants relate these *desired* elements to the deprivations they suffered in "the world". Socialization is a desired element that can be easily recognized; many who join new religious movements in general are discontented with their social status or their relationships.

The level of socialization and the number of interpersonal bonds attained in a communal setting are ideals widely held in society at large that are seldom achievable outside a commune. Most members have mentioned their discontent with their relationships or their lack of love and strong bonds in "the world". The TT seems attractive in this sense: a group of people that express their love for one another and aid each other in every aspect of everyday life embodies a utopian ideal usually unattainable in the larger society; its absence creates a sense of social deprivation for most (if not all) people. Thus, the seemingly idyllic communal culture of the group appeals to aspirants.

Members believe that by abandoning the selfishness that drives people in "the world" to competition and isolation, and by tending to the needs of others on a daily basis, the needs of every member will be met. This communal element is justified by the movement's theology:

> There are so many so-called gospels, but there is only one gospel that is a cause to live for. It is to bring about the end of the reign of selfishness. That is the purpose of community. Community is an all-out attack on selfishness. And if we can bring about the end of selfishness, we can bring about the end of Satan's reign, who is the great conspirator and perpetrator of the reign of selfishness. He can't be dealt with until selfishness is dealt with in us.[13]

This spirit of togetherness allows the group to function financially as a unit as well; even though tasks are divided based on skill and experience, every member is assigned work that accomplishes either community maintenance or provides

---

[13] The Confederation of the Twelve Tribes, Transcriptions of a meeting, 18.

income. For example, someone might be in charge of educating, or "training", the children while another works at the community's café; both have no income and handle no money, yet both receive the same accommodations.

Members discard personal financial responsibilities in the community. Most never handle any money, nor are they involved in financial decision-making. In each community, certain members are in charge of the treasury and some are in charge of shopping. In 2009, I went shopping with a sister in Vista, California. Her list included products from clothing to cleaning supplies to food and honey. I noticed that the Costco membership card and the credit card were both in her (Hebrew) name; members close their bank accounts and abandon their debts once they join the Community, leaving commercial and financial transactions to those in charge of specific tasks. This elimination of financial concerns would appeal to those whose lives in "the world" are characterized by poverty, financial instability, or debt. For such members, commonly desired stabilities regarding life's necessities replace financial deprivation.

These are some of the familiar, ideal, and desired cultural elements to which aspirants are initially exposed and through which they form opinions about the group. These elements in turn account for three components of the recruitment theory employed in this chapter: deprivation, (ameliorated by desired elements), interpersonal bonds, and cultural appeal. In seeking alternatives to society's standards and seclusion from the corruptions of "the world", many find the TT an ideal answer. Eventually, adherents are no longer attracted to the culture alone and theology begins to play a crucial role in how the individual functions in and perceives the Community. Cultural innovation and appeal persist, but do so in light of the movement's theology.

Adherents

Communal living, music as worship, and extravagant hospitality are not unique to the TT. A specific combination of these familiar yet distinct elements results in a "radical new culture". At first glance, the visual culture of the TT is unusual and distinctive. In fact, however, many of its elements are not new at all. For example, women look like Orthodox Jews, or the Bruderhof, or Israel Family members in dress and hairstyles. The simple, old-fashioned floral patterns, earthy colors, and loose-fitting clothing, along with the uncut hair parted in the middle, make them indistinguishable from women in these groups.

The TT has developed what Susan Palmer calls a "distinctive material culture, with a recognizable aesthetic and consistent standard of beauty in buildings, interior furnishings, costumes, food presentation and art forms".[14] In other words, what is old-fashioned is a standard. Vintage furniture, flowery patterns and decorations, and round-rimmed eyeglasses are ideal because members "don't want anything to do with the fashions of the world".[15] In this sense, the group's material and visual culture is neither new nor unique. The culture, however, has evolved over the years as a result of the process of cultural innovation that has not only shaped the community, but has remained tied to its theology as well: "We are *discovering* an ancient culture and will not be led along by the fashions, music, philosophies and religions of our surroundings".[16] Specific innovative practices, called "traditions" within the group, help bind the community and support its theology.

Paradoxically, the innovation of tradition in the TT justifies and is justified by its restorationist theology and its zeal for a return to the simple beginnings of Christianity. The TT's evangelistic publications refer to the Community as "a brand new culture" and "a radical new life"; and given that the group rejects conformity to conventional societal standards, membership in the TT requires conformity to the group's evolving culture. Members are encouraged to "correct" each other and confess their sins before others in minchahs (gatherings held twice a day in every community). Members use this time to reflect on their spiritual and social well-being, discuss scripture, confront each other if needed, confess sins, sing, dance, and pray.

I classify the innovation of tradition in the TT as multicultural, communal, and symbolic. *Multicultural* traditions serve to demonstrate the group's inclusion of people of different backgrounds by embracing racial and cultural diversity. For example, when the first Japanese sister joined the community, the tradition of eating with chopsticks began as a sign of respect and welcoming. Although forks are provided for guests and spoons for soup and yogurt, members eat with

---

[14] Susan Palmer, "The Twelve Tribes: Preparing the Bride for Yahshua's Return", *Nova Religio*, 13/3 (February 2010): pp. 59–80, 75.

[15] Interview with elders in Vista, California, 15 October 2011.

[16] Personal communication with a member, 25 March 2012.

chopsticks. Even though the menu depends on availability, ethnic foods are sometimes added and greeted with excitement. During most of my visits, members asked me to teach some of the sisters how to make an Iranian dish. I often cooked a sandwich spread and baked cookies, and wrote a recipe for them. They have never failed to inform me that they have tried the recipe after my visit.

Most often, they also ask me to prepare a short presentation on Iran during or after supper. In Sus, France, and in Chilliwack, British Columbia, supper was a special occasion one night with the addition of dessert, which rarely happens except on Fridays. I also presented in the geography class in the community in Valley Center, California. I have been told that these guest presentations are a tradition and have become an important part of the communities' education. Another example of a multicultural innovation is the composition of songs in different languages used to address guests of different backgrounds and aspirants in countries that "walkers", or missionaries, visit.

Communal traditions are also methods of proselytization, hospitality, and group bonding, supporting recruitment and the sustenance of the group. Merrymaking, for example, is a tradition of travel in buses for evangelization through singing and dancing in different cities. The refurbished double-decker buses attract attention because of their purple color. Merrymaking also provides an opportunity for members to travel together and visit other communities, an activity that not only serves as a source of entertainment, but also provides an opportunity for the single members to meet each other across communities. TT communities are secluded to a certain degree, the many visitors notwithstanding; many members and especially children have little exposure to "the world". Merrymaking provides a means for travel, which members have addressed successfully in custody cases that become an issue when one parent leaves the Community.[17] In response to allegations of seclusion and isolation, children testify to the many countries they have visited during these trips.

The evolving practice of Jewish rituals and holidays are also noteworthy as communal elements. Members of the Community emphasize the festive nature of Jewish holidays and the meaning attached to Jewish rituals. For example, the

---

[17] *The Messianic Communities in the European Union: An Issue of Parental Authority.* The Twelve Tribes: The Commonwealth of Israel Website. Available online at http://www.twelvetribes.com/node/56, accessed September 4, 2011.

TT considers Sukkot to be one of the many holy celebrations it must observe. In addition to the importance of observing the Law and retaining the Jewish rituals that were commanded in the Old Testament, however, members add that "we're learning that our Father needs people who are moveable. [Sukkot] shows us that we are flexible and willing to move" between tribes in order to meet the needs of individual clans (to run businesses, to learn farming, or to start new communities). They understand that objection to moving stems from selfishness and emotional attachments. Evidently, the abrupt relocation of families can be a problem in tight-knit communities. Sukkot is a test of members' flexibility and appreciation of shelter; it teaches them to build temporary dwellings and to live outside of their houses. It is also a celebration in which children participate, building booths and starting campfires. During my visit to the Vista community in October 2011, the children were overjoyed to show me their booths and even more excited to sleep in them. One member told me, "We haven't had time to take the children camping. I guess this is a great alternative." New traditions such as these, although theologically founded, seem to serve as a form of community bonding, entertainment, and cultural development.

The third type of innovative traditions, *symbolic* elements, is a subset of larger communal elements. They are symbolic of the theology, the Community, and even the status of the group as the "New Israel". For example, weddings are designed to symbolize the TT as the Bride reunited with Yahshua, the Bridegroom, as well as the holiness of the covenant made between husband and wife. Susan Palmer lists three functions that weddings serve in the group: "(1) they are a rite of passage for young couples entering the matrimonial state; (2) they serve as an evangelizing outreach method; and (3) they are dramatic pre-enactments of the last days, when Yahshua will return to claim his Bride".[18] Because of the emphasis on marriage in the Community, the involvement of members in weddings is crucially important, making weddings a communal element.

One of the most recent traditions to start in the TT requires men to roll up their pant legs upon entering the minchah. I witnessed this first in the summer of 2011 in Klosterzimmern, Germany, where I was told, "we are starting a new tradition to honor the minchah"; this was the first day this tradition was being implemented in the community. I had just arrived from the community in Sus, France, and had

---

[18] Palmer, "The Twelve Tribes," pp. 71–72.

not yet heard about this innovation. When I asked about the theological basis of this new tradition the young woman who was accompanying me claimed that she had no idea. I then remembered an incident in the community in Valley Center, California, in the spring of 2009, when brothers arrived for the minchah after a day of farming and were asked to change since their muddy pant legs were dirtying the floor in the meeting space; it was considered disrespectful that their pants were not only dragging on the floor, but that they were dirty as well. When I visited the community in Vista, in October of 2011, I inquired about the new tradition and was told,

> If pant legs are drooping down that is not our Father. We don't want anything to do with the fashions of the world ... we don't want to conform to the world. We don't want our clothes to be too tight. Pants carry in the leaven of the world into our minchahs.

In Germany, the tradition was still not perfected; some men would forget to roll their pant legs up and some were confused when it came to shorter pants. Although men do not wear pants that reveal the calf completely, a couple of the men wearing khaki capris did not roll them up since they would then be too short. It also took a couple of days for the children to be mindful of the tradition. It seems that the level of necessity in the innovation of this tradition is low. Nevertheless, it has quickly acquired meaning in its symbolization of purity and respect for the minchah. However, I feel that most importantly, it provides a male counterpart to practices required of women, who must wear headscarves during the minchah to symbolize their submission to their husbands, and in turn to God. The tradition had been well-established by the time I visited the community in Warsaw, Missouri in November, 2012.

Another symbolic element of the innovation of culture is a weekly event, the "Jesse Goodman Push",[19] during which every member of the community rises one hour earlier than usual to gather at 6 a.m., giving them an extra hour before the morning minchah. All members are assigned a task and participate in helping

---

[19] *The Sons of Jesse Goodman*, The Twelve Tribes: The Commonwealth of Israel Website. Available online at http://www.twelvetribes.com/parables/jesse-goodman, accessed August 13, 2011.

in the garden or on the farm; I have been assigned to pick up fallen fruit with the children, plant lettuce, and pick beans and strawberries for the Farmers' Market. The TT recalls Jesse Goodman's family working together in a parable, which members idealize as representing the perfect family unit. Hence "Jesse Goodman Push" is also meant to symbolize the togetherness of the Community in work and the sacrifices they are willing to make for each other by "doing just a little more", while providing communal participation.

Communities communicate these traditions in different ways. Apostles are skilled, long-time members who travel between communities to provide their expertise, playing an important role in unifying the group by tending to inconsistencies and implementing the same culture in every community. The Intertribal News (ITN), a monthly publication that includes teachings from Yoneq, members' testimonials, and reports from all TT communities, also accomplishes this. Music is also included in the ITN and communities learn each other's songs. The degree to which the TT is culturally unified is impressive; other than by language and accents, it would be difficult to distinguish among clans and tribes.

The different types of the innovation of tradition (multicultural, communal, and symbolic) foster cultural creativity among members, which allows members to engage in the development of the TT's culture. In other words, members collectively enhance the culture and its appeal. Together, the recycling of existing traditions and the innovation of tradition function to render the culture of the TT attractive in two phases: initially to aspirants and continuously to adherents. The second phase intertwines with the repeated justification of the theology, which in turn justifies the culture as well. The next section briefly discusses this process of theological justification, along with other functions of the culture of the TT.

Identity Formation and Legitimation

The group's attractive culture, a product of the theology and the ideal life of the Community, sometimes overshadows its millenarian and supernatural theology. The interdependence of culture and theology makes the latter appealing by association. Music, as one of the group's cultural developments, is an example of the theological foundation of the TT's culture.

Music reflects the group's emphasis on simplicity, distinction, and religiosity, and provides insight into the group's processes of cultural innovation and theological evolution. On 28 September 1997, Yoneq held a meeting at the community in Oak Hill, NY, after a wedding. The community was concerned with the song that the bridegroom dedicated to his bride at the wedding because he breathed into the microphone, changed his voice from its natural way, and played two instruments, which gave the song "the same beat that you might hear at the average rock concert".[20] In addition to the rejection of "music from the world" in order to keep the culture pure and unique, there are many theological precepts undergirding the disapproval of non-TT music:

> Music is spirit. It vibrates the airways. It comes from somewhere—a spirit, a source. The vibration is for good or for evil. As every breath you take is spirit, so is the sound of music (Mt 12: 33–37). Where music is concerned you communicate a spirit. Music played in purity, without drawing attention to yourself, drives away evil spirits.[21]

Biblical characters would agree: "David played pure music long ago. We have to reclaim music from Satan who stole it in the first place. We've got to reclaim it till the end of days."[22] Hence, technology in music has a negative impact; the electric guitar is not a "pure" instrument since it detracts from the simplicity of the message that the lyrics are communicating and since the music it produces is not "natural".

The "new and emerging culture" of the TT, a manifestation of its collective identity, "must be a Contrasting Society so that those who hate the corruption they see in the world will recognize a distinction and come out and be separate".[23] Being distinguished from other cultures helps members identify with the group; it is not only a large component of the TT's appeal, but it also serves the theological position that Yahshua will be able to tell TT members apart from others in the End of Days. Hence the group must be distinct, not only for the members to be able to

---

[20] *Music is a Spiritual Tool*. Transcriptions. 28 September 1997: Oak Hill, NY, p. 1.
[21] Ibid., p. 1.
[22] Ibid., p. 3.
[23] *A Brand New Culture*, A Twelve Tribes Freepaper, 6.

identify with it as different from "the world", but in order for members to be able to support their religiosity with their lifestyle by in turn supporting their lifestyle with their religiosity. One way this uniqueness is achieved is with the cultural syncretism and innovation discussed in this chapter.

Simply put, the collective identity of the TT is culturally unique and theologically supported. The culture reflects the theology, and the theology is credited for the success and appeal of the culture. In this sense, culture and theology are separate and distinct. However, as demonstrated in this chapter, their interdependence makes the two indistinguishable. According to Rhys Williams, "religion is implicit culture, a set of organizing principles. It is less about beliefs, than about meaning in the world."[24] In this religion-as-culture approach, the way religion and culture are intertwined becomes a requirement. Williams concludes that

> a culture of solidarity reinforces existing social relations, but challenges to the status quo also rely upon ritual, symbolism, and the production of collective identity. Locating either culture or ideology on only one side of any social cleavage misses the social processes they share.[25]

The TT's culture is not separate from its theology, but what the guests witness upon initial exposure to the Community is a visual and material manifestation of the theology that includes elements familiar to and idealized by aspirants. The integration of culture and theology allows aspirants to eventually merge their initial infatuation with the culture into the religiosity of the group.

The innovation of cultural elements, or "traditions", is the most fascinating aspect of the TT's developments. Like any new religious movement, the group has had to make itself culturally and theologically distinctive and does so by the innovation of "traditions":

---

[24] Rhys H. Williams. "Religions as Political Resource: Culture or Ideology?" *Journal for the Scientific Study of Religion*, 35/4 (1996): pp. 368–378, 370.

[25] Ibid., p. 372.

> That is what our traditions are there for. Traditions give us definition – the traditions of the Spirit who has been set apart to set us apart. That's what Yoneq has always taught us: "The Holy Spirit is set apart, and the only reason He is set apart is to set us apart."[26]

Evidently, the TT recognizes the need for a unique culture as a theological requirement. However, it is also evident that the development of a unique theology has required the group to be culturally distinctive as well. Although paradoxical, this two-layered process of innovation results in the sustenance of the group as a unified movement.

---

[26] The Confederation of the Twelve Tribes, 13.

Chapter 9

The Family International:
The Evolution of a Communal Society

Claire Borowik

In an era when business and government leaders urge themselves to "think outside the box," here is a group that lives its entire life outside the formal structures that constrain most people. Yet it has found a coherent and apparently satisfying way of life for its members. More than a mere counter culture, the Family is an alternative society.[1]

The Children of God (later to be known as the Family International) burst on the religious scene in the late 1960s as a fundamentalist Christian, world-rejecting movement, comprised in its majority of converted hippies. Rejecting the established churches of the day, the movement espoused communalism as representing the purest model of early Christianity. The Family International has evolved into a highly organized communitarian society that has thrived in the face of many challenges, arguably the largest surviving communal experiment engendered by the Jesus Movement. With its uncompromising message and challenge to drop out and forsake worldly possessions to serve God, in its early years the movement appealed primarily to young adults disaffected with modern society and welcoming of an alternative lifestyle. Its missionary zeal and purpose galvanized its members to circle the globe with the Family's unique presentation of the Gospel message and music. Members proved to be adept at acclimatizing to a diversity of cultures while consolidating the Family's societal structure within their communes.

---

[1] William Sims Bainbridge, *The Endtime Family: Children of God* (New York, 2002), pp. xii–xiii.

The Family International has been considered the most controversial of the communal societies to emerge from the Jesus Movement of the 1960s era. Its uncompromising anti-establishment message and denunciation of the "System" and its institutions would place it at the center of controversy. The introduction of sexually liberal doctrines and practices in the late 1970s would result in the marginalization of the movement from mainstream Christianity, as well as intense negative media coverage and official and public scrutiny. Despite the polemic and resulting negative profiling of the movement, Family members have been relatively successful in engaging local communities through their evangelistic and charitable activities.

The movement has experienced monumental shifts in its structure and discipleship paradigm throughout its history, shifts that have been reflected in its communal patterns and culture. It has faced the challenge of balancing two primary focuses: its core purpose of reaching the world with the Gospel, and its determination to maintain the integrity of its society and belief system. Hence, the organization has experienced trends of recurrent experimentation and adaptation to address new challenges, while subsequently introducing retrenchment programs to preserve its religious and societal imperatives, creating a culture of periodic innovation and change.

In 2008, the movement's historical communal model, in which most committed members lived in communal homes, came under consideration, resulting in the institution of the most sweeping reorganization to date in July 2010, known as the Reboot. A new model of membership was introduced with the intent of fostering greater personal autonomy for members and a more open, inclusive culture that would be conducive to the movement's current mission objectives. Previous requirements for communal living were effectively rescinded, and the former organizational structure was virtually dismantled. Although communal living is no longer required of members or systemically structured, the Family continues to uphold the foundational principles and values of the communal model, and many members continue to live in cooperative households.

Theological Underpinnings

The practice of communalism has been fundamental to the Family's belief system. From its inception, the movement has been organized as a religious society, guided by its doctrine, both traditional Bible-based and revelatory. As James Chancellor noted:

> While the Family can be viewed and examined from many perspectives, it is essentially a religious movement grounded in a clearly articulated belief system. The Family boasts an extraordinary range of educational, religious, cultural, ethnic and national backgrounds. Even so, the disciples are guided and sustained by a common vision and a coherent set of theological commitments.[2]

Theologically, two foundational principles have underpinned the Family's communitarian practices. First, a belief that the early church practice recorded in the Bible of "all who believed were together and had all things in common"[3] was meant to serve as the archetype for future generations of Christians. And second, based on biblical metaphors indicating that Christians are the bride of Christ,[4] the Family's doctrine maintained that members were part of a greater marriage and one family.

All Who Believed

Previous versions of the Family's statement of faith explained the movement's religious stance regarding Christian communalism:

> We believe that the New Testament's account of the lifestyle of the Early Church offers us not only a historical narrative, but an exemplary pattern and model, which God intended succeeding generations of believers to follow. The Early Church's unselfish, cooperative lifestyle, in which "all who believed were together, and

---

[2] James D. Chancellor, The Family International: A Brief Historical and Theological Overview, *Sacred Tribes Journal* 3/1 (2008): p. 19.
[3] Acts 2: 44, English Standard Version.
[4] See Romans 7: 4; 2 Corinthians 11: 2; Revelation 19: 7–9.

had all things in common" (Acts 2:44), proved to be exceptionally beneficial for the fledgling movement in terms of practical and economic concerns. Even more importantly, the close fellowship and spiritual unity fostered by this lifestyle provided the early disciples with needed support, fellowship, encouragement, and a spiritual haven. It was an example to nonbelievers that Jesus' followers could live together in harmony and cooperation—further proof of the love that they professed. Likewise, we today have found both the practical and spiritual benefits of cooperative communal living to be extremely advantageous in helping us achieve our goal of reaching all whom we can with the Gospel of Christ.[5]

The movement's founder, David Berg (1919–1994), understood from the accounts of the early church in the book of Acts that it was intended that committed Christian disciples would work together to develop a form of godly cooperative society. This would result in the believers sharing their material and intellectual resources for the benefit of all, and an equalitarian distribution to all so that none would lack.

We are doing what the Lord wanted the church to do in the first place, and which the church did in the first place, in the days of the Early Church where they lived communally and "no man called anything his own" (Acts 4:32) and "owe no man anything save to love him" (Rom.13:8) and shared all things, just as it says in Acts 2. They really lived communally and it worked, like it's working with us, because of the Lord and our love and sacrificial service and wanting to help others and help each other. It works.[6]

We are not trying to form colonies purely for selfish pleasure or just to prove the point that communal living works! We are banding together and spreading around the world in order to devote our full time and energies to preach the

---

[5] The Family International, *Statement of Faith* (2008). Copies in the archives of the Family International.

[6] David Berg, "Why Our Family Really Works", ML (Mo Letter) 2342 (Zurich, 1987). Works authored by David Berg not otherwise credited are located in the archives of the Family International.

Gospel to every creature and win their souls to Jesus Christ and their bodies to His service for others.[7]

Communes were to serve as faith-based centers where the believers could reside, nurture their faith, congregate, study, and build their outreach and ministry. In earlier years of the movement's history, Berg also envisioned the Family's cooperative lifestyle as serving as a testimony against what he perceived as the worldliness and lack of commitment of the established churches of his day:

> Our greatest witness is our example of dropping out and forsaking all, which is a condemnation of the churches. We are doing something that is phenomenal, almost unheard of—the way we're doing it is almost unheard of. There have been all kinds of communal groups before, but none with such a militant and active type of witness as we've had and continue to have.
>
> Preaching salvation is as old as the hills. Witnessing is ages old. Telling people about Jesus is eons old, but let me tell you right now, *living* the way God wanted people to live has not been practiced or tried very much, because not many people had faith to try it. Besides it was too revolutionary, too anti-System, too totally different. They were afraid to, they wouldn't be accepted, or respected, might even be persecuted, so why do anything different ... We're living witnesses against them. Ninety-nine percent of the church says, "It can't be done. You shouldn't do it. It's not for today. Do your own thing, and just go to church on Sunday."
>
> It's not by our preaching salvation, or Jesus or healing or the baptism of the Holy Spirit, but what makes us unique is that we are living like Jesus intended for His church to live. We are proving that it can be done and we have got to make it work.[8]

Integral to recreating this model of early Christian cooperatives was the doctrine of "forsaking all". Forsaking one's earthly possessions and secular pursuits was

---

[7] David Berg, "Public Relations", ML 142 (Zurich, 1971).
[8] David Berg, "Not a Sermon, but a Sample", ML J (Zurich, 1970).

pivotal to becoming a member of the Family through much of its history, based on the stipulations mapped out by Jesus for His disciples: "So likewise, whoever of you does not forsake all that he has cannot be My disciple." "No one can serve two masters. Either he will hate the one and love the other, or he will be devoted to the one and despise the other. You cannot serve both God and money."[9]

The monetary and in-kind donations obtained through this process of forsaking all accrued to the good of the local community and all its members equally, as described by the Apostle Paul in the Bible: "Our desire is ... that there might be equality. At the present time your plenty will supply what they need, so that in turn their plenty will supply what you need. Then there will be equality."[10] The rejection of the concept of personal ownership was both doctrinal in nature and foundational in practice to the economic structure of the homes and the organization.

Of equal importance to full-time discipleship was "dropping out", which represented a renunciation of the System, referred to in the Bible as the world. The movement embraced the anti-establishment message and values of the counterculture youth that comprised the majority of its founding members. Berg taught that modern churches and denominations had accommodated to the secular institutions surrounding them, and thus had compromised their beliefs and obedience to the Christian imperative to "love not the world, neither the things that are in the world".[11] His writings denounced materialistic pursuits and secular values, not dissimilar to the renunciation of the world espoused by Saint Francis of Assisi.

> Berg preached against the System, his name for the social, economic, cultural, and religious mainstream in the United States. The Family, by contrast, was the Revolution that stood against the System. Berg's opposition to the prevailing ethos of the day would characterize the Family throughout its history. Berg preached that the end times were near, when Christ would return to earth to initiate the final phase of history. He insisted on aggressive evangelization tactics aimed at saving as many people as possible through a personal relationship with Jesus Christ. Although these ideas were consistent with much of Protestant

---

[9] Luke 14: 33; Matthew 6: 24, New International Version.
[10] 2 Corinthians 8: 13–14, New International Version.
[11] 1 John 2:15, King James Version.

evangelicalism, Berg's later sexual experimentation and communal living arrangements were not.[12]

Berg challenged the status quo and viewed most established institutions with suspicion, as being in the hands of the ungodly world that Jesus warned His disciples against. He also challenged contemporary values and Christian culture and mores. His writings were iconoclastic in nature, often colorful, strongly worded, and colloquial in style. Portions of his writings espoused extreme viewpoints or theological speculations, which later would be renounced and expurgated. The Family's administrative body is currently in the process of assessing the writings previously published by the organization to identify those containing enduring principles, which will be preserved. Writings that are deemed to no longer reflect the organization's core beliefs and values will not be a part of its future official library.

One Wife and Law of Love Doctrines

Two of the most significant theological innovations that shaped the Family's communal practices were the One Wife and Law of Love doctrines. While the rationale for communal living lay in the model of the early church and the understanding that Christians were called to form intentional communities as part of their belief system, the One Wife and Law of Love doctrines would provide the foundation for the development of novel cultural and behavioral norms.

Based on the parable of the ten virgins told by Jesus in the Bible,[13] all of whom waited to enter the bridegroom's chamber, the One Wife doctrine extolled the larger marriage of the body of believers to Christ over private relationships. Berg further interpreted this parable as a metaphorical representation of the spiritual marriage of the believers to one another. Members were perceived as conjointly forming a greater marriage, the embodiment of the biblical conceptualization of the believers as the bride of Christ. While conventional marriages and nuclear families were upheld, broader relational ties were forged with other members of

---

[12] Dereck Daschke and W. Michael Aschraft (eds), *New Religious Movements* (New York and London, 2005), p. 164.
[13] See Matthew 25: 1–13.

the community, all of whom were understood to comprise the greater marriage of the believers. Berg explained:

> The history of communes shows that the most successful communes either abolished all private relationships entirely and required total celibacy, or abandoned the private marriage unit for group marriage—because they found that the private family group was always a threat to the larger family unit as a whole ... The family marriage, the spiritual reality behind so called group marriage, is that of putting the larger family, the whole family, first, even above the last remaining vestige of private property, your husband or your wife! We do not minimize the marriage ties, as such. We just consider our ties to the Lord and the larger Family greater and more important ... We are not forsaking the marital unit—we are adopting a greater and more important and far larger concept of marriage: The totality of the bride and her marriage to the Bridegroom is the Family! We are adopting the larger Family as the family unit: The Family of God and His Bride and children.[14]

Berg's subsequent introduction of the Law of Love doctrine in 1975 interpolated a singular dimension to this concept, in that it made allowance for sexual interaction between adult members of the movement without sin, regardless of marital status. Based on the Gospel of Matthew (22: 35–40), the Law of Love doctrine is founded on the principle that love of God and love for others fulfill biblical laws. Therefore, Christians are no longer held to the previous Mosaic laws, as long as their actions are carried out in unselfish love for others. As such, heterosexual relations between consenting adults were deemed permissible insofar as others affected by these actions were not hurt or offended.

With the introduction of the Law of Love, the greater marriage concept would evolve to encompass sexual relations outside of marital bounds, rooted in the understanding that if such acts met the criteria of being motivated by unselfish love and not hurting third parties, the biblical prohibitions of adultery were not applicable. Unselfishly giving of self to others, even in the sexual realm, was encouraged, in order to ensure that people who weren't married could have their needs for affection and intimacy met and to foster unity and oneness.

---

[14] David Berg, "One Wife", ML 249 (Zurich, 1972).

Needless to say, this doctrine of sexual liberality would serve to further separate the Family from the Christian mainstream. Conversely, it also empowered Family members to reach segments of society previously difficult to reach for many Christians.

> The distinctive guiding principle most known about the Family has been the Law of Love, derived from the Gospel of Matthew (22:36–40). As the Family interprets it, the command to love overrides and frees individuals from the strictures of the Mosaic law. At its most general level, this interpretation has extolled self-sacrifice to bring people the saving truth of the gospel. On a more practical level, it has allowed sexual contact between consenting adults as long as they meet the conditions of love (unselfishness) and do not act out of mere lust. Under the Law of Love, the Family went from conventional behavior concerning sex and marriage into a period of broad sexual experimentation. In the mid-1980s, it began a step-by-step retrenchment to return to something near its original stance, approaching a more conventional view regarding sex.[15]

The practice of this doctrine, while fostering a tightly knit culture, also posed a number of challenges – both internal and external – ultimately resulting in a great deal of controversy and negative media profiling. A number of negative outcomes resulted internally from the degree of liberality encouraged by Berg in his writings: cases occurred of disruption of marital relations and nuclear families, incidences of sexual advances to minors prior to 1986 when rules were instituted for the protection of minors, as well as behaviors that did not align with the principles of the doctrine. These were addressed and corrected over the years from 1986 onwards. A stringent child protection policy was adopted in 1989, rendering any sexual contact between an adult and a minor an excommunicable offense. Regulations were further introduced into the Family's Charter of rights and responsibilities in 1995[16] to demarcate the boundaries of sexual relations and avoid these causing hurt to third parties or disrupting nuclear families.

---

[15] J. Gordon Melton, *The Children of God: "The Family"* (Salt Lake City, 1997), p. 11.

[16] First instituted in 1995, the Charter has been recently updated to reflect sweeping institutional change introduced into the organization in July 2010. For the 2010 version of the Family International's Charter, see http://tficharter.com, accessed 23 August 2012.

Apologies for negative outcomes due to past practices were issued on several occasions, one as recent as 2010 by David Berg's wife and successor, Maria:

> Peter and I realize that there have been a number of difficulties, problems, and hurts that have occurred in many cases as a result of the sexual application of the Law of Love. We are very sorry if you have experienced any hurt, or strain on your marriage or committed relationship, or any other difficulty as a result of applying the Law of Love to sexual interaction. While the sexual application of the Law of Love is a precious gift from the Lord, it can also be very challenging to practice.
>
> As we go into the future, we need to recalibrate our understanding and implementation of the sexual application of the Law of Love. To create a more inclusive culture where people feel comfortable and welcome, we'll need to change some aspects of the culture of the Family. Some modifications are needed so that we will be more relatable to a broader membership. Some members will need to adjust how they interact with one another. In general, the sexual ethos of TFI needs some adjustment.[17]

In 2010, a new position was adopted by the organization which continues to maintain the viability of the Law of Love doctrine, while decisively deemphasizing its application to sexual practices. The current position relegates sexual practices to the realm of personal lifestyle choices as opposed to the previous doctrine that attributed spiritual merit to the practice. It also acknowledges and affirms the biblical concept of adultery, albeit making allowance for exceptions, not dissimilar to those expressed in situational ethics.

> Applying the doctrine of the Law of Love to sex is no longer something that we will promote or encourage members to practice as part of discipleship ... How members choose to live regarding sexual matters is meant to be a *discreet personal lifestyle choice*, and not a prominent part of our culture.[18]

---

[17] Karen Zerby (Maria Fontaine), *Applying God's Law of Love* (2010). Copies in the archives of the Family International.

[18] Ibid., emphasis in original.

Considering the lesser emphasis on communalism and the relegating of past sexual doctrines largely to the realm of personal lifestyle choices, it seems likely that such practices will diminish over time. Notwithstanding this more moderate approach, the Family's liberal position on sexuality continues to place it outside the mainstream of Christianity.

Cultural Implications

The practice of communalism resulted in the forging of a way of life that has endured throughout the Family's history. Although the movement has never exceeded 15,000 members, including children, it has effectively established a presence in over 90 countries and currently is comprised of members of over 100 nationalities. Family homes have been relatively successful in accommodating to local cultures, notwithstanding the highly mobile nature of the organization and the natural challenges of learning languages and cultural adaptation. Members have effectively incorporated people of different nationalities and customs into their homes, while sustaining a unified subculture. Homes in Japan, for example, could adopt a distinct Japanese flavor and be comprised mostly of Japanese nationals, and yet be readily identifiable as part of the Family culture.

> From turbulent beginnings as a loosely organized apocalyptic band of young hippies, The Family has evolved into a transnational religious community with its own clearly articulated culture that—regardless of variations in ethnicity, language, or prevailing customs of the host nation—has become standardized within communal homes located on every continent but Antarctica.[19]

> The Family is a remarkably diverse community. Its membership spans a wide range of economic, educational, religious, cultural, ethnic and national backgrounds. There is no such thing as a "typical" Child of God. Yet, in the

---

[19] Gary Shepherd and Gordon Shepherd, "Evolution of the Family International/Children of God in the Direction of a Responsive Communitarian Religion", *Communal Societies*, 28/1 (2008): p. 48.

midst of this diversity, the disciples are guided by a common vision. Although life in The Family is not uniform, it is coherent.[20]

Discipleship for Family members has represented an all-encompassing commitment, commencing with a religious commitment to devote their lives to Christ and the missions, and subsequently to share their lives with other members in a highly structured setting that regimented most aspects of the members' lifestyle. Organization-wide norms existed for many features of daily life and ministry, including child-rearing, discipline, education, nutrition, and religious indoctrination.

For most of its history, children were sheltered and schooled at home, and exposure to the outside world was generally conducted in supervised environments. Children were considered to be the shared responsibility of the members of the community and a uniform approach was adopted for their upbringing, with the active participation of all adults in the community. The Family generally espoused a "one household" style of communalism, with all the members living under one roof, or in the case of large communes, on one property or two or more adjoining properties. As a rule, the organization shied away from purchasing properties and encouraged members to retain mobility and be prepared to move on to other mission fields.

Unlike the trend in most fundamentalist Christian movements, the Family International adopted an egalitarian approach to gender and generational roles. Men and women have been equally able to adopt roles of leadership or ministry. Since the "coming of age" of its first set of teenagers in the early 1990s, the movement has actively strived to incorporate second-generation members into all aspects of community and organizational oversight and leadership.

Finances have been typically common-potted. Due to its adherence to the biblical mandate to "go into all the world and preach the Gospel"[21] and its belief in an imminent end-time, the Family International as an organization, and consequently its members, did not generally build or save for the distant future. Instead, members largely invested their limited resources in mission work and the

---

[20] James D. Chancellor, *Life in the Family: An Oral History of the Children of God* (Syracuse, 2000), p. 58.

[21] Mark 16: 15, English Standard Version.

immediate needs of communal home life. David Berg preached extensively of a soon-to-come end of the world. His understanding of the biblical apocalypse was that the systems of the world would come to an end and a millennial restoration of the earth would occur, ushering in a new and godly system.[22] As such, Family members were also generally uninvolved in political or social causes.

> We're not merely trying to revamp the existing systems! We want to see a complete and total and absolute change of systems, from man's systems to God's System—the Kingdom of God on earth, which is coming some day, when Jesus comes—a total and complete and absolute Revolution of the Spirit which will change the hearts of men, not mere governments, economics and religions![23]

The movement tended to eschew Christian and secular resources for much of its history, though this approach mellowed over time. Its separateness from the external society contributed to establishing a distinctive identity and richness in the culture, characterized by energy and creativity. Numerous original resources were created by members: original music and video productions that members successfully marketed to acquire revenue for the upkeep of the homes; Gospel publications for distribution; devotional and doctrinal publications; early learning scholastic materials and educational videos; Family-created art, particularly in the currently popular comic format, and novels and short stories. Such enterprises were made possible by the communal arrangements and collaboration between members and homes, which empowered individuals to combine talents and resources in creative ways.

By December 2008, Family members had distributed nearly 16 million CDs and DVDs of Family-produced music and drama, and over 990 million Gospel publications, all created in-house. These proved highly effective as instruments for sharing the Gospel message and providing much needed financial resources for the movement. Its signature magazine, *Activated*, containing both traditional Christian teachings and contemporary messages in prophecy, has been published

---

[22] The Family International, *Statement of Faith* (2010). Available online at http://www.thefamilyinternational.org/en/about/our-beliefs, accessed August 23, 2012.

[23] David Berg, "Backsliders", ML 140 (Zurich, 1971).

in 27 languages since its inception in 2001. As of December 2010, over nine million copies of *Activated* have been distributed worldwide.

Cultural Innovations

Innovation and change have characterized the Family International since its earliest days. In the process of evolving from a loosely knit USA-based collection of counterculture youth to a structured international missionary movement, it has experienced continual change, referred to internally as "revolutions". The movement's ability to reinvent itself periodically and introduce innovative solutions to the challenges of the day has empowered it to evolve at a rapid pace while remaining relevant to its members.

> If there has been any persistent truth about the Family during its several decades of existence, it has been its almost annual ability to introduce novelty and change into the routine into which its members would otherwise fall. This novelty makes the Family interesting to scholars, confounds its critics, and prevents even the most careful observers from predicting its future. It is expected that change will remain an integral part of the Family even as it moves to develop a more settled congregation-oriented lifestyle.[24]

Family members have been able to sustain continuous change due to the theological consistency throughout the organization's history. Its core purpose of preaching the Gospel to the world has remained unchanged, despite at times drastic internal restructuring. Its commitment to communalism has also been a constant (notwithstanding the most recent changes in 2010), regardless of the trends or pushes of the time. This has provided stability to the movement despite its prevailing state of change and flux.

Several factors have served as catalysts for change and adaptation throughout the movement's history. First, the difficult task of balancing the evangelistic imperatives of the movement with the internal societal needs and the preservation of its belief system would inform many of the changes introduced. The Family

---

[24] Melton, *Children of God*, pp. 61–62.

experienced monumental shifts over the years depending on the prevailing emphasis; at times it became more regimented in order to preserve the spiritual integrity of the movement, and at others, less regimented to facilitate the missionary activities of the members. At times, the average community size dropped to six members; at other times, the average approximated 40, with several communes consisting of around 100 members. The latest model of membership introduced in 2010 places emphasis on personal autonomy in order to empower members to more effectively minister without the limitations imposed by the previous structure.

The second factor which played a key role in fostering innovation and accommodation was the emergence of the second generation. This predictably introduced a new series of dynamics that would significantly impact the evolution and focus of the movement from 1990 to the present. The natural propensity of the second generation to look beyond the limitations of the communal lifestyle and doctrinal boundaries necessitated adaptation and ultimately a broader model of discipleship. Allowance would need to be made for lesser commitments, as well as for a larger diversity of opportunities for higher education and careers.

The movement's expansion and membership building programs also served as catalysts for change. In 1999, the Family began to shift its previous focus of primarily sharing the Gospel and leading souls to Christ, often by means of one-time encounters, to expanding its membership and building congregations. It became apparent that in order for the movement to grow its membership and influence base, it was necessary to reduce tension with the greater society and thus empower members to better relate to their target audiences.

In contemplating aspects of the Family doctrine, practice, and lifestyle that could sustain change in order to achieve the movement's growth and evangelization objectives, it became clear that its traditional communal model needed to be re-evaluated. After much analysis of a large volume of critiques and frank observations from leadership and members around the world, the conclusion was reached that the enforcement of the previous stringent communal requirements for full-time members would not be conducive to the Family's future success and growth.

Considering that communal living has been typically highly structured and normative for full-time members, this has imposed some limitations on the ability of individual members to pioneer innovative ministries. Although the

Family's *Charter* guaranteed the rights of the individual, the democratic vote of the community tended to override the individual on community matters or issues relating to their mission works. The larger the community, the more difficult it became to accommodate innovative enterprises, and domestic issues necessarily demanded a larger share of the members' attention and resources.

Time management was a driving factor in the decision to adopt a broader approach regarding communal households. The Family had developed complex theological and pragmatic norms over time, particularly for high-commitment members, resulting in a predominantly internal focus, despite its ongoing evangelization and humanitarian efforts. Family communities have served as education centers for homeschooling children, reception centers for visitors and the training of converts, missionary bases for humanitarian and charitable works, the community's place of worship and private residence, and more. They have been multifaceted, encompassing a number of diverse ministries, age demographics, and focuses, all of which tended to compete for the time of the resident members. In order to successfully navigate the transition from earlier evangelization models to flock-building and expanding its membership, it became clear that competing focuses were likely to develop. Changes in membership requirements and expectations would need to be adopted.

Through the Reboot, flexibility was incorporated into membership requirements, including adherence to and practice of the Family's unconventional doctrines, in order to enable Family members to explore different options for ministry and lifestyle choices. This change in approach was articulated as follows:

> While Family members have demonstrated that it's possible to have a successful Christian communal lifestyle in today's society, and that it can be a powerful witness in some situations, we also acknowledge that times have changed over the last 30–40 years. In today's world, communal living is not necessarily the best way to be a living testimony of Jesus' love in every country or culture, nor is it the only proof that His teachings can be lived in daily life.
>
> In some cultures, a communal home can be a beautiful and compelling testimony, one that is appealing or intriguing to those who are interested. In other cultures, communal living is not highly thought of, nor is it understood, and the very

foreignness of it can work against our members being accepted by the people they are trying to reach. In some areas of the world, housing that is adequate for a large communal home is often prohibitively expensive, or is located far outside the city, which can sometimes make it more challenging for members to engage in the mission.

Living communally can also be complex, particularly in larger homes. The bigger the communal home, the more must be invested in internal matters in order to help the home run smoothly. In some cases, the benefits of living communally equal or outweigh the time and effort that has to be invested to have a happy, harmonious home. In other situations, the internal workings and upkeep of a large communal home can become time-consuming or demanding in ways that make it difficult for the home members to give as much of their time and energy to mission-related focuses as they would like. In those instances, communal living is not contributing significantly to the mission, and in some cases, might even be detracting from fulfilling mission goals ... The reality is that it's not possible—or always best—for all members to live communally.[25]

Retirement

The modification of the Family's communal model has brought new issues to the fore, in particular the question of retirement. The care of aging members who have served in the communal structure for decades and therefore have little or no savings or preparations made for retirement and old age has become a notable concern. The previous expectation had been that the communal structure would absorb the care of aging members; limited provision had therefore been made for retirement. Peter Amsterdam, co-director of the Family International, commented:

> The care of TFI's older members who have served the Lord faithfully for many years, and what help will be available to them when they reach an age where

---

[25] The Family International, *Lifestyle* (2010). Copies in the archives of the Family International.

they need more assistance, is a topic of concern to Maria and me, as it is to many of you.

Those of you who have been in the Family for many years have spent those years investing in the lives of others. In most cases, you've given everything you had to further the work of the Family, helping others to find the Lord and know His love. Most of you have not kept much, if anything, materially and financially speaking, for yourselves. In addition, the Family's culture of the past 40 years did not encourage long-term financial investments or saving for retirement. We invested everything into the Lord's work and the needs at hand and trusted that the Lord would repay and provide all our needs.

… Maria and I understand that … the change in our discipleship model—including communal living no longer being required—and our move away from maintaining our own societal structure, has raised the question of what you first generation members will do when you reach an age when you need assistance.[26]

The results of a poll conducted in March 2011 identified retirement as an issue of primary concern for the majority of Family members.[27] In response, the organization has created a board devoted to the needs of members who will reach retirement age over the next decade. Resources have also been allotted to provide minimal support for elderly members as the need arises. Although this funding is currently limited, investment opportunities will be sought out and cooperative living arrangements developed for those in need of assistance. Additionally, many first-generation members are currently investing independently in creating resources for their own retirement. It is likely that in some cases second-generation members will take on the care of an aging parent. The Family's administration has committed to investing time and resources over the next years to develop a structured plan to provide viable solutions for the care of elderly members.

---

[26] Peter Amsterdam, *Care of Elderly Family Members* (2011). Copies in the archives of the Family International.
[27] Peter Amsterdam, *Snapshot of TFI Member Poll* (2011). Copies in the archives of the Family International.

Conclusion

The Family International has thrived as a communitarian culture for over four decades in numerous countries and cultures around the world. It has forged a way of life that has been embraced by its members and has served to nurture the movement's religious and missionary purpose. Communalism has proved to be a successful model for its goals of creating an alternative society whereby its non-traditional belief system and mission purpose could be nurtured. The Family's distinctiveness from mainstream Christianity has resulted in the development of novel approaches to evangelization that have provided an alternative representation of Christianity, as well as unique doctrines, notably the widespread use of prophecy amongst its membership. The movement embraces the belief that God continues to speak to His people to impart His direct messages, revelation, spiritual direction, and counsel through prophecy. The practice of receiving messages in prophecy has been applied routinely to members' daily lives, resulting in the creation of a "culture of prophecy", with members receiving daily spiritual messages for both individual and collective guidance.[28]

The challenges the Family International has faced, whether internal to the organization or those presented by external pressures, controversy, and opposition, have ultimately served to foster innovation and adaptability. The movement has proved adept at adjusting its policies to circumstances and developing innovative ideas and practices to accommodate to the needs and trends of the day. Notwithstanding the many changes it has sustained, the Family's core beliefs and mission purpose as expressed in its statement of faith have remained fundamentally unaltered.

Operating successful communes has been a hallmark of the movement and its unconventional form of Christianity. In the process of transitioning to a new model no longer based on the communal ideology that has been central to its culture and belief system, the Family has undertaken its most monumental reinvention to date. The redefinition of its core identity that this necessitates will doubtless give rise to new dynamics and challenges, in particular the need to identify and cultivate a new sense of identity and community. Developing new agencies for

---

[28] Gary Shepherd and Gordon Shepherd, "Grassroots Prophecy in The Family International", *Nova Religio*, 10/4 (2007): p. 38.

sustaining a vibrant community and spiritual life, which have been core to the Family International's existence, will be crucial to a successful transition to its new model and ongoing relevance to its members.

While the Family International no longer institutionalizes a structured model for communal households, its affirmation of the values and principles that underpinned its brand of communalism remains unchanged. Cooperation, collaboration, and the application of its Christian values and core beliefs continue to be fundamental to the organization. Considering that members have participated in a rich, shared culture for decades, it seems safe to surmise that new, less formal models of cooperative households will emerge in future years that will be forged by like-minded individuals bonded by common beliefs and objectives. As the movement strives to transition to a more expansive version of Christian community while retaining core elements of its unique culture and belief system, it has doubtless embarked on a new journey of innovation and change.

Chapter 10

How Many Arks Does It Take?

Chris Coates

[A]n ark is a symbol for a refuge in a time of trouble. Noah was warned of the disasters ahead; we also will require an ark in the time to come, and there is a small group of people now in London that has started building one ... There are great disasters ahead of us and we've got to prepare for them. There will be wars, political unrest, revolutions and all on such a scale that everything that humanity has managed to build up may well fall in ruins.[1]

On the surface of it there would seem to be very little that individual spiritually based intentional communities have in common with each other, except perhaps on a superficial level – they often have a charismatic leader/founder, vaguely similar practices (dance, meditation, etc.), and there are only a limited number of physical forms that any community can take. But when it comes to the philosophical ideas and backgrounds that underpin each community they can seem like chalk and cheese to each other. In studying a number of twentieth-century British communities I began to be intrigued by particular patterns that began to emerge when I was looking at them from a distance, so to speak – or when looking at them in comparison to each other.

It all began when I read a book called *Venture with Ideas* by Kenneth Walker, published in 1973, which is a record of his time spent studying the ideas of the Armenian mystic G.I. Gurdjieff in the period just before and after World War II with others at Lyne Place at Virginia Water in Surrey. As early as 1923 Gurdjieff had prophesied that there would be another war and that humanity would fall into ruin; he had spoken to his followers urging them to form arks in the event of a "flood of evil engulfing the world". As Neville Chamberlain delivered his message to the British nation on 3 September 1939 that they were once again at

---

[1] Maurice Nicoll in conversation with Kenneth Walker, 1924, in Kenneth Walker, *Venture with Ideas* (London, 1973).

war, the residents of Lyne Place were escorting their children to a heavily timber-reinforced basement that they had prepared. In the distance the wail of sirens could be heard. Plans for their "ark" had been in place for some time. In the grounds of the house the group had dug a large underground concrete bunker to store food in; it was well stocked with provisions of every kind: hams, dried fruit, jars of salted butter, sugar, oatmeal, flour ... Arrangements were in place for as many women and children as possible from the London connections of the group to be accommodated in the house and in the various cottages on the small estate.

Lyne Place had been bought in 1936 by Mr and Madame P.D. Ouspensky as a base to carry out plans for an esoteric school teaching ideas and practices that they had both learnt from Gurdjieff. The newly acquired property in Surrey came with extensive gardens, rhododendron walks, a small lake with a boathouse, a farm, greenhouses, pigsties, barns, stables, and a vegetable garden. It was in a poor state of repair and required three months of renovation before it was fit for anyone to move in. The Ouspenskys' plans for the new venture were to, "so far as was possible", create a self-contained, self-supporting community. The permanent residents set about learning how to grow their own fruit and vegetables in the extensive kitchen gardens and orchards. At weekends the numbers were swollen by visitors from London with as many as a hundred people sitting down to meals. By the end of two years in residence the group were growing their own wheat, milling it themselves into flour and baking their own bread. They had constructed a shed containing fruit-drying equipment and expanded their work into managing the woodland on the estate, felling timber and converting it in a "Heath Robinson" (ingenious but eccentric) sawmill that they had built themselves. Other members were kept busy with sheep and dairy farming. The core of residents of the new community were Russian – the Ouspenskys, the Savitskys, Mme Kadloubovsky, plus a handful of St Petersburg pensioners. Some of Ouspensky's senior English pupils had been drafted in to manage the household and grounds. By the autumn of 1937 the new community was thriving and Ouspensky's work was attracting the interest of a younger generation of the English intelligentsia.

All this activity was thrown into confusion by the outbreak of the war. As the esoteric refugees bunkered down in their Surrey Ark, Ouspensky meditated on the state of the world and came to the erroneous conclusion that Germany would quickly win the war, that this would spark a Europe-wide revolution supported by the Soviet Union, and that only America would evade the clutches of Communism. London meetings were eventually canceled due to the frequency of air raids, and work at Lyne became harder as members were called up for National Service. By 1940, with the Battle of Britain raging in the skies above Lyne and the Blitz having destroyed their London flat, the Ouspenskys decided to emigrate to America, leaving Lyne Place in the hands of trusted senior members of the group. With the departure of the two teachers, the group's work in England came to a standstill. In America, the Ouspenskys would try to recreate their English setup at Franklin Farms, Mendham, the former residence of the Governor of New Jersey. As they sat out the war in the States – P.D. Ouspensky spent much of the time in New York writing and lecturing, while Madame Ouspensky supervised the new community, teaching "the movements" (a ritualized form of group dancing devised by Gurdjieff) and gathering her own group of followers – the health of both started to deteriorate. Suffering some sort of existential crisis, Ouspensky started to drink heavily, no doubt not helped by his wife's Parkinson's disease diagnosis. Back in Surrey, as the end of the war approached those who had stayed behind awaited the return of the master with anticipation, seemingly unaware of his declining health and apparent spiritual malaise. Ouspensky delayed his return to England until January 1947. He returned to Lyne Place and became a near recluse, staying in his room and limiting contact to his secretary, a Miss Quinn, Rodney Colin-Smith, who had become a close confidant during the years in America, and a collection of cats. A series of what turned out to be final meetings were arranged in London at which Ouspensky shocked his followers by renouncing his own teachings, claiming that there never was any "system" and that they should all "begin again, starting from what he or she really wanted". Ouspensky died at Lyne Place on 2 October 1947.

What really intrigued me about this story was the use of the imagery of the Ark which continued to reappear throughout the work of Gurdjieff's followers during this period. Dr Maurice Nicoll, a Harley Street psychologist who had studied with Gurdjieff at the Château du Prieure at Fontainebleau in France and had been given permission to teach the "system" in England by Ouspensky for some years in the late 1930s, ran weekend courses and lectures at Lakes Farm at Rayne, near Braintree in Essex.

The house itself was old and had a delightful atmosphere. Along the back wall a verandah had been built where all meals were served during the summer. A long trestle table covered with gaily coloured cloth and equally gay china looked so delightful that it was a pleasure to sit down and eat the food that Mrs Nicoll provided.[2]

Gurdjieff's "Work" was an esoteric path to enlightenment, supposedly handed down from a mysterious Sarmoung monastery. Originally shrouded in obscurity, partly due to secrecy surrounding it and partly due to unorthodox teaching methods utilized by Gurdjieff, the Work consisted of various techniques to be practiced by adherents, with names such as self remembering, self observation, conscious labor, and intentional suffering.

The owner of Lakes Farm died in 1934 and bequeathed the farm to her goddaughter, Jane Nicoll. Soon afterwards, Dr and Mrs Nicoll came up with a plan for building a house on the land next to the Lakes Farmhouse that would be suitable for carrying out the group activities that were by then attracting more and more people down to the farm at weekends. The new house would have large activity rooms on the ground floor, with bedrooms above for the weekend guests. Plans for the building were drawn up by young architect George Kadleigh, and the Work weekends were transformed into spiritual self-build weekends. The group tackled pretty much the whole range of building works, digging the foundations, putting up timber frames, lath and plastering, carpentry, and even weaving their own stair carpets. Almost the only work done by actual builders was the thatching of the roof and sinking of a well. The finished house was named Tyeponds after the name of the field in which it stood.

The Nicolls heard about the imminent outbreak of war whilst on holiday with a small group of friends in Normandy in August 1939. The group rushed back to Essex where other members of the group had already started organizing the digging of trenches in preparation for expected air raids.

---

[2] Selene Moxon describing her first weekend at Lakes Farm, in Maurice Nicoll, *Psychological Commentaries on the Teachings of Gurdjieff and Ouspensky*, vol. 1 (London, 1952).

> We all thought that London would be bombed immediately. Friends came down in crowds and we found room for them all. Some brought their babies, others their dogs. Some came laden, feeling that they had left their homes for ever; others brought no possessions.[3]

Maurice Nicoll had always had in the back of his mind that Tyeponds would act as a refuge, or Ark, should Gurdjieff's predictions come to pass. In addition to the members of his weekend groups and their families, the farm was allocated a large number of evacuees. These very quickly filled up the accommodation in the houses and further people were crammed in any available space. A group of a dozen or so expectant mothers were put up in the carpentry shed; the music room was turned into a makeshift school room for the numerous child evacuees. The group rose to the task of looking after these "guests". Nicoll spent his own money on whatever was needed: prams for new mothers, extra stoves ... Numbers reached 50 within weeks; children were enrolled in the local school and more suitable accommodation was found for the pregnant women at Frinton. Numbers were further swollen at weekends as the group continued with the group work courses they had run before the outbreak of war. Life settled down for a few months until the residents were abruptly disturbed on 26 May 1940 by instructions that the area had been declared a military zone and that they had 24 hours to pack and leave the area. The following day, as the group packed to leave, across the channel the evacuation of the British Expeditionary Force from Dunkirk began. Nicoll and his small group found refuge for the duration of the war at a large Victorian house called The Knapp at Birdlip in the Cotswolds, and after the war re-established himself not back at Tyeponds, which had been pretty much destroyed by the military, but in a couple of locations close to London. He settled first at a house renamed Quare Mead at Ugley near Bishop Stortford, where he again started running weekend courses and the small number of permanent residents started a smallholding. When that building proved too small the group moved to Great Amwell House in Hertfordshire, where Nicoll carried on the Work until his death in 1951.

In the post-war years Gurdjieff's work was continued at another community set up by J.G. Bennett in the former British Coal Utilisation Research Association

---

[3] Beryl Pogson, *Maurice Nicoll: A Portrait* (London, 1961).

(BCURA) base on the seven-acre Coombe Springs estate at Kingston upon Thames in Surrey, where he had worked during the war researching coal-based alternatives to oil. Bennett started off running weekend courses at Coombe Springs in the immediate post-war years whilst still working for BCURA, but became increasingly worried about the possible collapse of civilization and a further global war. In 1948 Bennett and his friends started to look for a "Noah's Ark", a place where they would be secure from political, economic, and social turmoil. Somewhat strangely, in retrospect, they looked to South Africa as a possible refuge. Bennett went to Africa to assess the feasibility of moving there and setting up an independent community. In South Africa he met the Prime Minister, Jan Smuts, who was in the middle of issuing the Fagan Report that proposed relaxing the country's racial segregation laws – the reaction to which would usher in apartheid. In the end it was decided that Africa was not "the right place", and Bennett, his wife and 10 of his closest pupils formed the core of a new "research community" at Coombe Springs. Numbers were swelled at weekends by numerous visitors who came down to study not only the teachings of Gurdjieff, but over the years a whole selection of other esoteric teachers. In 1956, inspired by Sufi meeting houses he had seen on a tour of the Middle East, Bennett embarked on the construction of a fantastic building in the grounds of Coombe Springs. Instead of going for a building in any traditional architectural style, either eastern or western, it was decided to base the design of the new building on the mystical geometrical symbol of the enneagram, claimed by Gurdjieff to have great cosmic significance. The unique nine-sided 50-foot-high hall was designed and built by Bennett and a group of architects led by Robert Whiffen. Money for the project was raised through loans from members. The construction work was also carried out utilizing the largely amateur building skills of the membership. A small team of residents was swollen at weekends with up to 40 enthusiastic volunteers. The physical labor was incorporated as part of the spiritual Work of the volunteers. The central axis of the hall was laid out so that it pointed to Gurdjieff's grave at Fontainebleau. The hall had three levels: a concrete base, signifying the material world; timber structure and walls, signifying the living world; and a copper roof, signifying the spiritual world.

> I was asked to give a name to the building, and chose the word Djamichunatra, taken from Chapter 46 of All and Everything, where it is used to describe the place where the soul receives its spiritual nourishment.[4]

The group at Coombe Springs continued through until 1965 when, in a move with echoes of Ouspensky's renunciation of his own teachings, Bennett persuaded his followers to hand over the property to Idries Shah who promptly sold it, reputedly for £100,000, to a developer who flattened the whole estate – the main house, the amazing Djamichunatra, everything – in order to build luxury homes on the site.

Bennett later continued his spiritual research work, buying the rambling semi-derelict Sherborne House in the Cotswolds, and in October 1971, with the help of his wife and several assistants, he launched the International Academy for Continuous Education. Bennett thought that the old world was likely to disintegrate before the end of the twentieth century, but that the seeds of a new world could be nurtured in experimental communities and that the Academy could be a place where people who were starting to become aware of the coming changes could be "trained to perceive, to understand, and to withstand the strains of the world process". To do this, a year-long course was devised utilizing Gurdjieffian techniques and ideas alongside material from other sources. Bennett oversaw three of the year-long courses as part of a five year program after which his intention was to invite back the best pupils and take the "next step" with them. It would seem that the next step was to be some kind of self-sufficient community made up of Sherborne graduates. Due to the increasing price of land in England, Bennett started to look to the USA as a possible location for a community that could continue his work. At the fourth annual course started at Sherborne in October 1974 an agreement was signed between the Institute and The Claymont Society to lend them $100,000 to enable the purchase of Claymont Court, a farm and mansion on 400 acres in the Shenandoah Valley, Jefferson County, West Virginia, for the foundation of a psychokinetic community. Bennett would never see either the end of the five year program at Sherborne or the development of the community in the States. He died, aged 77, on 13 December 1974.

In some ways it is not surprising that a generation that had grown up in the shadow of one World War and just lived through a second should be driven by

---

[4] J.G. Bennett, *Witness: The Story of a Search* (London, 1962).

thoughts of impending doom and of founding refuges and "Arks". This mood of apocalyptic thinking would be sustained by the cold war through the 1960s and 1970s, casting a shadow over other spiritually based communities that started in that era. The story of the beginning of the Findhorn Community in the north of Scotland has been told many times. It was founded as a "community of light" through guidance received by Eileen Caddy and through the growing of giant vegetables by her husband Peter with guidance from plant "devas". Peter Caddy is portrayed in the early literature and reports about the Findhorn Community as a positive-thinking man of action enthusiastically putting into practice the guidance received by the mostly female "sensitives" or mediums that surrounded him. The focus over the years has fallen on Eileen Caddy as the source of this guidance, but in the early days of the group this certainly wasn't the case, nor was Eileen the first medium that Peter had listened to for guidance. After the war, whilst serving as catering manager for British Service personnel who were traveling by military aircraft, he found himself in the Philippines, where by chance he met "a grey-haired lady" called Anne Edwards known by her spiritual name as Naomi. Very quickly the two were deep in conversation ranging from discussing Tibetan Masters to the works of Alice Bailey. Naomi said she had been contacted on numerous occasions by beings from outer space who had instructed her to set up a group that could contact other groups around the world by telepathy and form a psychic network to channel extraterrestrial energies that were being poured down upon the earth by the Space Brothers. She told Peter that so far her group had been telepathically in touch with 370 other groups around the world. The meeting with Edwards would establish "an extraordinary bond" between the two of them. For years they would exchange up to two or three letters a week, and her revelations sparked a long-term fascination with UFOs in Caddy. Their contact would eventually lead to Edwards joining the Caddys at Findhorn in 1964. Peter Caddy's interest in UFOs, backed up by the messages from the Space Brothers being received by Naomi, prompted him in 1954 to write a report, *An Introduction to the Nature and Purpose of Unidentified Flying Objects*, explaining what lay behind the increasing numbers of UFO sightings that were being reported at the time. He received guidance to get 26 copies of the 8,000-word report and deliver them to a list of key persons including Winston Churchill, Clement Attlee, Prince Philip, President Dwight D. Eisenhower, and several other prominent military, scientific, and spiritual figures.

Messages continued to be received from outer space throughout the late 1950s, becoming increasingly apocalyptic as time went by. In one, Eileen Caddy saw the mysterious word LUKANO written in letters of fire. This was quickly confirmed by Naomi as the name of the captain of a spaceship from Venus who was planning a rescue mission to Earth should a nuclear holocaust occur. The messages from outer space kept coming, at times on an almost daily basis, with details of the proposed mission. In 1958, Eileen Caddy was told "this is not the only oasis from which people will be rescued when destruction comes. But it is the only one in this country."[5] In a story in *The Sunday Pictorial* on 20 September 1960 under the headline "The Martians Are Coming, He Says", Peter Caddy is reported as declaring that flying saucers from Mars and Venus were on the way to Earth to warn humans that they were on the brink of disaster.

> I believe they will offer people on Earth a chance to leave this planet with them before the catastrophe. They are like us in many ways, but the chief difference is that they have no understanding of such emotions as hatred, greed, jealousy or spite. Their only emotions are love and friendship.[6]

So convinced was he that an extraterrestrial rescue was imminent, Caddy cleared trees from a mound behind the Cluny Hotel in Forres, which he managed at the time, to create a UFO landing strip, and on Christmas Eve and again on New Year's Day a small group kept night-time vigils waiting for the spaceships to land. The little band of watchers were later informed that the landings had been attempted but had failed due to a combination of climatic conditions and the effects of radiation from atomic bomb testing.

In October 1962, as the Caddys moved their caravan first onto the Findhorn Sands Caravan Park and then the following month to the Findhorn Bay Caravan Park, the Cuban Missile crisis was unfolding, presumably adding to the bleak outlook and the group's apocalyptic mood. Extraterrestrial messages kept coming after the group had moved to the caravan park, alternating between visions of the Space Brothers:

---

[5] Eileen Caddy's notebooks, now in the Scottish National Library.
[6] Ibid.

> I have always seen our space brothers and the mothership or a craft, but tonight I seem to be taken to the natural garden with the building carved out of the rock with everything in harmony. It was on Venus. No windows in the building. There were people like us there tonight, but radiant people. I have never been with Lukano or seen him anywhere but on the ship, or flying saucer before. On Venus everything is in harmony.[7] (Elixir/Eileen Caddy 10 May 1963)

And apocalyptic scenes of planetary destruction

> I saw a great storm over Washington City, and all the buildings seem to be struck by lightning or thunderbolts as they lay shattered. All the people were dead and an awful darkness seemed to envelope the city. Then I saw thousands of small shadowy forms moving everywhere, and I saw they were black rats swarming everywhere consuming the dead, for there was no one left in the city to bury the dead.[8]

A fascination with UFOlogy would continue to be part of the ideas that attracted people to visit Findhorn until the early 1970s when it would slowly fade into the background, warranting little and eventually no mention in any community publications. The Caddys saw the community they were setting up as a refuge from the world, and the imagery of the Ark crops up in the community's publications written at the time.

> "The garden is like the ark I asked Noah to build. It is difficult for you to see the reason for it, for you cannot see into the future, but let Me assure you that it is vitally important."[9] (Elixir/Eileen Caddy, quoted in *The Findhorn Garden*)

And even as late as the 1990s Carol Riddel, writing about Findhorn, continued to use the Ark as a symbol to convey the idea of a new ecological threat and the lack of response to it.

---
[7] Ibid.
[8] Ibid.
[9] Andy Roberts, "Saucers over Findhorn", *Fortean Times* (December, 2006).

> We are all part of the same global Noah's Ark now, a leaky ark that needs a lot of repair to survive the floods of cynicism and disillusion that threaten to swallow us.[10]

Many of Gurdjieff's teachings come from Sufi Muslim sources, and the root of much of the early Findhorn ideology stems from esoteric Christian sources. That they should both use the iconography of the Ark led me to do a bit of digging around the general cultural background of stories about the flood and Noah and his Ark. Not only did I find out that the story appears both in the Bible and the Quran but that it also appears in Hindu mythology, recorded in The Mahabharata as the story of Vaivasvata, who is ordered by Vishnu to build a ship for himself and his family and to collect the seeds of every plant and a pair of every species of animal in order that they can survive a flood. Some have speculated that the Hindu myth is, in fact, the source of all following Ark stories. This led me to two further spiritual communal Arks.

By 1977 the Hare Krishna Movement had established over 100 temples worldwide, along with farms, restaurants, schools, a scientific institute, and a book company. They also had a number of communes or ashrams across the globe, including Bhaktivedanta Manor in the UK. Hare Krishna founder and guru A.C. Bhaktivedanta Swami Prabhupada died in November 1977, and despite his efforts to plan for his succession the movement entered a period of flux and uncertainty. Eleven new "gurus" had been initiated by Prabhupada, each with a regional remit. This contributed to various factions appearing, and during the same period the movement went through a somewhat apocalyptic phase.

> [M]ost of the eleven gurus embraced the revelation of an apocalyptic world war. According to the widely accepted scenario, only core ISKCON members, a few thousand chosen souls, would survive, with the insiders leading the others into an age of spiritual enlightenment ... Leaders implored devotees to stand by their posts on the front lines of preaching, collecting money, and selling books until, upon the Governing Body Commission's command, it would be time to retreat

---

[10] *The Findhorn Garden* (New York, 1975).

to rural strongholds. They said guns would be necessary to fight off looters and refugees[11]

This dose of cold war paranoia was prompted by interpretations of what was known as the "World War III tape", a recording of a conversation in 1975 in which Prabhupada discussed tensions between India and Pakistan and said "Next war will come very soon. Your country, America, is very much eager to kill these Communists and the Communists are also very eager. So very soon there will be war".[12] Asked what devotees would do while the war is going on, he replied "Chant Hare Krishna".

At the same time as the Hare Krishna devotees were worrying about the apocalypse, so too were followers of another Hindu Guru who had moved to the West and set up his own communes. The teachings of Bhagwan Shree Rajneesh had always had an apocalyptic thread running through them, and in the late 1970s he predicted that World War Three would start in 1993 in the Middle East, would last six years, and would destroy modern civilization except for a few Rajneesh communes which would survive to start the new world. Later this turned into a prophecy of a "great crisis" that would occur between 1984 and 1999, during which every kind of destruction would be visited on the Earth: floods, earthquakes, volcanic eruptions, nuclear war. In this cyclone of destruction Rajneeshism would create a "Noah's Ark of consciousness" to save humanity. It appears not to have been clear whether this great crisis was meant to be taken metaphorically or as a reality, though at least one of the group's leading therapists believed that Bhagwan meant that extraterrestrials would descend in their mother-ships to save them. This doom-laden message was heightened when AIDS broke out in the early 1980s. The reaction of the Rajneeshees to the threat of AIDS was quick and fairly draconian. Bhagwan announced that this was a sign of the great crisis and would wipe out two-thirds of mankind. Instructions were sent out from the Oregon headquarters:

---

[11] Nori Muster, *Betrayal of the Spirit: My Life Behind the Headlines of the Hare Krishna Movement* (Urbana, 1996).

[12] www.prabhupada.org.uk, accessed August 23, 2011.

> [W]e were told: in order that sannyasins would survive, a radical programme of preventative measures was to be introduced immediately. ... all sexual intercourse, with other sannyasins and between sannyasins and non-sannyasins, would take place using protection. Condoms, plastic gloves and dental dams were to be issued to every sexually active sannyasin. Plastic gloves had to be worn for all genital contact. Contaminated waste-bins would be available for disposal in the kitchens, toilets, and dormitories.[13]

Every member was tested for HIV and a system of colored beads on members' malas was introduced: a blue bead for those not tested, a yellow bead for those awaiting their test results, and a green bead for those who had tested negative. Anyone who had sex with someone without a green bead was to have his or her beads confiscated for three months. As it turned out, no one at the commune tested positive – had they done so they were to be placed in isolation and cared for by the community. In the 1980s the Rajneeshee communes would self-destruct in a scenario of their own making[14] rather than serve as Arks to survive an external apocalypse.

I find it somewhat surprising that the shadow of two world wars and the consequent cold war should cast itself so far and wide across intentional communities, particularly those with a spiritual basis to them. I could understand that influence on those communities formed during and after the war that had come from a pacifist and peace movement background, but to find a vein of what starts to look like paranoia running through such a spectrum of spiritually based communities has made me wonder if the machinations of the wider political world have more influence on the formation of alternative communities than we think and in ways that are not clear at first, or even second, glance.

---

[13] Tim Guest, *My Life in Orange* (London, 2004).
[14] See Frances Fitzgerald, *Cities on a Hill* (London, 1987).

Chapter 11

Religious Communes in America: An Overview

Timothy Miller

New religious movements do not limit themselves to innovative theologies and rituals, but often experiment with non-traditional forms of social organization as well. Thus it is that some organize their members into intentional communities, creating a lifestyle that tends to promote deep commitment and complete immersion in the group.

Communal groups are found all over the world and throughout history. Although some have a secular vision of a better society, a solid majority are religious in basis. What they have in common is high dedication and commitment among their members. Beyond that the pattern varies considerably. This chapter will provide a selective historical survey of religious intentional communities in the United States, highlighting a few of the many thousands that have existed over the years.[1]

The first independent intentional community after European settlement in what is now the United States was Swanendael, or Plockhoy's Commonwealth. A group of Dutch Mennonites led by Pieter C. Plockhoy arrived in Delaware in 1663, pursuing an elegant plan for a cooperative commonwealth. Unfortunately, the colony was short-lived due to warfare between the English and the Dutch.[2] Others followed, however. Followers of Jean de Labadie, a French Jesuit priest turned Protestant, established the Labadist colony at Bohemia Manor, Maryland, in 1683,

---

[1] Several good scholarly surveys of American intentional communities are available. Important are Donald E. Pitzer (ed.), *America's Communal Utopias* (Chapel Hill, 1997) and Yaacov Oved, *Two Hundred Years of American Communes* (New Brunswick, 1988).

[2] Leland Harder, "Pieter Plockhoy Revisited", *Mennonite Life*, 60:1 (March, 2005).

which endured until 1722 or later.[3] In 1694 a band of Rosicrucian hermits led by Johannes Kelpius founded a community known as Woman in the Wilderness near Philadelphia; it dissolved slowly after Kelpius's death in 1708.[4] In 1732 an ascetic named Conrad Beissel took up residence in rural Pennsylvania, and soon others joined him to form the Protestant monastic Ephrata Community, which lasted for nearly a century.[5]

In 1774 one of the best-known of all communal religious groups, the Shakers, arrived in the United States from England. These millennial enthusiasts soon founded about twenty colonies with thousands of celibate members living strictly disciplined lives. The Shakers are probably best remembered for their elegant architecture and furniture, but were also visionaries and social activists who worked for peace and racial equality. Over two centuries later one small colony of Shakers survives tenuously in Maine.[6]

While the Shakers were thriving, other communal movements came along as well. A prominent nineteenth-century example was the Harmony Society, a band of German Pietist immigrants led by George Rapp who settled in Pennsylvania, then Indiana, then Pennsylvania again as they awaited the Second Coming. When they left their second communal home, in Indiana, they sold their town, New Harmony, to the Scottish industrialist and social reformer Robert Owen, who turned it into a secular community. As a community the Owenite incarnation of New Harmony was short-lived, but Owen's vision of cooperation and humane working conditions has inspired social activists ever since.[7]

The Harmonists were only one group of German Pietists who crossed the Atlantic and settled communally in the United States. Another large group became known as the Amana Society, whose distinctive belief was that inspired prophets could exist in the present, not just the biblical past, and thus could carry

---

[3] Ernest J. Green, "The Labadists of Colonial Maryland, 1683–1722", *Communal Societies*, 8 (1988): pp. 104–121.

[4] Willard M. Martin, "Johannes Kelpius and Johann Gottfried Seelig: Mystics and Hymnists on the Wissahickon", PhD dissertation (Pennsylvania State University, 1973).

[5] Jeffrey A. Bach, *Voices of the Turtledoves: The Sacred World of Ephrata* (University Park, 2003).

[6] Stephen J. Stein, *The Shaker Experience in America* (New Haven, 1992).

[7] Karl J.R. Arndt, *George Rapp's Harmony Society, 1785–1847* (Rutherford, 1965); John F.C. Harrison, *Quest for the New Moral World: Robert Owen and the Owenites in Britain and America* (New York, 1969).

divine messages to believers. Under such inspired leaders the group moved from Germany to New York state, and then to Iowa, where they founded the Amana colonies and lived communally until 1932.[8] The villages and church endure, even though the communal economy has been dropped. Other similar groups, minus the inspired leaders, were the Zoar Society (founded in Ohio in 1817), the Bethel Colony (Missouri, 1844), and Bethel's offshoot the Aurora Colony (Oregon, 1856). For several decades German-speaking Pietists were prominent on the American communal scene.[9]

Around the middle of the nineteenth century the Oneida Community in New York state emerged to become one of the largest and most influential communities of its day. The Oneidans believed that they had achieved moral perfection. Their leader, John Humphrey Noyes, however, added an unusual twist to perfectionism: he taught that earthly marriage did not suit the new dispensation, and thus instituted what may have been the world's largest and longest-lived group marriage, which involved as many as 300 participants and operated smoothly for three decades. The Oneidans all lived in a huge single home, and at their peak opened several branch communities. They prospered by manufacturing animal traps, and later silverware. Eventually, however, external pressure and internal disagreements led to the community's dissolution in the late 1870s. But the silverware industry, still called Oneida, endures.[10]

The last third of the nineteenth century saw the rise of some of the largest communal movements of all. The 1870s constituted the heyday of Latter Day Saint, or Mormon, communalism. The Mormons had had flirtations with communitarian organization earlier, but when they finally settled in Utah in the late 1840s, they finally had a place to try it in earnest. Church president Brigham Young promoted what the Church called the United Order in 1874, and hundreds of cooperatives were organized soon thereafter. The textbook example was Orderville, in southern

---

[8] Jonathan Andelson, "The Community of True Inspiration from Germany to the Amana Colonies", in Pitzer (ed.), *America's Communal Utopias*, pp. 181–203; Peter Hoehnle, *The Amana People: The History of a Religious Community* (Iowa City, 2003).

[9] On Zoar see Edgar B. Nixon, "The Society of Separatists at Zoar", PhD dissertation (Ohio State University, 1933). On Bethel and Aurora see Robert J. Hendricks, *Bethel and Aurora: An Experiment in Communism as Practical Christianity; With Some Account of Past and Present Ventures in Collective Living* (New York, 1933).

[10] George Wallingford Noyes, *Free Love in Utopia: John Humphrey Noyes and the Origin of the Oneida Community* (ed. Lawrence Foster) (Urbana, 2001).

Utah, which in 1874 adopted a communal economy that endured for nearly a decade and had a peak membership of over 600. Following Young's death in 1877 the Church deemphasized communitarianism, but in some places it persisted. In 1890 the Church renounced its former endorsement of polygamous marriages, and many who believed that polygamy continued to be the divine order of things organized their polygamous families into intentional communities in remote parts of Utah, Arizona, and Idaho. Some tens of thousands of schismatic Mormons continue the practice today, often in communal settings.[11]

Just as the United Order was taking shape, the first Hutterites arrived in the United States, and with them came the largest and longest-lived communal movement, apart from the religious orders of the Catholic Church and other similar bodies, in American (and perhaps world) history. The Hutterian movement took shape with the Radical Reformation of the 1520s, which produced the Anabaptists who called for far-reaching ecclesiastical and social reforms. The Hutterites adopted complete community of goods in 1528, and their subsequent history fluctuated between persecution and toleration. In 1770 the Russian government offered the Hutterites special privileges, including exemption from military service, if they would move there as productive farmers. But a century later a different Russian government withdrew the privileges, and once again the Hutterites migrated, settling in South Dakota. Later, amid persecution occasioned by World War I, most of them went to Canada. But they have grown enormously since then, to over 50,000 members in some 500 colonies in the US and Canada. With their thoroughly communal economic and residential system, they have a remarkable history that now spans nearly 500 years.[12]

Nearly a century after the Hutterites settled in South Dakota, a neo-Hutterite movement established its own American presence. The Bruderhof had been founded in Germany in 1920 by Eberhard and Emmy Arnold, who, seeking to recover New Testament Christian living, moved with others into a communal

---

[11] The most comprehensive survey of Mormon communitarianism is Leonard J. Arrington, Feramorz Y. Fox, and Dean L. May, *Building the City of God: Community and Cooperation Among the Mormons* (Salt Lake City, 1976). The largest of the more recent polygamous and communal Latter Day Saints movements is the Fundamentalist Latter-day Saints Church; its history is recorded in Martha Sonntag Bradley, *Kidnapped From That Land* (Salt Lake City, 1993).

[12] Rod Janzen and Max Stanton, *The Hutterites in North America* (Baltimore, 2010).

farmhouse in Germany. They especially admired the early Hutterites and sought to emulate them. The pressures of Nazism and World War II made the Bruderhof a peripatetic movement, and it ended up in New York state in 1954. The movement has grown considerably since then, opening new colonies in the United States and other countries. With perhaps 2,500 members, the Bruderhof has become one of the largest independent communitarian religious movements in the world.[13]

Some of the communes of the latter nineteenth century subscribed to ideas that might best be described as exotic. One of them was the Koreshan Unity, which took communal shape with over 100 members in the 1880s in Chicago under the leadership of Cyrus Read Teed, who called himself Koresh, Hebrew for Cyrus. Teed's most distinctive teaching was that the earth was hollow and that we all live on the inside. In the 1890s the Koreshans moved to Florida, where they built a communal village and, among other things, conducted "scientific" experiments by which they hoped to prove their hollow-earth hypothesis. The celibate population reached more than 200, but declined after Teed's death in 1908.[14]

Thomas Lake Harris was an intriguing figure in American religious history. Remembered primarily as a Spiritualist, Harris and his following, known as the Brotherhood of the New Life, occupied four successive communal locations, the most important of which was Fountain Grove in California, founded in 1875. With a dairy and extensive vineyards, the community prospered for several years until hostile press coverage forced Harris to depart in the early 1890s. Enough colony members stayed on to keep some operations, including the winery, going until a final dissolution in 1934.[15]

The Theosophists were premier American community-builders. Following the death of founder Helena Blavatsky in 1891, their principal organization, the Theosophical Society, splintered. One faction regrouped under the leadership of Katherine Tingley, who oversaw the building of an elaborate intentional community at Point Loma in San Diego, California. The fabulous, mystical architecture of

---

[13] Yaacov Oved, *The Witness of the Brothers: A History of the Bruderhof* (New Brunswick, 1996).

[14] Lynn Rainard, "Dissolution as an Act of Creation: The Koreshan Unity", *Communal Societies*, 30:2 (2010): pp. 1–25.

[15] Herbert W. Schneider and George Lawton, *A Prophet and a Pilgrim: Being the Incredible History of Thomas Lake Harris and Laurence Oliphant; Their Sexual Mysticisms and Utopian Communities Amply Documented to Confound the Skeptic* (New York, 1942).

Point Loma reflected Theosophical ideas about form and color, and the residents enjoyed an active cultural life highlighted by Tingley's love of Shakespearean drama. Point Loma thrived for decades, finally declining after Tingley's death in 1929. In the meantime, however, other Theosophical branches had started communities of their own. Krotona was founded in Hollywood a few years after Tingley established Point Loma, and by 1913 it had attracted some 45 members. In 1924, amid financial problems, the communards sold their land and moved Krotona to Ojai, California. There they built a library and a retirement community, among other improvements, and a Theosophical community has operated there ever since.[16]

At about the same time a new branch of the Theosophical movement arose in Germany. Rudolf Steiner, an Austrian, joined the Theosophical Society in 1902 and became its ardent advocate, but in 1912 his differences with the movement's leaders led him to break away, and the following year he founded the Anthroposophical Society. A generation later, Scottish Anthroposophists started a community known as Camphill, and in 1961 the concept spread to the United States. In the Camphill communities, disabled and retarded young people are helped to lead productive lives in a communitarian setting – one in which they are members, not just patients. Now nearly a dozen Camphill communities are active in North America.[17]

Other unconventional religions were contemporaries of Theosophy. The House of David was founded in Benton Harbor, Michigan, by Benjamin and Mary Purnell in 1903. The movement was derived from the work of the English visionary Joanna Southcott, whose work had come a century earlier, and also had roots in the concept of British Israel, that the British people were the true descendants of the biblical Israelites. These new Israelites numbered around a thousand at their peak and were best known to the public for their barnstorming baseball teams with long-haired players (Purnell's followers did not cut their hair).

---

[16] For a survey of Theosophical communalism see J. Gordon Melton, "The Theosophical Communities and Their Ideal of Universal Brotherhood", in Pitzer (ed.), *America's Communal Utopias*, pp. 396–418. For Point Loma specifically, see W. Michael Ashcraft, *The Dawn of the New Cycle: Point Loma Theosophists and American Culture* (Knoxville, 2002).

[17] Jan Martin Bang (ed.), *A Portrait of Camphill: From Founding Seed to Worldwide Movement* (Edinburgh, 2010).

Purnell was arrested for statutory rape in 1926, and the community was ruled a public nuisance. But Purnell soon died and the issue was dropped. The movement split into two factions, both of which continue.[18]

While intentional communities have been continuously present for over three centuries, they were less visible than usual in the United States between about 1920 and the 1960s. Several of the older communal movements continued, as in the case of the Hutterites, and a few new ones were founded, but only quietly. In the wake of the Russian revolution a Red scare gripped the United States; after World War II that gave way to the cold war. In that atmosphere anything that had a name that resembled "communism", or even simply promoted cooperation, was suspect. At one point in the 1930s the federal government opened about 100 communitarian settlements, most of them rural, with clustered housing and cooperative industries, as a Depression-relief measure, but anti-communist sentiment in Congress eventually brought it all to a halt.[19] During World War II some conscientious objectors banded together in communes, partly for self-protection in a country that overwhelmingly reviled them, and they typically kept to themselves as completely as possible.[20]

A few religious communal groups did emerge, however, especially during the Great Depression of the 1930s, when communal economics helped some of the destitute survive. Perhaps the most visible example was the Peace Mission Movement of Father Divine. During the Depression years he created dozens of "heavens" (communal homes) and businesses from a base in New York's Harlem neighborhood. Father Divine, whose believers regarded him as God, led a predominantly African-American celibate flock and provided followers with essential social support in hard times.[21]

Less visible, but certainly important, was Koinonia Farm, an outpost of interracial harmony in Georgia established by the Baptist preacher Clarence Jordan

---

[18] Clare Adkin, Jr, *Brother Benjamin: A History of the Israelite House of David* (Berrien Springs, 1990).

[19] For the New Deal communities see Paul K. Conkin, *Tomorrow a New World: The New Deal Community Program* (Ithaca, 1959).

[20] One of the few good sources on the small, low-profile communities in the mid twentieth century is Wendell B. Kramer, "Criteria for the Intentional Community", PhD dissertation (New York University, 1955).

[21] Jill Watts, God, *Harlem U.S.A.: The Father Divine Story* (Berkeley, 1992); Robert Weisbrot, *Father Divine and the Struggle for Racial Equality* (Urbana, 1983).

and others in 1942. A racially integrated colony did not sit well with most white Southerners, and Koinonia experienced hostility and even violence for several years. Eventually, however, it became a model of racial cooperation. One Koinonia project was the building of houses for the poor, a program that eventually evolved into Habitat for Humanity, which now builds homes for those in need throughout the world. Jordan died in 1969, but the community continues its work.[22]

The low-profile communitarianism of the first two-thirds of the century came to an end rather dramatically in the 1960s. Early in the decade a few devotees of alternative culture – some of them beatniks, others psychedelic explorers, still others antiwar activists – began to create communal homes for like-minded souls. An early harbinger of the proliferation of communes that would come in the late 1960s was the establishment of Tolstoy Farm in Washington state in 1963. Huw "Piper" Williams became involved in antiwar activism in Connecticut early in the decade, and, inspired by the writings of Tolstoy and Gandhi, started a west coast outpost of nonviolence and noncoercion. They settled on Williams family land west of Spokane, and with the rise of the counterculture more and more people came. Tolstoy survives today as a community of self-sufficient residents and an ongoing commitment to living without rules.[23]

One notable part of the communal explosion of the 1960s was the rise of communes based in Asian religions that appealed to non-Asian converts. One of the first of them was the Himalayan Academy, established in 1962 in Virginia City, Nevada, by Master Subramuniya, who had studied in Ceylon (now Sri Lanka) in the 1940s. As the counterculture heated up in the mid 1960s his following grew, and in 1967 he moved to the Hawai'ian island of Kauai, where the group exists communally today.[24]

Another decidedly different kind of spiritual community was founded a year after the Himalayan Academy. In the early 1960s Timothy Leary, Richard Alpert, and a growing band of associates conducted pioneering experimentation with

---

[22] Ann Louise Coble, *Cotton Patch for the Kingdom: Clarence Jordan's Demonstration Plot at Koinonia Farm* (Scottdale, 2002); Tracy Elaine K'Meyer, *Interracialism and Christian Community in the Postwar South: The Story of Koinonia Farm* (Charlottesville, 1997).

[23] Timothy Miller, *The 60s Communes: Hippies and Beyond* (Syracuse, 1999), pp. 23–26.

[24] Richard Fairfield, *Communes USA: A Personal Tour* (Penguin, 1972), pp. 160–162.

psychedelic substances, and in 1963 they were offered the use of an extensive estate in Millbrook, New York. There they explored the inner world and the religions of the world until police pressure forced them out.[25]

1966 saw a flowering of countercultural communes. One of the best-known was Morning Star Ranch, a 31-acre former apple farm in Sonoma County, California. Lou Gottlieb, a popular folk musician, bought the place and soon declared it open land, going so far as to deed it to God. In its early period its residents were serious religious seekers who styled their premises the Morning Star Ashram; they read and discussed spiritual teachings, ranging from those of Aurobindo to Ouspensky to Lama Govinda. When word got out that the land was open to all, however, it was engulfed with young hippies and a few less desirable persons, mainly alcoholics and motorcycle gangsters. The neighbors became irate at what they saw as a hopelessly dissolute cesspool. Finally, county bulldozers razed the simple housing, and by 1973 Morning Star was finally finished. Some went to nearby Wheeler's Ranch, where Bill Wheeler had opened his much larger tract of land and organized the Ahimsa Church, but in due course the county shut that commune down as well.[26]

As the counterculture wound down after the Summer of Love in 1967, some hippies turned to religion. The largest numbers of newly religious hippies constituted the Jesus Movement, essentially conservative Protestantism with the outward trappings of hip (long hair, flamboyant clothing, and, often, ongoing use of marihuana and the psychedelics).[27] The largest network of Jesus Movement communes was the Shiloh Youth Revival Centers, which had its origins in a communal house in California in 1968, but soon moved its headquarters to Eugene, Oregon. Within a few years Shiloh had expanded to some 175 communal centers, and had a wide range of industries and services. Its inexperienced management

---

[25] Ram Dass and Ralph Metzner, *Birth of a Psychedelic Culture: Conversations About Leary, the Harvard Experiments, Millbrook and the Sixties* (Santa Fe, 2011), pp. 59, 106–205.

[26] Ramón Sender Barayon (ed.), "Home Free Home: The Story of Two Open-Door Sixties Communes, Morning Star and Wheeler's Ranch, as Told by Various Residents" (manuscript in the library at the University of California, Riverside; available online at http://www.diggers.org/home_free.htm, acccessed August 30, 2012.

[27] David Di Sabatino, "The Jesus People Movement: Counterculture Revival and Evangelical Renewal", MTS thesis (McMaster Divinity College, 1994).

ultimately failed to handle such a large operation, and Shiloh closed in the 1980s.[28] But many of the thousands of Jesus communes survived, some continuing in essentially the same form today. Jesus People USA, for example, purchased a hotel in Chicago and turned it into a communal residence that continues to house hundreds of members.[29]

Other new Christian communities were decidedly not of the hippie sort. The Community of Jesus, founded in 1970 in Orleans, Massachusetts, resembled a Catholic monastery, save for the fact that many of its members were married couples, sometimes with children – and were mostly Protestants. By the early 2000s it had grown to over 200 residents, including 50 children.[30] In the early 1970s several American L'Arche communities were founded, based on a French original, dedicated to serving the developmentally disabled and grounded in Roman Catholicism.[31]

Judaism has had its own communal expression from time to time. In the 1880s many of the swarms of East European Jewish immigrants were settled, with assistance from fellow Jews already resident, in cooperative farm settlements across the country.[32] More recently, during the communal heyday of the 1960s era, young Jewish idealists banded together in the Havurah movement, which had several communal encampments, most notably Havurat Shalom in Cambridge, Massachusetts, founded in 1968.[33]

In 1965 America's immigration laws were loosened, and greatly increased numbers of Asians, including many spiritual teachers, streamed into the country. One of the most colorful, and most controversial, was the International Society for Krishna Consciousness (ISKCON), whose members mainly lived in communal

---

[28] Joe V. Peterson, "The Rise and Fall of Shiloh", *Communities*, 92 (Fall, 1996): pp. 60–65.

[29] David Janzen, *Fire, Salt, and Peace: Intentional Christian Communities Alive in North America* (Evanston, 1996).

[30] Dave Jackson, "The Community of Jesus", *Coming Together* (Minneapolis, 1978), pp. 176–177.

[31] Michael William Hryniuk, "Growth in Communion: Spiritual Transformation in the Context of L'Arche", PhD dissertation (Emory University, 2001).

[32] Uri Herscher, *Jewish Agricultural Utopias in America, 1880–1910* (Detroit, 1981).

[33] Stephen C. Lerner, "The *Havurot*", in Jacob Neusner (ed.), *Contemporary Judaic Fellowship in Theory and Practice* (New York, 1972), pp. 121–138.

temples. Gradually, some of them moved to farm communes. Several ISKCON communal centers are still thriving.[34]

Other Asian-based religious intentional communities proliferated as well. The Ananda World Brotherhood Village, located in California, was founded in 1969 by J. Donald Walters (Swami Kriyananda), a one-time disciple of Paramahansa Yogananda, an Indian spiritual teacher who had come to the United States in 1920, and it has flourished since.[35] Several Buddhist organizations have established communal centers; for example, the Nyingma Institute of Tarthang Tulku, a Tibetan teacher in the United States, operates several communal residences and is building an elaborate rural community called Odiyan in northern California, and Shambhala International, founded by Chögyam Trungpa, similarly operates several communities among its many centers.[36] Yogi Bhajan, a Sikh teacher who spent many years in the United States, opened over a hundred communal ashrams there, some of them with hundreds of members.[37]

Not all religious communities have been related to long-established religious traditions; leaders who have attracted followers to their own distinctive spiritual views have created hundreds of independent communities in America. Perhaps the best known of them from the 1960s era, Stephen Gaskin, began to teach an eclectic spiritual philosophy to a following that reached into the thousands in San Francisco in the late 1960s. Eventually the group hit the road and ended up in Tennessee, where they built a community known simply as The Farm. Within a decade, The Farm had grown to some 2,000 acres in size and perhaps 1,500 members. Gaskin's teachings embraced virtually all of the world's religious and wisdom traditions. The Farm continues, among other things overseeing worldwide charitable and environmental programs.[38]

But Gaskin was hardly the only independent religious visionary to draw followers into community. In the early 1960s an independent preacher named

---

[34] E. Burke Rochford, Jr, *Hare Krishna in America* (New Brunswick, 1985).

[35] Susan Love Brown, "Community as Cultural Critique", in Susan Love Brown (ed.), *Intentional Community: An Anthropological Perspective* (Albany, 2002), Chapter 8.

[36] Rick Fields, *How the Swans Came to the Lake: A Narrative History of Buddhism in America* (Boston, 1981), pp. 304–308.

[37] Constance Waeber Elsberg, *Graceful Women: Gender and Identity in an American Sikh Community* (Knoxville, 2003).

[38] Rupert Fike (ed.), *Voices from the Farm* (Summertown, 1998); [Stephen Gaskin], *Hey Beatnik! This Is the Farm Book* (Summertown, 1974).

Daniel Wright began to gather followers who in 1966 moved to a farm near Bedford, Indiana, where they initially lived with little publicity, supporting themselves with a sawmill. But soon the community attracted large numbers of seekers. With the biblical name of Padanaram, it eventually reached a reported population of 200, half adults and half children, and expanded its landholdings to, eventually, over 3,000 acres. Wright was in many ways a traditionalist, supporting fairly conventional gender roles, for example. But until his death in 2001 he and his flock pursued "Kingdomism", a pursuit of the Kingdom of Heaven on earth. Today the remaining members continue to pursue Wright's vision.[39]

A rather different vision was the basis of the San Francisco commune called Kerista. Its members were secular hedonists, living exuberantly and practicing free love. Somewhere along the line they invented their own religion centered on a goddess named Kerista. Religion for the Keristans was as they thought life should be: a good time.[40]

As the 1970s wore on, the rate of creation of new communes declined, but commune building hardly ground to a halt. One distinctive new one that came on the scene in 1976 was Kashi Ashram, in Florida, founded by Ma Jaya Bhagavati (formerly Brooklyn housewife Joyce Green), who began a spiritual quest in response to a visionary experience. Ma's idiosyncratic teachings are all-embracing; on the grounds of the community are shrines representing most of the world's major religions. Among the community's social projects is an AIDS hospice.[41]

Several communities dedicated to the heritage and progress of African Americans emerged in the 1970s and thereafter. Oyotunji African Yoruba Village in Sheldon, South Carolina, for example, was founded by His Royal Highness Oba Oseijeman Adefunmi I, formerly known as Walter Eugene King; it was devoted to recreating and preserving African and Yoruba culture.[42] Tama-Re, begun in 1993 and located in Georgia, was a fantastic complex of mainly Egyptian-themed

---

[39] Rachel Wright Summerton, "Padanaram: The Valley of the Gods", in Bill Metcalf (ed.), *Shared Visions, Shared Lives: Communal Living around the Globe* (Findhorn, 1996), Chapter 2.

[40] Bluejay Way, Eden Zia, and Wise Sun, "Kerista: The Utopian Commune That Invented Polyfidelity", *Communities*, 71–72 (Summer–Fall, 1986): pp. 65–66.

[41] Vasudha Narayanan, "Gurus and Goddesses, Deities and Devotees", in Karen Pechilis (ed.), *The Graceful Guru* (New York, 2004), Chapter 6.

[42] Anthony B. Pinn, *Varieties of African American Religious Experience* (Minneapolis, 1998), Chapter 2.

buildings built by a group who called themselves Nuwaubians. It had as many as 500 residents, but in 2004 its leader, Dwight York, was sentenced to a lengthy prison term following a criminal conviction, and the property was sold.[43]

New Age communities have also proliferated in recent decades. In many cases inspired by the Findhorn Community in Scotland, they have worked for the improvement of the planet and the spiritual growth of their members. One North American network known as the Emissary Communities actually predates Findhorn, having opened its principal community, Sunrise Ranch in Colorado, in 1945, but the Emissaries enjoyed increased visibility and opened new communities as interest in New Age ideas spread.[44] Sirius Community in Massachusetts could be considered a direct descendant of Findhorn, having been founded in 1978 by former Findhorn members.[45]

Communities have continued to be started at a fairly steady pace ever since the great proliferation of the 1960s era, with hundreds, probably, emerging every year. The preceding paragraphs have provided only the lightest of samplings. Communities based in every conceivable religion from traditional Christianity to belief in flying saucers to wicca are alive and well. And beyond the thousands of religious communes in American history are large numbers of secular communities.

Although communal visions are diverse, a few themes recur frequently, and one is newness. In community after community, the members have a sense of building an entirely new culture together. Implicit in that drive, usually, is the conviction that the culture now prevailing in the world is hopeless, that a moral, environmental, or spiritual slippery slope is carrying the human race down to sure destruction. If the existing world is hopeless, then why not try to build a new one?

Sadly, perhaps, most groups think they must start from zero to do that building. Many commune builders are not familiar with the thousands of communal projects that have gone before, and therefore learn little, if anything, from their

---

[43] Julius H. Bailey, "The Final Frontier: Secrecy, Identity, and the Media in the Rise and Fall of the United Nuwaubian Nation of Moors", *Journal of the American Academy of Religion*, 74/2 (June, 2006): pp. 302–323.

[44] Michael S. Cummings, "Democratic Procedure and Community in Utopia", *Alternative Futures*, 3 (Fall, 1980): pp. 35–57.

[45] Corinne McLaughlin and Gordon Davidson, *Builders of the Dawn: Community Lifestyles in a Changing World* (Walpole, 1985), pp. 128–134.

predecessors. Besides, most predecessor communes have gone out of existence, so what is to be learned from them except that they "failed"?

That disinclination to learn from the past may have to do with the fact that a great many communes have short lifespans. Many observers note a high "failure" rate for communal ventures. But "failure" seems to mean simply that eventually the commune in question dissolved. As it happens, just about every human institution dissolves, sooner or later. Failure is not properly descriptive of any venture in which participants have had good times, learning experiences, good social relations, and spiritual satisfaction – just the kinds of things that communal life confers on its participants, even if it provides certain bits of dissatisfaction as well.

Many American communitarians seem to subscribe to a sense of American uniqueness, and do not learn from, or even become aware of, their counterparts overseas. How many communes realize that much of their social vision has already been enacted by the Israeli kibbutzim? How many independent spiritual communities are aware of the Grail movement, which has thousands of members and many centers, some communal, in several countries? Even within the New Age communities, many (probably most) have not heard of Damanhur, a pioneering Italian community featured in this volume, which is focused on the arts and arcane science, whose hundreds of members are trying to create a new way of life for a world that, as they see things, badly needs just that.

Insular vision may cause the typical American commune to be short-lived. But many other factors contribute as well, and generalizations about causes of communal longevity and closure are hazardous. One might suspect that a community founded on specific religious principles would have enough of a common center to enjoy a long lifespan, but both religious and secular communes can be found in lists of both long-lived and short-lived communities. Rosabeth Moss Kanter, in a well-known study, found that commitment mechanisms were essential to longevity. (Commitment mechanisms she noted included, for example, sacrifice, or giving something up as the price of membership; investment, or providing the member with some kind of stake in the community's outcome; and communion, or a strong sense of comradeship. A common religious commitment could be considered another such mechanism.)[46] Hugh Gardner, however, applying Kanter's theory to a group of more recent communes, found her analysis imprecise, at least.[47] A statistical analysis would undoubtedly reveal that the average commune has a fairly short life. But each communal story is different. Hundreds, at least, of American communities created over the last 200 years are still very much alive.

Intentional communities are founded and populated by people with different visions and principles. Why some achieve social cohesion and some do not is not determined by some sociological formula. Financial problems, for example, can sometimes lead to dissolution, while sometimes they strengthen the community by providing a sense of an external threat that can only be overcome by commitment to the common cause. Perhaps the safest generalization is that of Judson Jerome: "If you figure out who is going to carry out the garbage, everything else will seem simple."[48]

What can surely be said is that some Americans are not satisfied with prevailing social patterns and conditions, and yearn for a new and different way of life. More importantly, perhaps, a great many find a sense of community lacking in their lives and in the culture around them. People live their lives in private homes, private cars, between earphones, in front of televisions and computers – and all too little in the midst of supportive groups of people. As long as people see that other ways of life are possible, and as long as religious visions are there to drive them, communities will continue to dot the American – and world – landscape.

Note

I gratefully acknowledge support from the General Research Fund at the University of Kansas for the writing of this article.

---

[46] Rosabeth Moss Kanter, *Commitment and Community: Communes and Utopias in Sociological Perspective* (Cambridge, 1972).

Chapter 12

The Intersection of White-Racist Communes and the American Legal System

H.C. Lazebnik

Intentional Aryan communities and their members are actors in what may be termed a "white-racist milieu".[1] This chapter focuses on theoretical and actual implications of violence, freedom of speech, and freedom of religion with regard to American intentional white-racist, or "Aryan", communities and the law. The white-racist milieu includes, but is not limited to, white-racist nationalists, skinheads, Ku Klux Klan(s) members, national socialists, Aryan militants, neo-Nazis, neo-Pagans and Christians who are affiliated with various racist or hate groups and/or new religions. While white racism is the fundamental concept loosely connecting each group to the others, religion provides an additional means for holding together the white-racist milieu. Intentional Aryan communities have proven fertile ground for both violent speech and actual eruptions of violence.

The beliefs of the majority of biblically based white-racist groups are more or less entrenched in British Israelism, a religious movement that originated in nineteenth-century England and claimed that the British were the descendents of the "ten lost tribes" of Israel. Christian Identity, which developed in the 1930s and "represents one of the most powerful doctrinal statements of the Nazi cult in

---

[1] For Colin Campbell's characterization of the "cultic milieu", see Colin Campbell, "The Cult, the Cultic Milieu and Secularization", in Jeffery Kaplan and Heléne Lööw (eds), *The Cultic Milieu: Oppositional Subcultures in an Age of Globalization* (Lanham, 2002), p. 14.

contemporary society"[2] has, while still espousing the biblical concerns of British Israelism, significantly altered its doctrines. This highly fragmented group holds that the Jews are the offspring of Eve and Satan, and has contributed to various Aryan communes – including the Covenant, Sword, Arm of the Lord, and Aryan Nations.

The Covenant, Sword, and Arm of the Lord (CSA), also called Zarephath-Horeb, founded in 1976 by James Ellison, was an intentional community located in northern Arkansas. An evangelical preacher, Ellison converted to Christian Identity and was christened "King James of the Ozarks" by Pastor Robert Millar, a prominent Christian Identity cleric. Believing that Aryan Israel, a divine race, was predestined to inherit the Earth, Ellison cast Aryans as warriors caught up in a struggle against "lower" races that would culminate in an impending Apocalypse.[3] In order to protect themselves during the coming Apocalypse, members of the rural CSA commune militarized their settlement and offered paramilitary training to its members and other individuals of the radical right. A shooting range named Silhouette City, modeled after the FBI shooting range in Quantico, Virginia, included mockups of federal agents and Jews; in one mockup a state trooper wore, instead of a badge, a Star of David.[4] Members built factories dedicated to the manufacturing of grenades and firearm accessories and began to stockpile weapons, ammunition, explosives, and food to prepare themselves for the approaching apocalypse Ellison had foreseen in a vision.[5] While the community itself did not engage in physically violent acts, some CSA members committed crimes, at times violent, when away from the commune. CSA crumbled in 1985, shortly after it was raided by the FBI for firearms violations.[6]

Ellison's embracing of the teachings of Christian Identity meant the mutual enveloping of CSA in the theological and ideological arms of Christian Identity. In conjunction with Richard Butler, the head of Aryan Nations and pastor of the

---

[2] Nicholas Goodrick-Clarke, *Black Sun: Aryan Cults, Esoteric Nazism and the Politics of Identity* (New York, 2002), p. 234.

[3] Mattias Gardell, *Gods of the Blood: The Pagan Revival and White Separatism* (Durham, 2003), pp. 127–128.

[4] Jessica Eve Stern, "The Covenant, the Sword, and the Arm of the Lord", in Jonathan Tucker (ed.), *Toxic Terror* (Cambridge, 2000), p. 2.

[5] Stern, "The Covenant", pp. 2–3.

[6] Stern, "The Covenant", p. 1.

Church of Jesus Christ Christian, a Christian Identity Church based in Hayden Lake, Idaho, Robert Miles, a prominent member of the Michigan Knights of the Ku Klux Klan, and Louis Beam, a head ambassador of Aryan Nations, among others, Ellison developed a terrorist conspiracy to overthrow the existing US government, known as the Zionist Occupation Government (ZOG), and create an exclusively Aryan nation within the US.[7] The Order, a white-racist terrorist group created by Robert Mathews in the 1980s[8] and named after a terrorist cell in *The Turner Diaries*,[9] whose membership transcended group affiliations and included individuals from various walks of the white-racist milieu, included at least five members from CSA and others from the aforementioned groups. The main objective of The Order was "to hasten the racial crisis in America and cast society into a chaos out of which a new Aryan golden age would be reborn".[10] Members of The Order committed acts of murder, robbery, and bombing, and Mathews was killed by federal agents on 8 December 1984, a day referred to in Aryan revolutionary circles as the Day of Martyrs.[11] Many white-racist, including separatist, groups are modeled extensively after The Order.

The Aryan Nations, also known as the Church of Jesus Christ Christian, is a national socialist group founded by the late Richard Butler that was initially based in a heavily guarded compound in Kootenai County, Idaho. The organization, now based in Lexington, South Carolina, is dedicated to the creation of an Aryan homeland in North America. Although nominally a Christian organization, the Aryan Nations has non-Christian elements in its theology as well and may be properly understood as a type of racist neo-Paganism. Aryan Nations grew prominently during the mid 1970s when the influence of the Ku Klux Klan was declining.[12] The creation of an Aryan commune and its aspirations for an Aryan homeland in the Pacific Northwest is connected to the belief, common among white racists, that whites have "become an endangered minority in their traditional

---

[7] Stern, "The Covenant", p. 4.
[8] Intelligence Report, *The New Romantics*, Southern Poverty Law Center, 2001. Available online at http://www.splcenter.org/intel/intelreport/article.jsp?pid=436, accessed March 28, 2010.
[9] Stern, "The Covenant", p. 4.
[10] Gardell, *Gods*, p. 197.
[11] Gardell, *Gods*, p. 195.
[12] Nicholas Goodrick-Clarke, *The Occult Roots of Nazism: Secret Aryan Cults and Their Influence on Nazi Ideology* (London, 2004), p. 233.

ethnic homelands".[13] In an environment featuring "whites only" signs and Third Reich memorabilia, children are raised in a communal atmosphere that is not plagued by multiracialism and they rarely, if ever, see non-Aryan individuals; they are kept unaware of such things as the affirmative action programs found in mainstream society.[14]

Typical of white-racist religious movements, Aryan Nations emphasizes the need to protect and possess white women because racial mixing is "the greatest threat to the survival of the Aryan race"[15] and "the beauty of the white Aryan woman must not perish from the earth".[16] An Aryan Nations pamphlet titled "Endangered Species"[17] includes an image of a young, slender, bikini-clad blonde white woman with the adjacent statement, "Look long and hard, White man. Images like hers may soon cease to exist forever." While the *88 Precepts*, written by David Lane, an Aryan Nations member and incarcerated terrorist,[18] calls homosexuality "a crime against Nature", its more important contention is that the purpose of sex is for procreation and increasing the Aryan race. Males should be willing to "fight to death to keep and mate with their females" in order to assure the survival of the race. "The overpowering male sex drive must be channeled toward possession of females, as well as elements such as territory and power, which are necessary to keep them."[19] Consistent with this ideology, gender roles at the compound are very traditional. Men are required to provide for the women and respect them, while women are responsible for cooking, cleaning, and bearing children. One of the main problems Aryans are plagued with is the devaluation of these traditional roles. In mainstream society women are encouraged to make

---

[13] Goodrick-Clarke, *Occult Roots*, p. 232.

[14] Goodrick-Clarke, *Occult Roots*, p. 233.

[15] David Lane, *88 Precepts* (St. Maries, Idaho, 1990).

[16] David Lane, "Because the Beauty of Our White Women Must Not Perish from the Earth." Available online at http://www.whitenewsnow.com/white-culture-white-literature/2578-because-beauty-our-white-women-must-not-perish-earth.html, accessed November 27, 2012.

[17] "Endangered Species," Aryan Nations pamphlet, 25 January 2008.

[18] Intelligence Report, *The New Barbarians*, Southern Poverty Law Center, 1998. Available online at http://www.splcenter.org/intel/intelreport/article.jsp?aid=451, accessed November 27, 2012.

[19] Lane, *88 Precepts*.

money and have careers at the expense of child-bearing,[20] contributing to the decline of the Aryan race.

Adolf Hitler is referred to as the "Aryan Prophet",[21] and the organization advocates an "Aryan War", stating that the future depends on a "worldwide Kristallnacht".[22] Consistent with its view that the Aryan race is and has been marginalized for thousands of years,[23] Aryan Nations urges its members to take up arms, stating that "an unarmed or non-militant People will be enslaved".[24] Members of the Aryan Nations subscribe to the notion of the ZOG conspiracy and must agree to the "principles and position of violent, pan-Aryan revolution against the [J]ew".[25]

The Aryan Nations website[26] includes references to "the Gods of our people" and a Celtic blood oath; it frequently states that its deceased members are waiting for other members in Valhalla, which is the Norse mythological term for the "Hall of the Slain" ruled by Odin and located in Asgard, the Old Norse realm of the Æsir deities.[27] This embracing of Norse mythology illustrates the shift now apparently under way from biblically based white-racist beliefs to racist Neo-Paganism, which tend to view Christianity with contempt as a Jewish-based, Middle Eastern import that has played a primary role in the demise of white power and Western civilization.[28]

Odinism, a prominent form of white-racist Neo-Paganism, is a twentieth-century racist reconstruction of pre-Christian Norse paganism(s) from Europe, including Iceland, Scandanavia, and Greenland, that were traditionally called Asatrú. The Nordic/Teutonic mythologies of Odinism were foundational beliefs for Nazi Germany and played an integral role in the worldview of the Schutzstaffel (SS), which oversaw the network of Hitler's death camps, in addition to influencing the American Nazi Party. Militant racist Odinism is fragmented into various

[20] Goodrick-Clarke, *Occult Roots*, p. 232.
[21] *Aryan Nations*.
[22] "About Aryan Nations," *Aryan Nations*, 25 January 2008.
[23] *Aryan Nations*.
[24] Lane, *88 Precepts*.
[25] *About Aryan Nations*.
[26] *Aryan Nations*.
[27] Magnus Magnusson and Mark Harrison, *The Vikings: Voyagers of Discovery and Plunder* (Oxford, 2008), p. 121.
[28] Gardell, *Gods*, p. 153.

groups, although the foremost articulation of racist Odinism is Wotansvolk, a combination of esoteric Aryan nationalism and Jungian psychology that aims to redevelop Aryans' forgotten "folk consciousness". Militant racist Odinisms advocate racial cleansing, believing that the manifest destiny of Aryans is to become victorious over the "lower" races, eradicating them from the face of the earth.

David Lane and Louis Beam, influential individuals in the racist Right, were prominent Odinists. They championed the use of single individuals and cells to engage in terrorist activity, which, it is believed, will usher in Ragnarök, a final war that will culminate in the restoration of Aryans to power and produce a new golden age. Individuals killed or imprisoned in attempts to further the realization of Aryan domination, such as Robert Mathews, are idolized as martyrs. This martyrology is particularly unsettling for the government.

The concept of a leaderless movement has influenced several of the racist organizations. For example, in order to protect the Aryan Nations against infiltration by those wishing to destroy the organization or by the government (and "the [J]ew by proxy"), the organization "eschew[s] now and forever the model of top-down membership-based organization in favor of a permanent policy of decentralization and leaderless resistance under the radical banner of pan-Aryanism."[29] "The most recent example" of leaderless resistance, also referred to as the "lone wolf" model, according to Aryan Nations, "is the sharpshooter who wasted that Jew abortionist in New York".[30]

The practical value of a leaderless, organization-free movement became apparent in the case of the Aryan Nations, which was forced to pay a $6.3 million verdict in September 2000 for the assault and battery of two individuals[31] and was subsequently bankrupt (for a time).[32] The movement has regrouped, however, as the Aryan Nations Church of Yahweh, which has since introduced plans to create another communal settlement in John Day, Oregon, and was met with protesters

---

[29] *About Aryan Nations*.

[30] *Aryan Nations*.

[31] *Keenan v Aryan Nations*, CV-99-441, Dist. Ct. of the First Jud. Dist., Idaho (2000).

[32] Michael F. Leavitt, "CASENOTE: Keenan v Aryan Nations: making hate groups liable for the torts of their members", *Idaho Law Review*, 37 (2001): p. 604; *Keenan v Aryan Nations*.

there in March 2010.³³ Paul R. Mullet, Aryan Nations' current leader, intends to purchase two uninhabited buildings in the town in which to base the compound. Continuing the Aryan Nations' former legacy of providing members with paramilitary training, Mullet plans to use the forested lands in the area as survival training grounds, and to host a national convention in 2011. Mullet has threatened to sue the city should it not allow Aryan Nations to purchase the buildings for use as a communal settlement.

Another Neo-Pagan-influenced organization, meanwhile, has also attracted a small but dedicated following. Ukrainian-born Bernard Klassen, who held the title of Pontifex Maximus and was a Republican Florida State Legislator in 1966, founded the World Church of the Creator (COTC) or Creativity in 1973.³⁴ An offshoot of Christian Identity,³⁵ in the US the Creativity Movement is located in Illinois, Montana, Ohio, Connecticut, Colorado, and Wyoming. The movement also has followers in Croatia, Germany, Iceland, Slovakia, Portugal, Spain, England, Venezuela, and Australia.

The goal and purpose of Creativity is the purification of the white race, violent eradication of non-white "mud races", and the elimination of "all Jews from the earth because of their conspiracy to control the world economy."³⁶ Members, or Creators, are encouraged to engage in the violent annihilation of "mud races" in order to bring about a "whiter and brighter future",³⁷ and this will eventually culminate with a "Racial Holy War" (RAHOWA), a "total war against the Jews and the rest of the goddamned mud races of the world – politically, militantly, financially, morally and religiously".³⁸ Additionally, special forces called

---

[33] Joel Millman, "Oregonians Protest White Supremacist Compound", *Wall Street Journal*, 1 March 2010.

[34] Gardell, *Gods*, p. 129.

[35] Mark S. Hamm, *American Skinheads: The Criminology and Control of Hate Crime* (Westport 1993), p. 203.

[36] *Mansfield v Church of the Creator*, NO. 94-345-CA, Cir. Ct. Escambia County, FL (1994).

[37] *Creativity – Creed and Program*, The Creativity Movement, 1 October 2006. Available online at http://www.pacreator.com/US/index.php?option=com_content&view=article&id=60&Itemid=70, accessed November 27, 2012.

[38] *RAHOWA! Its Full Ramifications*, The Creativity Movement, 1 October 2006. Available online at http://www.creativitymovement.org/creator_library/english/rahowa-0.html, accessed November 27, 2012.

"White Rangers" and "White Berets" are given paramilitary training in an effort to advance the RAHOWA.[39]

The Church states the concept of RAHOWA is the "heart of [the] religious creed" and is "the most sacred credo of all".[40] RAHOWA is "a holy war to the finish". The Church states,

> no longer can the mud races and the White Race live on the same planet and survive. It is now either them or us. We want to make damn sure it is we who survive. This Planet is from now on all ours, and will be the one and only habitat for our future progeny for all time to come.[41]

The ultimate concern, then, is the creation of "a planet Earth devoid of mud races".[42]

The warrior archetypes and romantic, mythologized images of Aryan men and their beautiful, white women found in many white-racist religious movements may be understood as adoptions from Odinist traditions. These ideas contribute immensely to beliefs found in the white-racist milieu and tie together mythical historic narratives justifying violence. These beliefs and images help to solidify intentional Aryan communities and both justify and propagate violent behavior and hate speech.

The warrior archetype so common in white-racist religious and secular material provides white racists with a sense of collective purpose and has been realized in eruptions of violence.[43] As of 2008, the Southern Poverty Law Center (SPLC) determined that 926 hate groups were active in the US,[44] and members of white-racist groups have been involved in violent crimes against African Americans,

---

[39] *Mansfield v Church of the Creator.*

[40] *RAHOWA.US*, RAHOWA.US, 14 November 2009. Available online at http://www.rahowa.us/index2.html, accessed November 14, 2009; *RAHOWA! Its Full Ramifications.*

[41] *RAHOWA! Its Full Ramifications*; *RAHOWA.US.*

[42] *A Planet Devoid of Mud Races*, The Creativity Movement, 1 October 2006. Available online at http://www.creativitymovement.org/creator_library/english/rahowa-12.html, accessed November 27, 2012.

[43] Gardell, *Gods*, p. 11.

[44] *Hate Groups Map*, Southern Poverty Law Center, 2009. Available online at http://www.splcenter.org/intel/map/hate.jsp, accessed August 30, 2012.

Jewish Americans, Latinos, Asian Americans, and homosexuals;[45] some of these crimes were committed by members of Aryan communal groups. The religious tenets of white-racist groups often support violence and terrorism as acceptable means of combating both the perceived discrimination against and oppression of the white race[46] and terrorism and violence against and murder of "lower races". The aforementioned Louis Beam, a former Texas Klansman, Christian Identity member, and ally of Aryan Nations, has developed a system by which individuals are able to obtain points to become "Aryan warriors" by virtue of assassinating federal officials, civil rights leaders, Jews, blacks, gays, and others. In such a system, murder is not only justified but also functions as a symbol of honor.[47] Acts against the government are condoned especially in light of the concept of ZOG, which is a main feature of the white-racist milieu that is prevalent in the belief systems of white-racist religious groups.

The recent decentralization of the white-racist milieu and its religious groups has led to the development of the previously mentioned "lone wolf",[48] "leaderless resistance", and "phantom cell" models in which individuals act alone or with a small cell to commit acts of violence or terrorism against individuals or the government[49] in order to recreate the "golden age" of white world domination or end the pollution of the country or world by non-whites. Leaderless resistance, according to Beam, means "all individuals and groups operate independently of each other, and never report to a central headquarters or a single leader for direction or instruction".[50] These tactics are useful because, as white-racist religious groups observe, "the last thing federal snoops want ... is a thousand different small phantom cells opposing them ... such a situation is an intelligence nightmare".[51] WOTAN (Will of the Aryan Nation) is the paramilitary arm of Wotansvolk that is intended to operate in small, phantom cells and utilize various tactics including,

---

[45] Josh Adams and Vincent J. Roscigno, "White Supremacists, Oppositional Culture and the World Wide Web", *Social Forces*, 84/2 (2005): p. 759.

[46] Tanya Telfair Sharpe, "The Identity Christian Movement: Ideology of Domestic Terrorism", *Journal of Black Studies*, 30/4 (2000): p. 616.

[47] Sharpe, "The Identity Christian Movement", p. 617.

[48] Adams and Roscigno, "White Supremacists", p. 759.

[49] Sharpe, "The Identity Christian Movement", p. 617.

[50] Gardell, *Gods*, p. 200.

[51] Ibid.

but not limited to, terrorism, guns, bombs, fire, and destruction to bring about a revolution.[52] Providing members with paramilitary training as well, the Creativity Movement encourages its "White Rangers" and "White Berets" special forces "to use any means necessary, including violence and criminal acts, to bring about an end to the 'mud races' and the perceived 'Jewish conspiracy'".[53]

Enforcement of civil rights and the prosecution of perpetrators of racially motivated hate crimes may generally only be realized through civil lawsuits.[54] Two civil cases against communal white-racist groups have been brought to the courts: Aryan Nations, as mentioned above, was forced to pay a $6.3 million verdict in September 2000 for the assault and battery of two individuals[55] and was subsequently bankrupt (for a time),[56] and, in 1994, the Creativity Movement was fined $1 million for the murder of an African American Navy Shipman.[57] In both cases, the plaintiffs were represented by the Southern Poverty Law Center (SPLC), which, instead of suing the individual perpetrators of hate crimes, represented the plaintiffs in bringing suits against the organizations with which the perpetrators of the hate crimes were affiliated.[58] Legal scholar Michael Leavitt notes that "these lawsuits often result in effectively bankrupting these larger organizations ... leaving them without property or resources to continue promulgating their racially-motivated beliefs".[59] The effect of the SPLC's method has resulted in severely compromising the financial stability of the larger groups, including the Aryan Nations and COTC. Theoretically, this method has the potential to shut down the white-racist religious groups whose members engage in criminal activity; a tort can be brought against them without violating their constitutional guarantee of free exercise of religion. *Theoretically*, because the nature of the white-racist milieu is such that when a group dies, other groups will absorb those beliefs of the defunct organization and those beliefs will continue to circulate; also, the demise

---

[52] Ibid.
[53] *Mansfield v The Church of the Creator.*
[54] Joanne Doroshow and Amy Widman, "The Racial Implications of Tort Reform", *Washington University Journal of Law and Policy*, 25 (2007).
[55] *Keenan v Aryan Nations.*
[56] Leavitt, "CASENOTE", p. 604.
[57] *Mansfield v Church of the Creator.*
[58] Leavitt, "CASENOTE", p. 604.
[59] Ibid.

of a group might mean the creation of a new set of "lone wolves". Additionally, there is the danger that the group's members might be held as symbolic martyrs, evidence of the government's ongoing crusade to destroy, marginalize, or oppress the white race.

In *Keenan v Aryan Nations*,[60] SPLC and the plaintiffs, Jason and Victoria Keenan, sued three individuals in the Aryan Nations defense force for physical assault. Richard Butler, the head of Aryan Nations, and Michael Teague, property owner and former chief of staff for Aryan Nations, were sued for engaging in negligent and reckless hiring, retaining, and supervising of individuals on the defense force who committed the assaults. Finally, they sued Richard Butler, the Aryan Nations, and Sapphire, Inc., owners of the Aryan Nations property, for vicarious liability.[61] Similarly, the Church of the Creator was sued for damages related to the murder of Harold Mansfield, an African American Navy Shipman killed by a COTC member. The Church was held liable for the murder of Mansfield by the Reverend George Loeb who "carried out [the murder] to further the Church's goal of 'purifying' the white race by any means necessary", and was sentenced to life in prison in July 1992.[62] Following the murder, COTC congratulated Loeb for the murder and awarded him a medal of honor, and Steve Thomas, another Church minister, helped Loeb flee the area and was convicted in February 1992 of being an accessory after the fact. The Church was additionally held liable for crimes perpetrated by its members; all were honored by the Church for committing crimes carried out to further the mission of abolishing "mud races" and Jews. The crimes included Ohio bank robberies and the bombing of an NAACP (National Association for the Advancement of Colored People) branch headquarters. As a result of the Church's criminal activity and the criminal activity of its members with respect to their acting in accordance with the Church's mission, it was fined $1 million.

In both *Mansfield v The Church of the Creator* and *Keenan v Aryan Nations*, the defendants were required to pay large sums of money and the causes of action were based largely on crimes committed by members of the groups and, particularly with regard *Keenan v Aryan Nations*, the beliefs they subscribed

---

[60] *Keenan v Aryan Nations*.
[61] Leavitt, "CASENOTE", p. 610.
[62] *Mansfield v The Church of the Creator*.

to and the communication of those beliefs. "In bringing such a cause of action against them," Leavitt states, "the judicial system is effectively telling them, 'you can't preach what you preach.'"[63] The First Amendment to the US Constitution guarantees freedom of speech, within limits. One of the limits on freedom of speech targets speech that "is directed to inciting or producing imminent lawless action and is likely to incite or produce such action".[64] While it might be argued that groups like the Creativity Movement and Aryan Nations were simply exercising their right of free exercise of religion and free speech, the litigation was not directed to the speech of the groups in general "but toward the words that resulted in members perpetrating violence against other people".[65] The large damages awarded to the plaintiffs reached beyond compensating them for those damages and punishing the perpetrators: they were aimed at eradicating the groups from society by financially crippling them,[66] a notion that Leavitt admits "might make legal theorists squirm".[67]

The heightened sense of danger in the country following the 11 September 2001 terrorist acts and the government's efforts to suppress possible domestic terrorism has had an impact on white-racist groups. Following 9/11, terrorism was redefined to include acts that are "dangerous to human life that are a violation of the criminal laws of the [US] ... [and] appear to be intended to intimidate or coerce a civilian populations".[68] Although the Patriot Act was written in such a way as to target only "terrorists", the new definition expanded greatly the groups of individuals that might be suspects[69] and allowed the federal government to monitor religious groups.[70] White-racist religious groups that advocate the violent overthrow of the government or seek to harm non-white individuals can now be

---

[63] Leavitt, "CASENOTE", pp. 631–632.
[64] Ibid., p. 632.
[65] Ibid., p. 633.
[66] Ibid., p. 634.
[67] Ibid., p. 637.
[68] Steven H. Aden and John W. Whitehead, "Forfeiting 'Enduring Freedom' for 'Homeland Security': A Constitutional Analysis of the USA Patriot Act and the Justice Department's Anti-terrorism Initiative", *American University Law Review*, 51/6 (2002): pp. 1092–1093.
[69] Aden and Whitehead, "Forfeiting 'Enduring Freedom'", p. 1092.
[70] Ibid., p. 1091.

regarded as terrorists, and charges of seditious conspiracy may be brought against them.[71]

As a result of these new American anti-terrorism laws, the speech of some intentional Aryan communities whose belief systems support violence and terrorism may endanger their freedom of religion.[72] The discussion of violent tactics to harm non-white individuals or disrupt or overthrow the government by committing acts of domestic terrorism could be labeled dangerous, and some groups not only advocate committing such acts but provide members with special training to do so. Should such speech be proscribed, the government could, in effect, outlaw some groups.

Some argue that instead of focusing on regulation of hate speech, governmental attention should be given to regulation of the underlying thought and behavior that generates hateful acts.[73] In this framework, legal scholar Edward Eberle states, "bias-motivated thought that transforms to harmful overt conduct ... can be proscribed as hate crimes".[74] In adhering to the doctrine of content neutrality, the court separates itself from judging the quality of the material and "delimits official power over estimation of ideas",[75] thus allowing speech by white-racist religious groups that advocates, for example, racial purification or the overthrow of what they see as the ZOG.[76] This speech may be proscribable, however, if it fits within the government's category of unprotected speech that is "imbued or

---

[71] John Alan Cohan, "ARTICLE: Seditious Conspiracy, the Smith Act, and Prosecution for Religious Speech Advocating the Violent Overthrow of the Government", *St. John's Journal of Legal Commentary*, 17 (2003): p. 205.

[72] Cohan, "ARTICLE", p. 205; Edward J. Eberle, "ARTICLE: Cross-burning, Hate Speech, and Free Speech in America", *Arizona State Law Journal*, 36 (2004): p. 953; Elisa Kantor, "Note: New Threats, Old Problems: Adhering to Brandenberg's Imminence Requirement in Terrorism Prosecutions", *George Washington Law Review*, 76 (2008): pp. 762–763; Joseph Grinstein, "Jihad and the Constitution: The First Amendment Implications of Combating Religiously Motivated Terrorism", *The Yale Law Journal*, 105/5 (1996): p. 1354; Leavitt (2001).

[73] Eberle, "ARTICLE", pp. 956–957.

[74] Ibid., p. 957.

[75] Ibid., p. 963.

[76] Erin J. Cox, "COMMENT: Freeing Exercise at Expression's Expense: When RFRA Privileges the Religiously Motivated Speaker", *UCLA Law Review*, 56 (2008): p. 196.

closely linked with harm".[77] Speech that incites violence, then, is not protected under the First Amendment.[78]

Generally limited to speech or conduct,[79] seditious conspiracy does not require an overt act in order to be prosecuted; it is completed when two or more persons agree to commit an unlawful act.[80] In the words of the legal scholar Tracy Higgins, "seditious conspiracy deals with a crime of the mind … You don't have to do anything; you just have to think it."[81] The statute does not mention the types of content that qualify as seditious speech,[82] thus allowing for the criminalization of religious speech determined to be seditious.[83] The absence of an overt act requirement presents the courts with the difficulty of distinguishing between religious speech and beliefs that employ metaphors as opposed to advocating concrete action, as well as the danger of criminalizing a particular religion or religious speech.[84] Additionally, the courts have often used "clear and present danger" or "imminence" tests in seditious conspiracy cases. While some forms of sedition might be interpreted as "abstract doctrine" and thus not satisfy the "clear and present danger" test, "'language of incitement' is not constitutionally protected when the group is of sufficient size and cohesiveness [and] is sufficiently oriented towards action … [as] to justify apprehension that action will occur".[85] The Creativity Movement's White Berets or the Wotansvolk WOTAN might satisfy the imminence test as well. Furthermore, the Aryan Nations' embracing of phantom cells and "lone wolves", coupled with the requirement that all members agree to the principles of a violent pan-Aryan revolution against Jews and by proxy the Zionist Occupied Government, might count as seditious conspiracy.

As previously mentioned, for the purpose of this chapter religion is understood to be collective as opposed to individual; it is not an abstract entity but a matrix of belief systems that hold together groups' ideas of white racism with their

---

[77] Eberle, "ARTICLE", p. 963.
[78] Kantor, "Note", p. 757.
[79] Cohan, "ARTICLE", p. 206.
[80] Ibid., p. 210.
[81] Ibid., p. 206.
[82] Ibid., pp. 208–209.
[83] Grinstein, "Jihad and the Constitution", p. 1347.
[84] Cohan, "ARTICLE", p. 213.
[85] Ibid., pp. 217–218.

conceptualizations of the divine. An important component of white-racist religions is the process of attracting adherents, which is carried out through promulgation of religious ideas largely through the internet and other forms of speech. The government has, in the past, rarely monitored or controlled the content of religious speech, although Joseph Grinstein, a legal scholar, notes that this is because there has until recently not been a compelling enough reason to do so. The post-9/11 wartime climate and concern with domestic terrorism, however, has provided the government with that reason.[86]

Religious speech, according to the *United States v Rahman* decision that involved the preaching of a Muslim cleric, must be classified as conduct as opposed to belief in order to be proscribed.[87] The nature of religious sermons,[88] that is, discourses delivered by religious leaders, oral or written, that expound on religious tenets, belief, or behavior, among other things, for the purpose of instruction, are, according to John Alan Cohan, an attorney and legal scholar, such that they are not "mere speeches[89] that advocate ideas in the abstract",[90] but are constructed explicitly to incite followers to carry out certain actions. The endeavor of those delivering sermons is to persuade members to take those actions being taught, and, for Cohan, members listen to the religious teachings of the organization to which they belong to draw motivation to take those actions encouraged.[91]

The matter of preaching, then, is more complex than Cohan would suggest. While those delivering sermons do aim to incite followers to undertake those actions being taught in the sermons, a subset of individuals receiving the sermons, the seekers, might not intend to act upon those teachings. This is not a small issue; if a seeker who is a member of a group commits a crime, with or without overt action, he or she might or might not have been acting in his or her capacity as a

---

[86] Grinstein, "Jihad and the Constitution", p. 1367.

[87] Ibid., p. 1365.

[88] The term "sermon" evokes those religious speeches delivered by Protestant pastors, although it should be noted that "sermons" or "sermonizing" might also be understood as commentaries offered by religious leaders on tenets of belief offered in religious services, as well as outside of formal religious services in the form of newsletters, videos, or lectures. Thus, a sermon might be delivered as an oration or in written form.

[89] For the purpose of this chapter, "speech" used in "sermonizing" is understood as being delivered not only by means of oration but also in written form.

[90] Cohan, "ARTICLE", p. 204.

[91] Ibid.

member of that group, in which case the courts would be required to understand the capacity in which the perpetrator was acting. To charge a preacher or white-racist religious group with inciting unlawful action would be unconstitutional should that particular group or preacher not have been the direct cause of incitement.

Particular beliefs of a group would effectively be abolished should sedition and terrorism charges against white-racist religious groups or their leaders be realized, as such a situation would result in the criminalizing and censoring of certain religious speech. If beliefs central to violent white-racist religions were to be eradicated, the idea goes, those groups would cease to exist. Damages litigations, aimed at financially ruining an organization, have the potential of arriving at the same ultimate result of purging certain religious groups from society. However, religious white-racist beliefs, criminalized or otherwise, will continue to circulate in the cultic and white-racist milieux. Additionally, those defunct groups might be heralded as symbolic martyrs for the cause of white racism. Particularly if speech, a necessary component of religious belief not included in the Supreme Court's conception of religion, is proscribed without overt action(s), the goal of preventing terrorism and other unlawful action has the potential to backfire. White-racist religious groups may understand the government's actions to be in furtherance of the perceived discrimination against and oppression of Aryans; as yet another operation by ZOG to eliminate or compromise the pure Aryan race. Such perceptions are firmly rooted in the white-racist milieu. These beliefs, especially when coupled with the archetype of the Aryan warrior, have the potential to recapitulate the fears of violence against the government and non-whites. For group members, already having been instructed by religious leaders to form phantom cells or act as lone wolves, such actions by the government might actually incite terrorism rather than quell it.[92]

Conclusion

The Order, a terrorist group that included individuals from prominent white-racist intentional communities, influenced Odinist groups, both communal and non-communal, Aryan Nations, and Creativity, and has been used as a template

---

[92] Kantor, "Note", p. 778.

for other white-racist religious groups. Aryan Nations and Creativity have been held responsible for outbursts of violence on the part of their members, resulting in damages large enough to dissolve the groups. Protection of national security in the post-9/11 wartime state has led to the criminalization of religious speech and indictment of religious leaders based upon certain religious teachings they have propounded. According to the new definition, white-racist religious groups may be considered terrorist organizations, and should terrorism charges be brought against them, particularly with respect to sedition, the beliefs of certain groups could be criminalized. According to legal theorists, this would potentially remove those beliefs or groups from society and from the marketplace of ideas. The beliefs of white-racist religious movements do not, however, have a large presence in the marketplace; instead they circulate in the cultic and white-racist milieux. The nature of these milieux is such that those beliefs would not be eradicated, but instead be absorbed and reabsorbed by other groups that would perhaps use the criminalization of that speech to affirm that which they have been arguing all along: the Aryan race has and is being oppressed by the government, and the antidote is to embody the warrior ideal of their ancestors.

Chapter 13

Communes and Kibbutzim: Towards a Comparison

Henry Near

This is not a summary of a completed piece of research, but an outline of thoughts and tentative conclusions which serve as a basis for a research project on this subject which is still in progress.

The kibbutzim recently celebrated their hundredth year, and many communes have an even longer history; and in both cases scholarly research is almost as old as the communities or movements themselves. On the whole, however, research has been conducted on two separate tracks – one for communes and one for kibbutzim. This paper is a first tentative attempt to ask whether this division is justified. With the help of Timothy Miller I have drawn up a preliminary list of those communes and communal movements which have existed for a generation or more – about 30 years – and are still existing today. On the basis of this list I shall ask to what degree the factors which brought these communities into existence and sustained them until today are similar to those which engendered the growth of the kibbutz movement. In a word, are we dealing with two different types of community; is the kibbutz movement *sui generis*, or is it simply one species of the genus "commune" – at any rate from the point of view of the historical circumstances in which the two types of community grew up and survived?

My choice of research object is partly based on longevity. But is longevity important? It seems to me that the thrust of a very widely accepted theory, Donald Pitzer's theory of developmental communalism, is to deny this, or at any rate to play it down. Speaking as a long-term communitarian, I cannot accept this view. Whatever the *ex post facto* estimates of detached scholars, there are two principal criteria for the success of a commune: its survival, and the maintenance of its communal framework. However many refrigerators Amana has produced over the years, *as a commune* it was still a failure from 1932, when it abandoned its communal structure; and the thousands of communes which vanished shortly after their foundation constitute an interesting, perhaps even an important, historical phenomenon; but each one of them has to be considered a failure. Moreover, in terms of their contribution to historical development, communes as such have no special significance as against other successful forms of settlement. Communalism must be judged on its own terms; and longevity is one of the main criteria by which it must be judged. The other, of course, is part of the basic definition of a commune – that its members share their finances and manage them jointly. So, from the many thousands of ephemeral communes to be found in the literature – though no longer on the ground – I shall discuss a representative, though not entirely exhaustive, sample of 22 communes or communal movements which have survived and lived communally for a generation or more, and it is they which I shall compare with the kibbutz movement – see Table 13.1. As for the kibbutz movement itself, I have confined myself to the "classical" kibbutz, before the far-reaching changes of the late 1980s. Although these changes have undoubtedly initiated a major, and important, new phase in kibbutz history, it seems to me that it is as yet too early to see them in the perspective required for deep historical analysis.

Most of these communes were not known, or scarcely known at all, to the theorists and scholars of the kibbutz, most of whom relied principally on Hebrew language publications. Until the publication of the Hebrew versions of Yaacov Oved's researches on the historical American communes, the Bruderhof, and, very recently, the communes of the second half of the twentieth century,[1] and Yossi Katz's book on the Hutterites, their main source of knowledge was Shalom Wurm's book *Communes and Their Ways of Life*, published in 1968.[2] This is mainly a detailed account of the historical American communes – ending, of course, apart from the Bruderhof and the Hutterites, in failure or privatization.

---

[1] Yaacov Oved, *Two Hundred Years of American Communes* (Ef'al, 1986 [Heb.]); Yaacov Oved, *Distant Brothers: The Bruderhof and the Kibbutz Movement* (Ef'al, 1993 [Heb.]); Yaacov Oved, *The Witness of the Brothers: The History of the Bruderhof Communes* (Ef'al, 1996 [Heb.]); Yossi Katz, *In Their Faith Shall They Live: The Hutterite Communes in North America, 1874–2006* (Ef'al, 2007 [Heb.]).

[2] Shalom Wurm, *Communes and Their Ways of Life* (Tel Aviv, 1968 [Heb.]).

Table 13.1 Contemporary long-lived communes – comparative table

	Name and Location	Foundation Date	Population	Number of Communities	Ideology / Faith	Charismatic leader?	Communal meals?	Education
1	Hutterites International, many locations	1528	40,000	458	Anabaptist	+	Most. Limit of 150 per village	Own ps No high school or university m-g
2	Kibbutzim, Israel	1910	117,000	268	Zionist, socialist	+ −	Most	Schools at all levels and university m-g
3	Bruderhof, International, several locations	1920	3,200	28	Fundamentalist Ch.	+	Most	Own ps and hs College permitted m-g
4	Koinonia Farm, Georgia, US	1942	32	1	Nondenominational Ch.	+	Most	Donations to balance budget No school
5	Riverside, NZ	1942	34	1	Protestant → secular	−	No	No school
6	Communautés de L'Arche, France, Italy, Canada	1964	160	4	Spiritual, pacifist	+		hs
7	Braziers Park, UK	1948	23	1	Pagan	−	Most	No school
8	New Creation Christian Community (Jesus Army), UK	1957	600	60	Evangelical Ch.	−	Most	No school
9	Reba Place Fellowship, Chicago	1957	64	1 plus links with several other communities, not all coms	Evangelical Ch.	−	Many	No school; hs

Table 13.1 Continued

	Name and Location	Foundation Date	Population	Number of Communities	Ideology / Faith	Charismatic leader?	Communal meals?	Education
10	La Poudrière, Brussels	1958	60	3	Ecumenical Ch.	–	Most	No school
11	FIC, Twin Oaks, East Wind, US	1967	175	2	Ecological, pacifist	–	Most	No school; hs
12	Auroville, India	1968	2,100	1	Spiritual	+	Few	?
13	Alpha Farm, Oregon	1972	15–25	1	Secular, ecological	–	Most	No school
14	Jesus People, USA	1972	500	1	Evangelical Ch.	–	Most	Own ps
15	Twelve Tribes, International, multiple locations	1972	?	18	Evangelical Ch.	–	Most	hs
16	Findhorn, Scotland	1972	1,200	1	Spiritual	+ –	Many	No school
17	Comunidad Los Horcones, Mexico	1973	24	1	Radical behaviorism	+	Most	hs
18	Sandhill Farm, Missouri	1974	9	1	Ecovillage	–	Most	Outside school and hs
19	Damanhur, Italy	1975	600 (200 in coms)	8–10	Ecovillage, New Age	+	Few	Own schools and public schooling m-g
20	Svanholm, Denmark	1977	140	1	Organic farming	–	Most	No school; kindergarten
21	Elim, Holland	1981	13	1	Missionary		Some	
22	The Family International (Children of God), International	1986	8,000 (not all in coms)	13	Fundamentalist Ch.	+	Some	Own ps and hs, also outside school m-g

Notes: Data for communities still existing in 2010. Abbreviations: Ch = Christian; hs = home schooling; ps = primary school; m-g = multi-generational community; com. = commune, communal.

So the general belief among Israelis was that, with few exceptions, the kibbutz was a uniquely successful communal movement. Wurm says, in the conclusion of his book:

> In the solidarity and mutual responsibility between all parts [of the kibbutz movement] it is immeasurably superior to all the communal movements which have existed in the near and distant past.

This has been, and perhaps still is, the accepted view among kibbutzniks in general. But is it in fact true?

I shall take the historical development of the kibbutz movement as my starting point, and, after a brief description, compare it with the communes in my list, emphasizing particularly those highlighted – each of them indicating a group, or movement, of communes – since they are the closest parallel to the kibbutz *movement* rather than individual settlements.

I start with the usual suspects. One, which I shall not discuss in detail here, is economics. Both the kibbutzim and all of the communes on my list have been economically successful – some even very prosperous. The reasons for this are extremely complex: they involve geographic location, the availability of basic resources, leadership skills and strategies, the cultural and intellectual standards of the members, and more – often including a considerable element of luck. But in this chapter I shall take this as given, an attribute common to kibbutzim and long-lived communes, without which, by definition, they could not have survived. Historians, including myself, have also attributed the success and longevity of the kibbutz, as compared with other communes, to a number of factors: the ideological steadfastness and physical tenacity of its members, particularly the founding generation; its part in the building of Jewish Palestine and the State of Israel; its unique educational system; and the Zeitgeist, which, especially in the period when the kibbutz was most successful – from 1936 to 1948 – favored Socialist and revolutionary social philosophies. Of these, I myself have emphasized two factors in particular: first, what I have called the contract between the kibbutz and the Zionist movement (and, thereafter, the State of Israel) whereby the kibbutzim played a predominant part in the fulfillment of Zionist strategy – primarily settlement and defence – and, in exchange, were permitted to conduct their internal affairs, including their unique social structure, without interference, and afforded support at times of crisis; and, secondly, perhaps even more important, the existence of a huge reserve of actual and potential manpower in the Zionist youth movements.[3]

Others have pointed out other factors which seem to make the kibbutzim unique among communes. One is the fact that, in contrast to most of the communes and communal movements, they have never attempted to withdraw from surrounding society, but have always been involved in political and social activities: in fact, two of them actually created political parties of their own.[4] There are few parallels to this among long-lived communes, which have typically been withdrawn from the society around them. Many kibbutz theorists have attributed the success of the kibbutz to its unique educational system, and to the influence of the kibbutz-orientated youth movements.[5] Others again lay stress on the strength of kibbutz ideology, and the kibbutzniks' belief that they were creating a new society morally superior to that in which they themselves had grown up. Another stream of thought emphasizes the internal dynamics of kibbutz society, and the influence of the social solidarity (the "communal experience" in one formulation) which is inherent in its day-to-day way of life.

These, then, are the factors which are thought to have led to the success of the kibbutz movement: the support of the Zionist movement and the State of Israel; the youth movements; the kibbutz educational system, and its success in building a multi-generational society; the strength, persistence, and deep ideological conviction of its members, from the individual kibbutznik to the leaders of the kibbutzim and the kibbutz movements; its participation in the life of the surrounding society; and the role of the communal experience in buttressing communal life.

As I have said, this is only a preliminary report, and there are many important factors missing. One is a detailed demographic analysis of these communes. This is clearly of great importance, for we would like to know to what extent they

---

[3] Henry Near, *The Kibbutz Movement: A History*, vol. ii (Oxford and Portland, 1997), pp. 314–318.

[4] Baruch Kanari, *Hakibbutz Hameuchad – Mission and Reality* (Tel Aviv, 1989 [Heb.]); David Zait, *Pioneers in the Maze of Politics* (Jerusalem, 1993 [Heb.]).

[5] Yuval Dror, *The History of Kibbutz Education: From Practice to Theory* (Tel Aviv, 2002).

have managed to absorb their own children, or have to rely on recruitment from outside to compensate for leaving and death. The general rule among communes is that the younger generation does not join the community as adults. The known exceptions are the kibbutzim, the Hutterites, the Bruderhof, Damanhur, and the Family International, all of which are multi-generational. It is no doubt of some significance that all of these have their own primary schools. The claim that the commune's educational system contributes to its longevity seems to be substantiated in these cases, all of which are among the most successful groups of communes.

Another important factor is the size of the communes. A few kibbutzim have a population of some 2,000, but the great majority have no more than about 600, and several are very much smaller. All the communes are much smaller: the Hutterites split their communities when their population reaches 150, and found new settlements. Two communities – Auroville and Damanhur – aim at maximum expansion; but insofar as their members live communally (and not all of them do) they live in small communes within a wider federation. It seems, then, that most of the long-lived communes have learnt from experience or been forced by necessity to limit their populations. I shall discuss the implications of this a little later.

On the question of involvement in the outside community, there is no general rule, but most of the Christian communes do good works for the local community, collect for and donate to charity, do missionary work, and so forth. As for the kibbutzim, their chief involvement with the outside community has been their part in the process of nation-building: settlement, defence, and cultural creation. But they have also been active in politics, though since 1977, when an election made the political complexion of Israel radically more conservative, this activity has decreased substantially, and today they are far more concerned with the struggle for survival than with playing an active role in Israeli society.

I have left three major questions until the end. First, is there any parallel in the historical development of the communes to the contract between the kibbutzim and the Zionist movement? Second, how have the long-lived communes survived and, in many cases, flourished, without the backing of a youth movement? And third, what parallels are there between the ideologies of the kibbutzim and those of the long-lived communes?

In many cases the answers to these questions can be found in the ideological complexion of the communes. Of the 22 contemporary long-lived communes and communal movements – that is to say, those which are still in existence – 15 define themselves as Christian or spiritual (including two which are described as pagan – a variety of spiritual belief). These communities are not alone in the world. They have the psychological support of millions who share their beliefs, though some have an unorthodox view of what those beliefs entail. And this support is not only psychological. I shall quote two paradigmatic cases from among many. I have not included monasteries and nunneries in my list, although they are clear examples of completely communal societies, since I did not want to swamp the list of research objects by adding more than 300 more-or-less homogeneous communities. But the monasteries and nunneries have the spiritual, political, and financial backing of the Catholic Church, which is far more rich and powerful than the Jewish Agency before 1948, or even than the State of Israel today.

The same applies to many smaller and less orthodox communes and communal movements. In 1930, Eberhard Arnold, the leader of the Bruderhof movement in Germany, went to America to strengthen the Bruderhof's links with the Hutterites. Although a good deal of his time was devoted to theological questions, he also tried to raise contributions to a total of $25,000 – no small sum in those days – from the Hutterite communities in order to save the Bruderhof from financial collapse. In this he was unsuccessful, and the movement was only saved when a wealthy family joined a commune, bringing with it all its possessions. But the notion that a commune engaged in beneficent Christian activities could itself be a worthy object of charity was not foreign to the way of thinking of either movement.

So, although there was no standard official channel through which the Christian churches helped the communes as the Jewish Agency helped the kibbutzim or the Catholic church helped the monasteries, the Christian community often provided financial backing in times of crisis, as well as the moral certainty resulting from the Christian communards' beliefs. Moreover, many of the communes state that they regularly derive some income from charity – in addition to that which they collect in order to help families in need, and so forth.

It may also be observed that the case of the Bruderhof typifies a way in which the communes differ from the kibbutzim: in many cases, they profit from their members' social background, whether through contributions from the members themselves or (as often happened in the case of the American hippy communes) from their families. The kibbutzim have only very rarely received such help; but they have had official backing at many stages, from the allocation of land for settlement to the cancellation of accumulated debts. Thus, both the communes and the kibbutzim enjoy institutional support which helps them survive at critical periods.

No less important to communal survival is the question of demographic growth. We have seen that in four cases, and perhaps more, the communes have succeeded in absorbing enough of their children for the community to be described as multi-generational. The Hutterites and the Family International use only this method, while the Bruderhof are open to recruitment from outside their ranks. The kibbutzim, too, are multi-generational societies in this sense, but in another sense too: the recruitment of young people from outside the kibbutz through the Zionist youth movements. On the face of things, it seems that none of the communes or communal movements has similar backing.

I would like to maintain that this is not entirely so. Almost all of the long-term communes (with the exception of the Hutterites) continue to recruit members from outside their ranks, and those which have succeeded neither in doing so nor in absorbing their own children – as, for instance, Riverside in New Zealand – are clearly in a decline. Whence do these recruits come to them? A historical parallel with the hippy communes of the sixties is instructive. The communes multiplied by the recruitment (more accurately, self-recruitment) of tens of thousands of young people who, although they held no membership card and did not subscribe to a clearly formulated ideological program, belonged to a movement: a movement which saw in the commune one way of achieving its sometimes quite vague objectives. The hippy movement subsided, and with it the wave of communes it produced. But there still exist movements in this sense – groups of like-minded young people seeking a way to put their ideals into practice; and a few of them have made a substantial contribution to the demographic growth, for instance, of the communes of the Fellowship for Intentional Community (Twin Oaks and East Wind), whose publicity and public activities are aimed at such people. This is even more true in the case of the Christian communes, which are in touch with youth groups and evangelical movements which form a fertile ground for recruitment.

In absolute numbers, these recruits are quite few. But, in proportion to the size of the communes, which are themselves quite small, they make a substantial contribution to their demographic well-being – as do the youth movements to the kibbutzim, although the number of dropouts from them is, as it has always been, very high. So here again, the kibbutzim are far from being unique in having a more or less assured demographic backing; the differences are organizational and ideological. These factors certainly affect the number of recruits, and strengthen the impression that in this respect the kibbutzim are unique among communes; but this impression is far from completely accurate.

As for ideology, Christianity is certainly no less of a motivating force than Zionism or socialism. And nobody who has participated in a meditation session at Damanhur or any of the other spiritual-type communities can doubt the strength and attractiveness of joint spiritual experience. There remain the ecovillages (including those of the FIC). These are among the youngest of my group of communes, and it remains to be seen whether the fervor with which ecosystemic creeds have been advocated in the past will remain when, as seems to be the case, sustainable building, organic crops, and the like become part of the social norm. In any case, in the majority of cases religion and spirituality constitute an effective parallel to kibbutz ideology.

Thus, the principal factors which have preserved and strengthened the kibbutz movement are paralleled, *mutatis mutandis*, in the case of the majority of the long-lived communes. I would add one more comment. One of the central factors in the preservation of a communal society is the collective experience which binds the members together. In kibbutz life this is consciously fostered, whether in cultural events, the workings of face-to-face democracy, or the simple fact of eating together. I have no doubt it also exists in the long-lived communes, though without more detailed research I cannot give a reasoned account of it. But, as a first step, I have noted that in all of them meals are often – sometimes always – eaten together; this is an event which, in the religious communities, can even have a sacerdotal aspect. This is another aspect of the kibbutz which is paralleled in the long-lived commune – though, sadly, there are many kibbutzim in which common dining has been abolished as part of the privatization process. It is also of some significance that all the long-lived communes are relatively small: in some cases (as the Hutterites) deliberately so, and in others as a result of social developments within the overall organization. The communal experience is easier to foster and maintain in a small group.

As remarked above, I have confined myself in this paper to the classical kibbutz. And it seems that all of the factors to which its stability and growth are usually attributed are paralleled in the long-lived contemporary communes. There is a great deal of research yet to be done in order to obtain a complete picture, and this may be very different in various respects from the impressionistic sketch I have presented here. And how the privatized kibbutz will develop, and which of the classical characteristics of the kibbutz will be preserved, is a subject for further research – or speculation. So I shall conclude with a short and tentative, answer to the question I posed at the beginning of this paper: yes, in terms of their historical genesis and preservation kibbutzim and communes are two species of the same genus.

Select Bibliography

Introduction

Brown, Susan Love. 2002. *Intentional Community: An Anthropological Perspective*. Albany: State University of New York Press.
Metcalf, Bill. 1996. *Shared Visions, Shared Lives: Communal Living Around the Globe*. Forres: Findhorn Press.
Rexroth, Kenneth. 1974. *Communalism: From Its Origins to the Twentieth Century*. New York: Seabury.

Chapter 1: Damanhur

Buffagni, Silvia (Esperide Ananas). 2006. *Damanhur: Temples of Humankind*. Berkeley: North Atlantic Books.
Del Vecchio, Gianni and Stefano Pitrelli. 2011. *Occulto Italia*. Milano: Rizzoli.
Introvigne, Massimo. 1996. "Damanhur: A Magical Community in Italy", *Communal Societies*, 16: 71–84.
Merrifield, Jeff. 2006. *Damanhur: The Story of the Extraordinary Italian Artistic and Spiritual Community*. Santa Cruz: Hanford Mead.
Pesco, Stambecco (Silvio Palombo). 2011. *La Mia Damanhur: La Più Grande Comunità Spirituale Italiana Raccontata da Chi Ci Vive*. Reggio Emilia: Altriparaggi Edizioni.

Chapter 2: Mandarom

Introvigne, Massimo. 2004. "Holy Mountains and Anti-Cult Ecology: The Campaign Against the Aumist Religion in France", in *Regulating Religion*, edited by James T. Richardson. New York: Kluwer Academic.

Roncaglia, Florence and Bernard Nicolas. 1995. *Mandarom: Une Victime Temoigne*. Paris: TF1 Editions.

Zoccatelli, Pierluigi. 2005. "Notes on the Aumiste Religion", in *Controversial New Religions*, edited by James R. Lewis and Jesper Peterson. New York: Oxford.

Chapter 3: Brahma Kumaris

Hodgkinson, Liz. 2002. *Peace and Purity: The Story of the Brahma Kumaris, a Spiritual Revolution*. Deerfield Beach, FL: Health Communications, Inc.

Ramsay, Tamasin. 2012. "Brahma Kumaris: Purity and the Globalization of Faith", in *Flows of Faith: Religious Reach and Community in Asia and the Pacific*, edited by Lenore Manderson, Wendy Smith and Matt Tomlinson. Dordrecht: Springer.

Walliss, John. 2002. *The Brahma Kumaris as a 'Reflexive Tradition': Responding to Late Modernity*. Aldershot: Ashgate.

Whaling, Frank. 2012. *Understanding the Brahma Kumaris*. Edinburgh: Dunedin Academic Press.

Chapter 4: New Kadampa Tradition

Bluck, Robert. 2006. *British Buddhism*. London: Routledge.

Cozort, Daniel. 2003. "The Making of the Western Lama", in *Buddhism in the Modern World: Adaptations of an Ancient Tradition*, edited by Steven Heine and Charles S. Prebish. Oxford: Oxford University Press.

His Holiness the XIVth Dalai Lama (trans. Graham Woodhouse). 2009. *Direct Instructions from Shakyamuni Buddha: A Gelong's Training in Brief*. Dharamsala: Institute of Buddhist Dialectics.

Kay, David. 1997. "The New Kadampa Tradition and the Continuity of Tibetan Buddhism in Transition", *Journal of Contemporary Religion*, 6(1): 277–294.
Kay, David. 2004. *Tibetan and Zen Buddhism in Britain*. London: Routledge Curzon.
Lopez, Donald. 1998. "Two Sides of the Same God", *Tricycle: The Buddhist Review*, 7(3): 67–76.
Waterhouse, Helen. 1997. *Buddhism in Bath: Adaptation and Authority*. Leeds: Community Religions Project, Department of Theology and Religious Studies, University of Leeds.
Waterhouse, Helen. 2001. "Representing Western Buddhism: A United Kingdom Focus", in *From Sacred Text to Internet*, edited by G. Beckerlegge. Aldershot: Ashgate.
Waterhouse, Helen. 2005. "New Kadampa Tradition", in *The Encyclopaedia of New Religious Movements*, edited by P.B. Clarke. London: Routledge.

Chapter 5: Tamera

Dregger, Leila. 2010. *Tamera: A Model for the Future*. Wiesenburg: Meiga.
Duhm, Dieter. 2006. *The Sacred Matrix: From the Matrix of Violence to the Matrix of Life: The Foundation for a New Civilisation*. Wiesenburg: Meiga.
Duhm, Dieter. 2012. *Towards a New Culture: From Refusal to Re-Creation: Outline of an Ecological and Humane Alternative*. Wiesenburg: Meiga.
Lichtenfels, Sabine. 2006. *Grace: Pilgrimage for a Future without War*. Wiesenburg: Meiga.

Chapter 6: Camphill

Bang, Jan Martin (ed.). 2010. *A Portrait of Camphill*. Edinburgh: Floris Books.
Hudd, Christopher Boughton. 1996. *Rudolf Steiner, Economist*. Canterbury: New Economy Publications.
Jackson, Robin (ed.). 2011. *Discovering Camphill*. Edinburgh: Floris Books.
König, Karl. 1993. *The Camphill Movement*. Whitby: Camphill Books.

Luxford, Michael and Jane. 2003. *A Sense for Community*. Whitby: Camphill Books.

Steiner, Rudolf. 1974. *The Inner Aspect of the Social Question*. London: Rudolf Steiner Press.

Chapter 7: The Farm

Fike, Rupert (ed.). 2012. *Voices From The Farm: Adventures in Community Living*. Summertown, TN: Book Publishing Company.

Gaskin, Stephen. 2005. *Monday Night Class*. Summertown, TN: Book Publishing Company.

Gaskin, Stephen. 2007. *The Caravan*. Summertown, TN: Book Publishing Company.

Lapidus, Patricia. 2011. *Sweet Potato Suppers: A Yankee Woman Finds Salvation in a Hippie Village*. New York: Walking Tall Tales Press.

Stiriss, Melvyn. 2011a. *Voluntary Peasants Book 1: Holy Hippies and the Great, Round-the-Country, Save-the-World, School Bus Caravan*. San Francisco: Hot Button Press.

Stiriss, Melvyn. 2011b. *Voluntary Peasants Book 2: The Enlightenment Trip*. San Francisco: Hot Button Press.

Chapter 8: Twelve Tribes

Bozeman, John M. and Susan J. Palmer. 1997. "The Northeast Kingdom Community Church of Island Pond Vermont: Raising Up a People for Yashua's Return", *Journal of Contemporary Religion*, 12(2): 181–190.

Palmer, Susan J. 1994. *Moon Sisters, Krishna Mothers, Rajneesh Lovers: Women's Roles in New Religions*. Syracuse: Syracuse University Press.

Palmer, Susan J. 2010. "The Twelve Tribes: Preparing the Bride for Yashua's Return", *Nova Religio*, 13(3): 59–80.

Chapter 9: The Family

Bainbridge, William Sims. 2002. *The Endtime Family: Children of God*. Albany: State University of New York Press.

Chancellor, James D. 2000. *Life in the Family: An Oral History of the Children of God*. Syracuse, NY: Syracuse University Press.

Melton, J. Gordon. 1997. *The Children of God: "The Family"*. Salt Lake City: Signature Books.

Shepherd, Gary and Gordon Shepherd. 2008. "Evolution of the Family International/Children of God in the Direction of a Responsive Communitarian Religion", *Communal Societies*, 28(1): 27–53.

Chapter 10: How Many Arks Does It Take?

Guest, Tim. 2004. *My Life in Orange*. London: Granta.

Muster, Nori. 1996. *Betrayal of the Spirit: My Life Behind the Headlines of the Hare Krishna Movement*. Urbana: University of Illinois Press.

Nicoll, Maurice. 1952. *Psychological Commentaries on the Teachings of Gurdjieff and Ouspensky*. London: V. Stuart.

Pogson, Beryl. 1961. *Maurice Nicoll: A Portrait*. London: V. Stuart.

Riddel, Carol. 1990. *The Findhorn Community*. Forres: Findhorn Press.

Chapter 11: Religious Communes in America

Arrington, Leonard J., Feramorz Y. Fox and Dean L. May. 1976. *Building the City of God: Community and Cooperation among the Mormons*. Salt Lake City: Deseret.

Janzen, David. 1996. *Fire, Salt, and Peace: Intentional Christian Communities Alive in North America*. Evanston: Shalom Mission Communities.

Janzen, Rod and Max Stanton. 2010. *The Hutterites in North America*. Baltimore: Johns Hopkins University Press.

Oved, Yaacov. 1988. *Two Hundred Years of American Communes*. New Brunswick: Transaction Books.

Pizer, Donald E. (ed.). 1997. *America's Communal Utopias*. Chapel Hill: University of North Carolina Press.

Stein, Stephen J. 1992. *The Shaker Experience in America*. New Haven: Yale University Press.

Chapter 12: White-Racist Communes

Gardell, Mattias. 2003. *Gods of the Blood: The Pagan Revival and White Separatism*. Durham: Duke University Press.

Goodrick-Clarke, Nicholas. 2002. *Black Sun: Aryan Cults, Esoteric Nazism and the Politics of Identity*. New York: New York University Press.

Goodrick-Clarke, Nicholas. 2004. *The Occult Roots of Nazism: Secret Aryan Cults and Their Influence on Nazi Ideology*. London: Tauris Parke.

Hamm, Mark S. 1993. *American Skinheads: The Criminology and Control of Hate Crime*. Westport: Praeger.

Chapter 13: Kibbutzim

Dror, Yuval. 2001. *The History of Kibbutz Education: Practice Into Theory*. Bern: P. Lang.

Near, Henry. 1997. *The Kibbutz Movement: A History*. Oxford: Oxford University Press.

Oved, Yaacov. 1993. *Distant Brothers: History of the Relations between the Bruderhof and the Kibbutz*. Ramat Efal, Israel: Yad Tabenkin.

Index

Abgrall, Jean-Marie 34
About-Picard law 30
Adamites 3
Ahimsa Church 199
Airaudi, Oberto ("Falco") 19, 20–21, 23, 25–8
Alfassa, Mirra 7
Alpert, Richard 198
Alpha Farm 228
Amana Society 192–3, 226
American Nazi Party 211
Amish 3
Amory, Christine 34, 40–41, 46, 48
Amsterdam, Peter 166, 173–4
Anabaptists 3, 4, 8, 194, 227
Ananda World Brotherhood Village 201
Animal Project 89
Anthroposophy 7, 103–19, 196
Apostles of Infinite Love 9
Arnold, Eberhard 194, 232
Arnold, Emmy 194
Aryan communities 207, 219
Aryan Nations 208–13, 215–18, 222–3
Aryan Nations Church of Yahweh 212
Asatrú 211
Assassins 5
Association du Vajra Triomphant (AVT) 37, 41, 46, 48
Attlee, Clement 184
Aumisme 29–49
Aurobindo, Sri 7, 199
Aurora Colony 193
Auroville 7, 228, 231
Auschwitz 95

Bailey, Alice 184
Bainbridge, William Sims 142–3
Barkun, Michael 12
Bates, Albert 121–38
Beam, Louis 209, 212, 215

Beckford, James 35
Beissel, Conrad 192
Benedict of Nursia 2
Bennett, J.G. 181, 183
Berg, David 160–66, 169
Berg, Peter 137
Berry, Brian J.L. 12
Bestor, Arthur 17, 27
Bethel Colony 193
Bhajan, Yogi 201
Bhaktivedanta Manor 187
Bhaktivedanta Swami Prabhupada, A.C. 187–8
Bible Evening 106, 108–9, 111, 113–14
Biodynamic farming 104–5, 109–10
Blavatsky, Helena 7, 195
Bogomils 2
Bonnet, Yves 42, 45
Bourdin, Gilbert 29–32, 34, 39, 42–4
Brahma Baba, *see* Kirpalani, Lekhraj
Brahma Kumaris Spiritual University 51–64
Brard, J.P. 38
Braziers Park 227
Briggs, John 85
van den Brink, Margarete 116
British Israel 196, 207–8
Brotherhood of the New Life 195
Bruderhof 147, 194–5, 226–7, 231–3
Buddhist Sangha 1
Butler, Richard 208–9, 217

Caddy, Eileen 9, 184–6
Caddy, Peter 184–6
Camphill House 103, 109
Camphill Villages 7, 103–19, 196
Carmathians 5
Carroll, T.C. 132
Cathari 2
Catholic Church 103, 194, 232

Catholic Traditionalists 9
Catholic Worker 8, 10
Chamberlain, Neville 177
Chancellor, James 159
Children of God, *see* Family International
Christian Identity 207–9, 213, 215
Church of Jesus Christ Christian 209
Church of the Creator, *see* Creativity movement
Churchill, Winston 184
Claymont Society 183
Cohan, John Alan 221
Colin-Smith, Rodney 179
Colonia Dublan 6
Colonia Juárez 6
Colonia LeBaron 6
Comenius, Amos 113
Communauté du Chemin Neuf 9
Communautés de L'Arche, *see* L'Arche communities
Comunidad Los Horcones 228
Community of Jesus 200
Coombe Springs 182–3
Cosmoplanetary Messiah 29, 31–2, 45
Covenant, Sword, and the Arm of the Lord, the 208
Creativity movement 213, 216–18, 220, 222–3
Cultural Association of the Pyramid Temple 46

Dalai Lama 66–7, 71, 74
Damanhur Federation 15–28, 204, 228, 231, 234
Day, Dorothy 8
Degania 8
Delcourt, Alain 34–5, 42, 44
developmental communalism 225
Diggers 4, 137
Divine, Father 197
Djamichunatra 183
Dorje Shugden 67, 71, 73–5, 77, 80–81
Doukhobors 5–6
Duhm, Dieter 86, 95–8, 100
Dumas, Mireille 42

East Wind 228, 233
Eberle, Edward 219
ecovillages 10, 228, 234
Edwards, Anne 184
Ehrenpreis, Charly Rainer 95–7
Eisenhower, Dwight D. 184
Ekta, V. 39
Elim 228
Ellison, James 208–9
Emissary Communities 203
Emmaus International 10
Ephrata Community 6, 192
Esalen 134
Eurotopia 10, 12

Falco, *see* Airaudi, Oberto
Family International 157–76, 228, 231, 233
The Farm 13, 121–38, 201
Fellowship for Intentional Community 12, 228, 233–4
Ferrato, Robert 34–5, 40, 41, 45
Findhorn community 9, 184–7, 203, 228
Fountain Grove 195
Fontaine, Maria 166, 174
Franklin Farms 179
Frery, Bernard 45

Gardner, Hugh 205
Gandhi 198
Gaskin, Ina May 122, 127, 130–33, 136
Gaskin, Stephen 13, 121–38, 201
Gestalt therapy 134
Ginsberg, Allen 137
Giraldo, Javier 101
Gisler, Paul 92–4
Glasl, Freidrich 118
Global Campus Initiative 89, 92, 100–101
Global Ecovillage Network 22, 123
Gnosticism 109
von Goethe, Johann Wolfgang 109
Goodman, Jesse 151–2
Gottlieb, Lou 199
Govinda, Lama 199
Grad, Francine 44
Grail movement 204
Green, Joyce 202
Grinstein, Joseph 221
Grogan, Emmett 137
Grouès, Henri 10
Gurdjieff, G.I. 177–83, 187

Guyard Report 30, 36, 48

Habitat for Humanity 198
ha-emeq, *see* Spriggs, Marsha
Hamsananda Sarasvati, Shri Swami 30–32
Hare Krishna Movement 187–8
Harmony Society 6, 192
Harris, Thomas Lake 195
Havurah movement 200
Havurat Shalom 200
Heinlein, Robert A. 134
Helms, Chet 130
Herrnhutter communities 113
Hierokarantine 32
Higgins, Tracy 220
Himalayan Academy 198
Hitler, Adolf 130, 210
Holzer, Sepp 89–91
Los Horcones, *see* Comunidad Los Horcones
House of David 196
Hus, John 3
Hussites 3
Hutter, Jacob 4
Hutterites 4, 6, 11–13, 194–5, 197, 226, 227, 231–4
Huxley, Aldous 124

Identity movement, *see* Christian Identity
INFORM 13
Institute for Global Peace Work 89
International Academy for Continuous Education 183
International Communal Studies Association 22
International Society for Krishna Consciousness (ISKCON) 200
Israel Family 147

Janki, Dadi 54, 57, 59, 64
Je Tsongkhapa 67, 73, 80
Jerome, Judson 205
Jesus Movement 157–8, 199
Jesus People USA 200, 228
Jewish Agency 232
Jordan, Clarence 197–8
Jouret, Luc 39

Kadleigh, George 180
Kadloubovsky, Madame 178
Kanter, Rosabeth Moss 204–5
Kashi Ashram 202
Katz, Yossi 226
Keenan, Jason 217
Keenan, Victoria 217
Kelsang Gyatso, Geshe 65–75, 77–82
Kerista 202
Kerouac, Jack 132
kibbutzim 8, 204, 225–35
King, Walter Eugene 202
Kingdomism 202
Kirpalani, Lekhraj 52–4, 62
Klassen, Bernard 213
Kleinwächter, Jürgen 92–4
Klüver, Silke 91
Knights of the Golden Lotus 31, 39, 45, 46
Koinonia Community (Koinonia Farm) 11, 197–8, 227
König, Karl 103, 106, 108, 111–15, 117
König, Tilla 113
Koresh, *see* Teed, Cyrus Read
Koreshan Unity 6, 195
Kriyananda, Swami 201
Krotona 196
Ku Klux Klan 207, 209, 215
Kuten Lama 74

de Labadie, Jean 191
Labadist colony 191
Lane, David 210, 212
Lang, Fritz 134
L'Arche communities 200, 227
Latter Day Saints 6, 118, 193–4
Law of Love 163–6
Leary, Timothy 198
Leavitt, Michael 216, 218
Leleux, Jean-Pierre 44
Lennon, John 124
Lewis, Sam (Sufi Sam) 130
Lichtenfels, Sabine 95–7, 99–101
Loeb, George 217
Lofland, John 142
Love School 89
Luxford, Jane 119
Luxford, Michael 119

Ma Jaya Bhagavati 202
Macioti, Maria Immacolata 16, 18
Madhuban ("Forest of Honey") 54, 57
Manarah, Hamsah 29, 31–2, 34, 35, 37, 39–45, 48
Mandarom 29–49
Mansfield, Harold 217
Margulis, Lynn 85
Mathews, Robert 209, 212
Maurin, Peter 8
Melton, Gordon 131
von Mendelssohn, Benjamin 101
Mennonites 3, 8, 191
Millar, Robert 208
Millbrook commune 199
Miller, Timothy 15, 225
Mime Troupe 137
Mollison, Bill 136
Monastic orders 2, 3, 81, 192
Monday Night Class 121, 123–6, 128, 130–31, 133, 135–6
Monte Cerro Peace Education program 101
Moravian Church 3, 112–13
Mormons 6, 118, 193–4
Morning Star Ranch 199
Movement for a New Society 10
Müller, Bernd 91
Mullet, Paul R. 213
Münster 4

Naomi 184–5
Natural Rights Center 122
New Age communities 203–4
New Kadampa Tradition (NKT) 65–82
Nicolas, Bernard 40–42
Nicoll, Jane 180
Nicoll, Maurice 179, 180–81
Nofziger, Margaret 130
Noyes, John Humphrey 134, 193
Nuwaubians 203

Odinism 211–12, 222
Odiyan 201
Ökodorf Sieben Linden 10
Olcott, Henry 7
Old Colony Mennonites 8
Oneida Community 6, 134, 193
Open University 130

Order, the 209, 222
Order of the Magnificat of the Mother of God 9
Orderville 193
Ordre du Temple Solaire (OTS) 30, 37, 39, 40
Oseijeman Adefunmi I. 202
Ouspensky, P.D. 178–9, 183, 199
Ouspensky, Sophie 178–9
Oved, Yaacov 226
Owen, Robert 113, 118, 192
Oyotunji African Yoruba Village 202

pacifists 4–5, 11, 189, 227–8
Padanaram community 202
Palmer, Susan 148, 150
Paulick, Silke 89
Peace Mission Movement 197
Peace Research Center 91
Peace Village San José de Apartadó 100–101
Peat, F. David 85
Peccei, Aurelio 84
Pentecostalism 9
Philip, Prince 184
Pitzer, Donald E. 17, 225
Place of the Children 89
Plenty International 122
Plockhoy, Pieter C. 191
Plockhoy's Commonwealth 191
Point Loma community 195–6
Politicyl Ashram 89
La Poudrière 228
Prajapita Brahma, *see* Kirpalani, Lekhraj
Price, George 129
Publishing House Meiga 89
Purnell, Benjamin 196–7
Purnell, Mary 196
Pyramid Temple, *see* Cultural Association of the Pyramid Temple

Quakers (Friends) 9, 10
Qarmathians 5
Quinn, Miss 179
Qumran 1

Radical Reformation 3, 194
Raja Yoga 54

Rajneesh, Bhagwan Shree 188–9
Reba Place Fellowship 227
Reybaud, Roger 34–5, 38
Riddel, Carol 186
Riverside community 227, 233
Roncaglia, Florence 41–4
Rosenthal, Bob 131
Rosicrucians 109, 192

Sandhill Farm 228
Savitskys 178
School of the Americas 11
Scorn, John 129
Seven Lindens Ecovillage 10
Shah, Idries 183
Shakers 6, 192
Shambhala International 201
Shantivanam 7
Shi'ite Muslims 5
Shiloh Youth Revival Centers, 199–200
Shugen, *see* Dorje Shugden
Sirius Community 203
Sivananda, Swami 30
Smelser, Neil 35
Snyder, Gary 132, 137
Solar Temple, *see* Ordre du Temple Solaire (OTS)
Sons of Freedom Doukhobors 5
Southcott, Joanna 196
Southern Poverty Law Center 214, 216
Space Brothers 184–6
Spiritualism 195
Spriggs, Elbert 139–40, 152–3, 155
Spriggs, Marsha 139–40
Starhawk 91
Stark, Rodney 142–3
Steiner, Rudolf 7, 96, 103, 109, 110, 112–15, 117, 196
Subramuniya, Master 198
Sufis 5, 130, 182, 187
Sunrise Ranch 203
Suzuki Roshi 124, 127, 130
Svanholm 228
Swanendael 191

Tabor 3
Tama-Re, 202
Tamera 83–101
Tarthang Tulku 201
Tavernier, Janine 33–4
Teague, Michael 217
Teed, Cyrus Read 195
Testfield for a Solar Village 83, 87, 92–4
Theosophical Society/Theosophy 7, 109, 195–6
Thomas, Steve 217
Tingley, Katherine 195–6
Tolstoy Farm 198
Tolstoy, Leo 198
Trijang Rinpoche 66
Trouslard, Père 33–4
Trungpa, Chögyam 201
Twelve Tribes 139–55, 228
Twin Oaks 228, 233

Union nationale des associations de defense des familles et du l'individu (UNADFI) 32–3, 35, 36, 41
Unitas Fratrum 3
United Order 6, 193–4

Vatican II (Second Vatican Council) 9
Vedhyas Vishti 41, 46
Vine Christian Community 139
Vine House 139
Vishti, V. 46

Waldensians 2
Waldo, Peter 2
Waldorf Schools 109
Walker, Kenneth 177
Walters, J. Donald 201
Watts, Alan 131–2, 137
Wheeler, Bill 199
Wheeler's Ranch 199
Whiffen, Robert 182
Williams, Huw "Piper" 198
Williams, Rhys 154
Woman in the Wilderness 192
World Church of the Creator, *see* Creativity movement
Wotansvolk 212, 215, 220
Wright, Daniel 202

Wurm, Shalom 226, 229

Yogananda, Paramahansa 201
Yoneq, *see* Spriggs, Elbert
York, Dwight 203
Young, Brigham 193–4
Youth School for Global Learning 87, 89

Zarephath-Horeb 208

ZEGG (Zentrum für experimentelle Gesellschaftsgestaltung) 99
Zerby, Karen, *see* Fontaine, Maria
von Zinzendorf, Count Nicolaus Ludwig 112–13, 115
Zionism 7, 8, 227, 229–31, 233–4
Zionist Occupation Government (ZOG) 209–11, 215, 219, 220, 222
Zoar Society 193